SOULMATES

SOULMATES

Resurrecting Eve

Juliana Geran Pilon

Transaction Publishers
New Brunswick (U.S.A.) and London (U.K.)

Library of Congress Catalog Number: 2011006068
ISBN: 978-1-4128-4249-5
Printed in the United States of America

Library of Congress Cataloging-in-Publication Data

Pilon, Juliana Geran.
  Soulmates : resurrecting Eve / Juliana Geran Pilon.
      p. cm.
  Includes bibliographical references and index.
  ISBN 978-1-4128-4249-5
  1. Sex role—Religious aspects.   2. Equality—Religious aspects.
3. Eve (Biblical figure)   4. Religions—Relations.   5. Abrahamic
religions.   6. Sex role.   7. Equality.   I. Title.
  BL65.S4P55   2011
  201'.615533—dc22   2011006068

To my late parents Charlotte and Peter Geran, prototypal soulmates.

Return, fair Eve;
Whom fliest thou? Whom thou fliest, of him thou art,
His flesh, his bone; to give thee being I lent
Out of my side to thee, nearest my heart
Substantial life, to have thee by my side
Henceforth an individual solace dear;
Part of my soul I seek thee, and thee claim
My other half.

Milton, Paradise Lost IV: 481–488 (1674)

Contents

Overview

The story of Adam and Eve is arguably the most influential cultural metaphor in history. The fact that all three Abrahamic religions, Judaism, Christianity, and Islam, despite so many radical differences, understood the *Genesis* narrative in remarkably similar ways is extraordinary and fortuitous, offering an excellent opportunity for constructive dialogue. Each monotheistic sect originally considered man and woman to have been designed together in the image of God, their intimate relationship reflecting the holy, loving communion between humans and their Creator, Who is defined not anthropomorphically but spiritually. "He" is not a superman, but the Force, the Spirit, the Unthinkable.

Over the centuries, however, the original message of human creation was distorted, in a distinctly misogynist direction. "Resurrecting" Eve is necessary not only to restore the moral and spiritual justification for equality among the sexes intended by the one God, but to recapture the central meaning of human as well as divine love. As a first step, this requires refuting the myth that Eve was a satanic temptress responsible for igniting the wrath of God and the subsequent expulsion of humanity from the Garden of Eden.

When God created mankind, male and female, in "His" image, what emerged was the first soulmate relationship. The *I–Thou* connection among men and women, and among human beings as such, is an image of the relationship between human beings and their Creator. The resurrection of Eve thus constitutes not only a reiteration of woman's true place along her male partner; it is indispensable to attaining a true appreciation of love and faith.

At no time is this reexamination of the creation story more relevant than it is today. For soon after the demise of atheist Soviet-style communism, which had substituted "the masses" for God, a new threat was quick to emerge, courtesy of zealots bent on murder who invoked the name of Allah, determined to annihilate all infidels in order to establish Islam as the universal creed. The West, and America in particular, jolted out of its self-satisfied conviction that history had come to an end with the demise of the USSR, scrambled to find ways of engaging in interfaith dialogue, and found it in the shared ancestry of Abraham. Nobody thought of going further back. And few seemed to remember that before we even think about engaging in an inter-civilization dialogue, we need to first pay attention to Islam's majority population: women.

While their inferior status is obvious especially in highly authoritarian Muslim societies, such practices as female genital mutilation and old men marrying prepubescent girls are not uncommon throughout the Muslim world. The violent Taliban, a mutation spawned by the horrific Afghan War against the Soviets during the 1980s with American, Saudi, and Pakistani backing, are practically at war with the sex.

As long as fanatics mistreat and even torture their own wives and daughters, there is little hope for the rest of us. Revisiting the basic concept of human reciprocity, which underlies the *Genesis* account of creation adopted by the Quran, in fact addresses the entire spiritual basis of ethical conduct.

At the risk of seeming to imply moral equivalence (nothing could be further from the truth), I must note that the pathology of feminine identity poisons even the self-righteously liberal West. Of course, the United States, the leader of modern civilization, has come farther than any other nation in history in celebrating human potential, embracing God's creation to its fullest. But success is not always conducive to spirituality, and America's complex legacy has left us searching for our true identity. Many modern American women—and men for that matter—are confused. Oscillating between male envy, which we might call androphilia (from the Greek words for man, *andro,* and love, *philo*), at one extreme and male hatred—androphobia—at another, the underlying reason may well be an unwarranted sense of inferiority. It is hard not to have been affected, even subconsciously, by a millennia-old antifeminine bias. We tend to forget that even in America women did not obtain the right to vote until the first quarter of the twentieth century—many decades after the African American male minority. I believe that American women would do well to revisit, as indeed would their male counterparts, their biblical prototype, Eve, whom Adam honored as "the giver of life."

Recent scholarly studies by Jewish, Christian, and Muslim scholars convincingly demonstrate the egalitarian description of *Genesis* in the Jewish Bible—the Tanakh, known to Christians as the Old Testament—as well as in the Quran. The latter is especially fascinating in light of Salafi, Wahhabi, and other "fundamentalist" interpretations of Islam that, however debatable, have come to be widely accepted. Reconsidering the idea of mutual love and respect among men and women and a commitment to intimacy and connection as central to Islam's beginnings provides an important conceptual basis for reform in that culture.

Finally, this book draws upon a wide variety of sources from the history of religion, comparative mythology, psychology, and literature in order to draw out the emotional and ethical relevance of the twin nature of the soul. Notable among them is the "Psyche-Eros" aspect of the *Genesis* narrative, based on the Greek myth about the marriage of beautiful Psyche ("soul" in Latin) with the God of Love (known as Cupid to the Romans), son of Aphrodite (Venus to the Romans), Goddess of Beauty. The wonderful prebiblical story of Gilgamesh and Enkidu, among other spiritual antecedents, will also help us better understand the context of the *Genesis* narrative. Intimacy and empathy, compassion, and respect form the basis of morality and spirituality.

If there is any hope for civilization, for an uplifting, ennobling, and worthwhile human community to emerge out of the current cacophony of strife, debasement, nihilism, and fanaticism, I believe we must start by revisiting the original vision of our two fore-parents. And that means we must start with resurrecting Eve. Without her, Adam would have been without a soulmate, or as the Bible puts it, a "fitting helper." To love another as himself, Adam had to start by loving his kin spirit, figuratively if not indeed literally, flesh of his flesh—soul of his soul. And since God had simultaneously whispered the infinite Spirit of Creation into both of them, did they not in turn become God's soulmates? An awesome, humbling thought, but so it is—and so it can be, again.

Prologue

I encountered my first Bible without knowing what it was. In communist Romania where I grew up, Hebrew was outlawed. (That is not a joke. When my curious little sister happened on my father's secret grammar book—he was teaching himself Hebrew in case we would ever be allowed to emigrate to Israel, though after some fifteen years of waiting, he had pretty much given up hope—he told her it was Chinese.) So its strange, beautiful letters meant little to me. But I understood how much they meant to my grandmother, who would fetch the tiny jewel of a book on Friday evenings before she lit candles in near darkness, keeping it nearby without actually opening it—almost as if the little book were a kind of witness.

She would first cover her white hair with an intricately embroidered kerchief that I never saw her wear on any other occasion. Then, she would slowly run her hands over the candles that flickered high in the tall golden candleholders, while she softly murmured, eyes closed, tears flowing quietly over her light cheeks. She shook a little as she cried without as much as a sound, but since it didn't take much for my grandmother to start crying, I didn't worry. She even seemed to smile sometimes as she cried; it never crossed my mind that she did so for my sake—perhaps to prevent my asking any questions. Then came the magical book: she would take it up closer to the flame to see better, and then she would start reading. Or maybe she seemed to be reading, I wasn't quite sure, since she could hold the book open and speak while her eyes would close again. It seemed to me that the book had a power beyond the text itself, though I couldn't fathom how. Eerie, I thought, confirming once again my grandmother's magical credentials already established beyond dispute in both the culinary and the healing arts.

It was a gorgeous object: hardly larger than a cigarette case, the pages of the minuscule tome had golden edges that glittered in the dim light of the Sabbath candles. Its cover was of thick ivory with an intricate carved scroll, finer than the broach my mother kept in a small blue velvet box, and its filigreed old clasp closed gently like a bracelet. I was afraid that if I opened such a clasp, I might not be able to shut it again, though I would have loved to know what the little book contained: Maybe even pictures? I asked my grandmother, but she didn't answer; instead, she hugged me close to her and said I didn't have to think about it yet. I had no idea what I was supposed to wait for. When would it be the right time?

The time did come, eventually. But not before I learned other stories that helped me navigate the oceans of experience, steering my little boat while the winds of unexpected storms threatened to run me off course, whatever that may have been. I found a compass in magical myths. I found it in the wise story of Psyche, the ballads of my home country, the hills of Transylvania, the fables of Aesop, and folk tales. After immigrating to the United States as a teenager, I discovered the novels of Nathaniel Hawthorne, Edith Wharton, and John Steinbeck; the poetry of Walt Whitman and Edna St. Vincent Millay; and creation utopias used both in earnest, as by Immanuel Kant, and ironically, by Mark Twain. And I finally read The Book itself: *Biblia Sacra*. The simple, tectonic first sentence shook with symphonic thunder: "IN THE BEGINNING . . . ." A mere lifetime later, I would finally come to understand why the book had meant so much to my grandmother.

Where better to seek the meaning of human existence than in its first pages: the magical narrative of Adam and Eve. This story captures as does no other, before or since, the profound moral drama that has defined the purpose of humanity. Nowhere is the intimate relationship between man and God, as mirrored in the first marriage, described more ingeniously than in the words of that brief yet amazingly complex biblical narrative. Viewed in its full historical and cultural context, it helps us find a universal common human link capable of bridging seeming differences between the great monotheistic religions where originally none existed—and none should.

This is not to imply that ultimate "peace on earth" is a realistic possibility; we humans are an angry, passionate lot and, for all our genius, pretty stupid. But I put my trust in the unquenchable human thirst for meaning and purpose. No other species seeks and needs transcendence as we do. *With Thee, I am; without Thee, I am nothing.*

Salvation may not be for everyone, but without even its hope, there seems no point in living. Each one of us can feel that being is its own argument: I am, therefore I cannot help but yearn for God.

But who is God? And why has God created me? Why me, and why now? We cannot help wondering, lest we should wander aimlessly, to nowhere in particular. Man is a traveler in need of destination, and the story of *Genesis* can lead the way. What other reason need there be to revisit our first ancestors?

More specifically, let us start with Eve. But don't get me wrong: it's not *all* about Eve, anymore than it was ever all about Adam. Indeed, there precisely is the rub: it was never about Eve *as opposed* to Adam. Revisiting our first ancestors requires revising the picture of Eve that dominates the whole of Western culture today. Without claiming anything like an originalist or "fundamentalist" interpretation, I suggest reading the impetus behind the creation of the first couple as representing the inseparable, twin image of God.

The battle of the sexes and Eve's preeminent role in damnation came later, after *Genesis* was recast by some of its misguided interpreters in a skewed image projected on to an anthropomorphized figure of the "Father" Creator. The result has been nothing short of tragic—for men nearly as much as for women. Denigrating some members of the human family as inherently inferior affects the rest. Failure to appreciate the true reasons for the sanctity of life and the dignity of every human being is, after all, at the core of all violence. While degrading Eve comes close to moral suicide, resurrecting her permits not only a more accurate reading of the original story, it also helps recapture the true essence of our common humanity which, without her, is quite simply inconceivable.

This is obviously true in communities that purport to observe Islam most faithfully. It entails abolishing the barbaric—and definitely *not* Muslim—practice of what is known euphemistically as female circumcision, the prohibition against women attending school and working, to say nothing of the unfathomably barbaric practice of being killed by their own brothers and fathers for the "crime" of having been raped. Eventually, Muslim women may be granted civil and political liberties equal to their male compatriots. But reinstating woman to her rightful place as man's soulmate is intimately linked to man's inhumanity to other human beings in general: both result from utter disregard for the spiritual basis for life. To be sure, spirituality is difficult to define and harder still to experience, feel, trust, and apply it. Difficult, yes, but not impossible.

The approach I take in this book has evolved slowly. So slowly, in fact, that at times, it looked like the writer's version of my grandmother's theory of the *matzo* ball. (That theory was quite simple. Enervating to impatient onlookers like me and my sister, she would roll each little ball around and around in an elusive quest for a Platonic Idea of Absolute Roundness, till we were so hungry we would steal into the pantry and OD on pickles.) One thing I was certain: I wasn't interested in simply resurrecting woman as against man, but understanding how both had been created in God's image—which is to say, woman *alongside* man. Would I be fated to unearthing stories of competition, where *she* was victorious over *him*? Naturally, I loved those stories. History is replete with tales of gutsy, brilliant, wild wolf women and sundry goddesses that make for terrific mother–daughter bonding anecdotes, to say nothing of bibliographic ammunition against otherwise overbearing males who are yet easily intimidated by such overwhelming evidence of deep erudition. But it wasn't anywhere close to what I was really seeking.

I was frustrated by those militant feminists who urged women to overthrow the yolk of oppression by men, at one extreme, and by antifeminists, content with playing second fiddle to their macho mates, at the other. Even the so-called middle ground which holds, sensibly, that men and women are equal and unequal, respectively, in all the right places misses the point. For it is neither a question of which is better, A or E, nor whether A = E, but that A and E are spiritually *one* before their infinite Creator. It is neither A nor E but a mutual transformation through a transcendent relationship that itself was created in God's image.

Disillusioned with all traditional religions for what they see as their ineradicable misogyny, some feminists have opted for the obverse—an unrepentant, if not outright pathological, misandry (hatred of males). In his 1985 book *Eve: The History of an Idea*,[1] John A. Phillips describes feminism in at least one of its more activist forms as "the truly revolutionary movement of the twentieth century, because it cannot be reconciled with Western religion" as evidenced by its irrevocably jaundiced view of Eve. Unfortunately, writes Phillips, they go even one step further, selecting to "discover among themselves what they could not find in the company of men." How tragic; for if the result is Adam-hatred in the place of Eve-hatred, what has been gained? Two irreconcilable gender teams; score: zip–zip. No game. No winners.

Phillips warns that irredentist feminists "could fall victim to various ideologized forms of self worship."[2] Viewed in that light, the feminist project to resurrect the Great Goddess (in fact, a plurality of such goddesses, in different premodern cultures) allegedly "killed" by the One Male God who took Her place is hardly a spiritual advance over its corollary—glorification of the masculine. Writes Phillips:

> Man was reminded in the Old Testament that God was God and not Man, but feminists have not been ready to tell themselves that Goddess is not Woman. To these criticisms, feminists reply that the Goddess image is indispensable; it frees women from the damaging image of the male God and provides the focal point for the construction of a nonsexist alternative religion.[3]

Yet surely "religion" is not the right word for what is at bottom a battle for symbolic supremacy. By contrast, the true traditional function of religion is spiritual, personal nourishment. Rejecting the possibility that Goddesses can be resurrected at will, Phillips's own conclusion is chillingly Nietzschean: if God is dead, how much more so is the Goddess, whose demise preceded his by centuries.

> It would appear that the two religious events are inseparable: The Death of God, and the Death of the Goddess. Since the history of Eve was so closely bound to the latter, the religious experience of women over several thousand years should tell us something about the former. If it is true that God is dead, Eve and feminism will still have much to teach us about the future possibilities of religion and our common life.[4]

In effect, this amounts to spiritual capitulation. The allegedly self-evident assumption that both the God and the Goddess are "dead" is replaced by no discernable transcendent core. Why call this "religion" at all? It looks more like sociology.

If God is conceived in anthropomorphic terms, some theory of "His" sexuality is inescapable. And if a humanoid God is neither a He nor a She (setting aside, at least for now, the theory that God is both), the only alternative would be that God . . . does not exist at all. Yet instead of rejecting the Creator's existence, shouldn't we rather question anthropomorphism itself? That was in fact what Judaism thought it was doing: the Torah specifically warns on several occasions against too literal an interpretation of language that is metaphorical at its very core. God as the Author of the world and the Creator of mankind is not a superhuman creature, a kind of Zeus without an entourage.

Judaism introduced a revolutionary idea—namely, a spiritual, nameless, yet personal Creator—later adopted by both Christianity and Islam. And while all three monotheisms recognized spiritual intermediaries, from Moses and Abraham to Christ and Mohammed, the same Infinite First Mover suffuses all three faiths, informing their conception of human purpose guided by an ultimately inconceivable (i.e., unimaginable) Higher Being. In order to understand the latter, therefore, what we must revisit is the concept of spirituality linking mankind to God, as mirrored in the relationship between man and woman. Put more simply, the connection of soul and soulmate explains the relationship of soul and Soul Source. But how could we better grasp its meaning once again in a contemporary context in a manner that addresses twenty-first century political and cultural challenges, in terms that would inspire the climactic ecstasy of recognition?

At last I got lucky and stumbled upon a few seminal discoveries. Among the deepest insights came from fellow University of Chicago alumni, professors Amy and Leon Kass, co-authors of a wonderful anthology about marriage and courtship. Leon's bestselling *Beginning of Wisdom: Reading Genesis* truly opened my eyes. Next came the joyous surprise of both C. S. Lewis's *Four Loves* and Michael Novak's essay about *caritas*, "The Love that Moves the Sun." I knew then that I was finally on the right track.

No less inspiring were the writings of several extraordinary Muslim women, notably the witty, insightful Moroccan scholar, writer, political reformer Fatima Mernissi; the courageous Ayaan Hirsi Ali, who revealed her personal trauma to help us understand the plight of tortured little girls fated to become women mutilated in both body and soul; and the fiercely independent Muslim professor of comparative literature Azar Nafisi, who refused to wear a veil and opted to quit her post at the university under the tyrannical late Ayatollah Khomeini, eventually emigrating to the United States where I had the pleasure of meeting her.

In her masterfully written bestseller *Reading Lolita in Tehran*, Nafisi revealed the universal appeal of genuine love, the insatiable desire to know and be oneself, as well as the psychopathology of fanatic radical Islamism. Hirsi Ali exposed the danger of misguided multicultural Western liberalism that gives shelter, however inadvertently, to brutality against fellow human beings under the guise of religious tolerance. And finally, Fatima Mernissi, in her brilliant slim volume *Scheherazade Goes West: Different Cultures, Different Harems*, chides with subtle insight and even a touch of humor the Western inability to appreciate fully how insidious is the deeply entrenched double-standard lying just under the surface of presumed sexual equality in the West.

Yet Mernissi does not opt for a strident feminism; instead, she argues in favor of reconsidering what true intimacy really means, even suggesting that the West can actually learn a thing or two from classical Islam. I was especially taken with her autobiographical classic *Dreams of Trespass: Tales of a Harem Girlhood*, whose main theme is the desire to leave the prison of home through what she calls "trespassing" – meaning, *to learn all about* the world, to be a part of it, to feel, to be fully human. "To know or not to know?" For Mernissi, the question answers itself and leads not to damnation but, quite the contrary, to salvation.

It was in the "Note to the Western Reader," from her immensely popular book *Beyond the Veil: Male-Female Dynamics in Modern Muslim Society*, however, that she explains her methodology most clearly: "I am not concerned with contrasting the way women are treated in the Muslim East with the way they are treated in the Christian West. I believe that sexual inequality is the basis of both systems. My aim is not to clarify which situation is better, but to understand the sexual dynamics of the Muslim world."[5]

This is not moral equivalence; she does not deny that there are differences, indeed great ones, between the two civilizations. Nor is it relativism, which uses the pretext of open-mindedness and holier-than-thou cultural so-called sensitivity to obliterate moral standards. Rather, Mernissi is making a perfectly legitimate philosophical and psychological point that she proceeds to defend through a series of marvelous books and a lifetime of activities that speak for themselves. She explains her approach in *Beyond the Veil*: "Nor am I concerned with analyzing women as an entity separate from men; rather, I try to explore the male-female relation as a component of the Muslim system, a basic element of its structure."

> It appears to me that the Muslim system is not so much opposed to women as an entity separate from men as to the heterosexual unit. What is feared is the growth of an involvement between a man and a woman into an all-encompassing love satisfying the sexual, emotional and intellectual needs of both partners. Such an involvement constitutes a direct threat to man's allegiance to Allah, which requires the unconditional investment of all his energies, thoughts, and feelings in his God.[6]

The Jewish Essenes and Christian Shakers come to mind. Mernissi advocates taking a second look not merely at Eve but at Eve *and* Adam, as created *together* in God's image. Aha! The *matzo* ball was ready to be dropped in my literary chicken soup.

To resurrect Eve is to redefine the nature of human love not only for one another but for man toward his—and her—Creator, which restores meaning to all life. It's about God creating a soulmate for "Him"self as well as for us, God's human children, for one another.

Eve taught Adam many things just as he did her, but above all, they taught each other how to face the hardest possible knowledge: that inescapable awareness of the reality and inevitability of death, and the compensatory beauty of the world—more exquisite for our brief presence in its mist. The realization of temporality can lead to madness or saintliness, to evil and murder or to boundless compassion and generosity. But when the Creator is invoked to justify the most unspeakable cruelties, turning to hatred in the name of divine love, to torture in the name of Creation, when men defile, humiliate, and even kill their own women in the name of "morality," when spirituality is a cover for bloodlust, when suicide is glorified and death is worshipped with barbaric pleasure, revisiting one of the most cherished sources of human identity so as to revive its original message is not merely edifying: it is urgent.

Notes

1. John A. Phillips, *Eve: The History of an Idea*, 174.
2. Ibid., 175.
3. Ibid., 176.
4. Ibid.
5. Fatima Mernissi, *Beyond the Veil: Male-Female Dynamics in Modern Muslim Society*, 8.
6. Ibid.

Part I

Male and Female He Created Them

1

Once upon a Time

Myth is not the same as history; myths are not inspiring stories of people who lived notable lives. No, myth is the transcendent in relationship to the present. . . . And the problem is to open the words, to open the images so that they point past themselves.
Joseph Campbell, Pathways to Bliss

Myth as Sacred Metaphor

The magic of the incantation "once upon a time" has coaxed into Dreamland many a toddler determined to defy the ridiculous insistence of adults on going to sleep just as goblins are ready to play tricks. Nothing works magic quite as effectively as an invitation to pretend we are in another world, and "once upon a time" has just the right ring to it: once, never again, yet always; upon a time—any time, every time our imagination is ready to take on wings again . . . and again.

The equivalent of this fairy tale prologue in my melodic native Romanian[1] reads something like this: "There was once, as if there had never been, because if it had not, it wouldn't be told." Yes, it is just as awkward in Romanian, but the charming Latin rhythm and rhyme almost lull you into overlooking the possibility that maybe, just maybe, "it" didn't *really* happen: "As if there hadn't been" . . . . Acknowledging the intrusion of doubt, the attempt to dispel it rests on the subtly ironic, obviously shaky argument that if "it" had been mere fiction . . . it wouldn't have been told! (Full disclosure: it's not much funnier in the original . . . just mildly mischievous enough to amuse a toddler.)

And yet, deep wisdom lies hidden in that little stanza. For if something has been told, perhaps for centuries, doesn't that fact alone reveal a truth far more profound than any mere objective observation of a humdrum occurrence? Doesn't an entrenched narrative contain an essence of priceless wisdom, a moral, a hidden reality revealed by

3

means of pictures and suspense, through fantastical conflicts and their equally fantastical resolution?

The world we live in—which we could call modern, except that just about every generation has thought of itself that way at least since the Renaissance—has trouble with that kind of reality. One thing seems manifest: seduced by empirical observation, addicted to prediction, self-described modern man has embarked on a dogged, almost desperate quest for the Holy Grail of science and technology. It almost looks like he's getting his revenge by making the best of it in the here and now, implicitly getting back at the God who seemed to promise us blissful, or at any event, uneventful, paradise only to snatch it away almost immediately. And what had been our crime? Yes, it's true; we foolishly partook of an especially delicious-looking and manifestly nourishing item not on the menu, yet highly endorsed by a smooth-tongued reptile. And yes, it is true that the Chief Chef had expressly forbidden us to touch it. But did we deserve such a terminal punishment?

To make it worse, our Author simultaneously rendered us fully aware of our own mortality while expelling us. Can it be that the obsessive human search for answers to question after empirical question is really our way of attempting to master the universe by establishing our supremacy over the elements, by using our quasi-divine Reason to conquer the mysteries—and thus, in the most important sense, "*rule over*" —dumb Nature in imitation of our Holy Godparent?

Modern—or, if you prefer, "postmodern"—man fancies that he takes fate into his own, presumably rational hands. However, worshipping Reason and nothing but Reason is dangerous: if "I think therefore I am" is turned on its head to mean "Unless I think, I am not," we may find ourselves ignoring our most important assets: the instruments of heart and soul. While searching for answers, we may forget why we asked the question in the first place. To rely on reason alone, we may lose it altogether.

Not that we moderns or even postmoderns don't like taking time off from reasoning, to play. No man, however civilized, can survive without at least occasionally turning off the logic machine and resort to diversions, to what some like to call "entertainment." But at the end of the day, almost no one can really do without some kind of purpose, however subconscious. Beyond reason, and certainly beyond entertainment, there is the question of value and purpose, morality and meaning. For such matters, we tend to turn to religions, customs, and traditions, invoking history and family, the comforts of home—in short, whatever seems to rescue our pitiably lost selves. To invoke the title of a clever recent movie by secular philosopher and jazz-loving producer–actor Woody Allen: *Whatever Works.*

We try hard. We pray to be delivered from the demons of uncertainty—such a shameful abyss. There is at least one sure, albeit temporary, solution: if you cannot bear to be lost, declare yourself found, and call the place sacred: "Drive-in" salvation at a discount. Alas, it doesn't work for everybody! Most of us have trouble kidding ourselves about God's purpose. We cannot help asking and re-asking the question: Why us? Why is there mankind?

And so we should. Each one of us has to learn how to be human, as if we were each created anew from metaphorical dust. Every baby's world looks miraculous to its incredulous, astonished little eyes—and, with a little luck, stays that way for a long time. But each of us soon becomes overwhelmed in due course by the recognition of the irreversible, irrevocable end. We have to reinvent or rediscover or rename—pick your word—the Creator, as well as—for each of us—a brand *new* world, as best we can.

Millennia of wisdom may come in handy, but without a money-back guarantee of success, especially if we insist on using nothing but logic and fact. Those tools are powerless when the bell tolls late into the night, and tolls for you. To accept God's grace, what is required is not literal language, not number and causality. The faculty best suited for transcendence is not reason—certainly not reason alone. Called "imagination" by some, "the wings of soul," or simply "the heart," catching a glimpse of some nuggets of wisdom, the self asks each of us to step beyond. Like it or not, we all stand in need of—what else?—*metaphor*: the transformation of "as if" into "*really* is—even if I cannot exactly see what, or where." Reality transcends perception: to be is not merely to be perceived. It is to be felt, in the core of your very being.

The fundamental questions of value and human purpose, which we certainly can't "see" in any ordinary sense of the word, are impossible to capture by descriptive names or labels. If all we care about is the "what," we won't understand the "why." Nature alone can disclose no clear purpose, no matter how exquisite its stormy oceans, how awe-inspiring its glaciers and crystals, or how color-blessed a moonlit valley carpeted with intricate, delicate flowers. Descriptive language goes far, but stops at the gate of the soul. And the soul is left still longing for meaning.

The hidden caverns of the subjective, found only very deep within each heart, dissolve if subjected to the blinding light of plain cold fact. Facts drain reality of all but the bare necessaries to communicate without ambiguity and to accumulate information. What is, just . . . *is*; no more. Plain-talk scratches only the surface of plain-being. The deeper, inner caverns are not impossible to reach, but they reveal themselves rather through parables and double meanings in stories that are not quite what they seem, and in histories that happened long ago or foreshadow what might still be—usually both at once. Fortunately, prodded even a little, the soul readily responds to the magic of myth.

Aah, the seduction of myth . . . At first, *mythos* in ancient Greece denoted little more than a narrative or plot, basically a sequential ordering of words. But it was not long before the word resonated with poetry, as a *mythological narrative* came to refer to a story relating events in the lives of the deities. It soon described not just any plot but a particular genre of fantastic tales with spiritual content, what today we call a particular culture's mythology—Greek, Egyptian, Assyrian, and so on. Narratives, in turn, became further differentiated into "histories," on the one hand, and "stories," on the other: the former involved personalities (whether human or divine) whose narratives ran parallel to a sequence of external events that might be uncovered by archeologists, while the latter appeared to be constructed for their own sake. In other words, the former were objective while the latter were subjective—that is to say, fictional. A *history*, then, took place against a background of "real" events, while a *story* was basically made-up or imagined—as in "a likely story" (wink-wink).

With the advent of rationalism and modernity, history rose in prestige even as stories sank to the lowly status of mere *make-believe*—"make" implying deliberate deception. The celebrated literary critic Northrop Frye observed that, in time, myth "tended to become attached only to the latter [i.e., fictional stories], and hence to mean 'not really true'" (Read: lies). This, he argues, is "a vulgarism for many reasons":[2] for, above all, it misses a crucial aspect of human psychology, the religious sentiment that enriches and sustains the soul. By demoting myth to the status of falsehood, even semi-falsehood, when so-called objective reality alone is recognized as legitimate, what mankind lost is the ability to adequately express yearning and possibility. Yet are those not the ingredients of wonder, terror, and hope?

For the sake of historical perspective, Frye reminds his readers that among the stories of ancient, preverbal cultures, some had greater social significance than others. The most influential were "stories that tell a society what is important for it to know, whether about its gods, its history, its laws, or its class structure. These stories may be called myths in a secondary sense, a sense that distinguishes them from folktales—stories told [purely] for entertainment or other less central purposes." Writing in *The Great Code: The Bible as Literature* in 1981, Frye argued that myths are "sacred" stories, as distinguished from the latter "profane," suggesting that "[i]n Western Europe the Bible stories had a central mythical significance of this kind until at least the eighteenth century."[3]

Describing the most revered book in Western civilization as a myth, however, is not meant to belittle it but to capture the fact that at issue is a very different, indeed *higher*, kind of truth. Far from considering biblical and other similar stories to be in any sense fact-challenged, Frye emphatically asserts that the opposite is the case: a sacred myth "means being charged with a special seriousness and importance."[4] What *is* transcends what *seems*. What touches the heart, touches the soul. And what am I, if not my soul?

Frye's entire career was devoted to emphasizing the importance and validity of *all* types of literary discourse; he argued passionately that no story, no matter how "profane," is entirely devoid of truth. At the same time, he insisted that sacred stories or myths are *especially* true, for they are far more significant and life-changing than mere literal discourse. Calling them myths simply clarifies their far wider reach, beyond literal truth to the profound reality of emotion. It does not denigrate them; on the contrary, it sets them on the highest pedestal. They give us not merely descriptions, as does science, but explanations and meaning. For fact, we live; for meaning, we are ready to die.

Admittedly, most people associate mythology with ancient primitive cultures, with the image of illiterates huddling in caves, hunting and gathering to survive. "Primitive" certainly has a negative connotation: we, heaven forbid, are anything but that! So when Frye dares to suggest that modern humans share primal fears and desires with their, well . . . primitive ancestors, he is on dangerous territory. Taking aim at fellow academics first, Frye charges that "it apparently takes social scientists much longer than poets or critics to realize that every mind is a primitive mind, whatever the varieties of social conditioning."[5]

But rather than meaning to offend, he pleads for equal tolerance of poetry and mystery.

After all, what makes us so smugly certain that only "objective" reality is true? On the contrary, "objective" and "subjective" are little more than poles at the extremities on a continuum along the spectrum of *human experience.* That continuity should justify the profound relevance of such sacred texts as the book of *Genesis* not only for faith-challenged agnostics but even self-proclaimed atheists. Argues Frye, "whenever we move from the obviously legendary to the possibly historical, we never cross a clear boundary line. That is, the sense of historical fact as such is simply not delimited in the Bible, anywhere."[6] In other words, what we think happened, what has come down through the ages as commonly held belief about what happened, and what "actually" happened in the distant past of human history cannot be differentiated with ironclad precision. Tradition is a rainbow from one end of the human horizon to the other, the heavens reflected throughout, within every heart.

In brief, the Bible is not true or false in the way that a chemistry text may be said to contain true or false statements. To think otherwise is not only to trivialize the great book but to endanger its ability to be taken seriously, let alone inspire. Frye is justified in applying the word "myth" to stories whose import has influenced the way millions of people, for thousands of years, throughout the globe understood and organized their lives by finding meaning and purpose in special narratives. *Genesis* in particular has captured the imagination of our forefathers as well as our foremothers (a word whose comical ring is most unwarranted) as have all of the stories, narratives, and folktales cited in this book. They are all significant precisely because they have been *thought* to be such. As the Romanian incantation has it: "If it hadn't been, it wouldn't be told." What is more, the telling makes it be again, and again, every time it is retold.

The truth of a mythical narrative is reflected in the telling and the re-telling, enriching the lives of those to whom they are sacred. This is by no means to embrace relativism, or an "anything-is-true-if-someone-thinks-it-so" nihilism. That would be to repudiate the distinction between good and evil altogether, and with it any ability to distinguish civilized from uncivilized life—in other words, relegating humans to the status of beasts. I categorically reject such a position, not only for being sacrilegious but as intellectually bankrupt. The fuller story, to paraphrase Scheherazade, will be told on another night. For now, a metaphor will have to suffice.

That metaphor is the story of human creation, which I take to be a spiritual response to the central human question: *why mankind?* Unable entirely to forget about it, each of us is endowed with the magical ability to transform the frustrating interrogation into a thrilling quest. That quest is much enhanced by a pithy fable that may guide us along the unmarked, unpaved road of life. And sacred stories that might differ a little from one religion or culture to another yet share a common core should not be condemned as irreconcilable, as proof of inevitable civilizational clash; instead, we should rejoice in their similar underlying message. Different sacred stories may well diverge in details; but what they have in common is of far greater essence. We each cover the hole in our hearts as best we can, with different garments; still the hole gnaws at us all.

But what about the most important claim of all, made by deeply religious individuals, that a sacred book contains the precise words of God? I will not quarrel with such a claim, noting merely that its recorders were themselves human. In other words, even a sacred Word must be rendered into human language, which can only be imprecise, and subject to human interpretation, which comes in multiple versions. However perfect our Author may be, we cannot escape our selves, our minds, and our imperfections, no matter how hard we try and how eagerly we wish it.

While sacred stories may carry their own special truth, they reveal an even deeper message: protagonists of one may appear clad in very different garments and walk along seemingly divergent paths than do those of another, yet all arrive at what is at root the same destination. A sacred mythological narrative that helps us transcend despair, hatred (including, not least, self-hatred), and fear allows human beings to share their common fate as intelligent, creative mortals, with gratitude and compassion. Such a narrative is *Genesis*.

Psychology Tackles Metaphor

Sacred myth satisfies the psyche as no empirical hypothesis, which resorts to nothing but hard data, ever could. The science of the mind, which happens to be the literal meaning of "psychology" (in Greek, *psyche* and *logos* refer to, respectively, the mind, and science or study)—is in fact not so much science as art. Though a young discipline, psychology has long struggled to penetrate the paradoxical nature of the mind, which is at once a biological product and a ghostly other substance.

It seems highly ironic that Fascism and Nazism arose in civilized Western Europe roughly simultaneously with the most innovative advances in the understanding of mental phenomena. How could Austria, the land of chocolate and Mozart, have spawned the diabolical, genocidal Fuhrer at the same time as the brilliant, empathetic student of autism Bruno Bettelheim? And it was another fellow-Austrian, Sigmund Freud, along with his erstwhile Swiss colleague Carl Gustav Jung, who revolutionized the discipline that delved into the subconscious catacombs of the human personality with its unfathomable potential for evil.

Could it be that just as irrationality reached its peak in the political arena, others were trying to grasp its monumentally devastating powers of destruction? Western civilization almost succumbed to the Satanic monster, whose eventual suicide provided far too merciful an exit. At the same time, countless martyrs risked everything to help others—to shelter a child from the executioner, or bring a piece of bread to the skeletal inmate of a concentration camp—defying instant execution. How could the human brain spawn both mind-boggling evil and saintly sacrifice?

While both Jung and Freud sought to decipher man's inner life through dreams and other products of the imagination, the differences between these two giants of the new discipline were profound: while Freud started with neuroses, the pathological, the warped mind, rather than the "normal," Jung focused on the healthy psyche, positing a vigorous subconscious life which cannot be neglected without missing the engine of creative emotional reality. Freud viewed the *id* (his word for the unconscious) as capable of tormenting the human soul. Near the end of his life, as he lay dying of cancer, which coincided with the perverse anti-Semitism that failed to alert the West to its own malignancy, he posited the existence of a death instinct alongside the life-enhancing *libido*.

By contrast, Jung applauded the active subconscious, the powerful imagination, for organizing action by defining the fundamental categories of positive, life-enhancing purpose. Paraphrasing Blaise Pascal's dictum that *"la raison a des raisons que la raison ne connait point"* (reason has reasons that reason doesn't know), Jung argued that we all possess insights we cannot notice unless we take off our blinders. The way to reach the unconscious, indeed the "collective unconscious" shared by all humanity, according to Jung, is through archetypes that reveal basic, universal feelings and thoughts.

Those archetypes, suggests Jung, are found in sacred texts—their sacredness is a reflection of a deep psychic resonance and truth that both inspires and illustrates their timeless validity. He writes, "It is of especial importance for me to know as much as possible about primitive psychology, mythology, archaeology and comparative religion, for the reason that these fields afford me priceless analogies with which I can enrich the associations of my patients."[7] These priceless analogies are the currency of subliminal communication—interpersonal and, no less important, intrapersonal: we discover ourselves no less than one another, in mystery and myth. We know who we are by learning who mankind is and was.

Analogy as metaphor is indispensable even to the data-worshipping scientist. We may progress into deeper knowledge only by transcending the present, visible, and superficial. In order to formulate new hypotheses heretofore deemed absurd, we must resort to metaphor, and not just occasionally. The astronomers' incomprehensible black hole, for example, has virtually nothing in common with the pitch-dark tunnel I helped my friend dig in his backyard when his grandma wasn't looking, yet what an apt description of a "break" in the universe that—most counter-intuitively—sucks in matter and turns it into energy! Stephen Hawking's mind-bending explanations of the unbounded-yet-finite universe, and the pairing of matter with antimatter, stretch language to its limits.

To be sure, coming up with analogies and new meanings for old words should be done sparingly in the natural sciences—only when necessary to navigate across categories for the purpose of resetting connections, or to advance and test a whole new theory when the old one no longer does the job. Fortunately, the same hesitancy need not apply to exploring life within: here, by contrast, metaphor, as the very engine of poetry, is absolutely key.

Without metaphor there is no way to capture yearning in words, no dream, no spirituality. We escape the mundane on wings of fancy. The soul, even more than astrophysics, defies the truth–values of classic symbolic logic—true versus false, 1 versus 0 in computer lingo—with no middle ground. The soul basks in metamorphosis like a fickle butterfly, dismissing tight-knit syllogisms in exchange for casual

11

ambiguities, and delighting in vagueness with abandon, as if diving into a wind-torn cloud. The soul feeds on the stuff of great literature and timeless sacred text: without such nourishment, it shrivels without a whimper and too easily becomes outright demonic.

So we may turn to *Genesis* once more to learn not how but *why*, to learn not who the first mother or father was, exactly, but rather whom we must emulate to be not merely alive but fully human. Then we should find that Eve embraces each of her symbolic daughters, and Adam all his sons, with the comfort of ritual.

Each of us rehearses in our own life the first marriage, if only sub-liminally, sometimes so unlike *Genesis* that we can hardly recognize the link. Yet in ways that may not reveal themselves readily, we are their kin and, just like them, God's image on this earth.

And God Said, "Let There Be . . ."

God is day and night, winter and summer, war and peace, satiety and
want.
Heraclitus, Fragments *(c. 500 BCE)*

What must have it been like in the beginning of time, before there was time, before there was a beginning, before there was night, or anything at all? The mind has to stretch to accommodate the thought. Anyway, what does it matter how and why it all got started? Not everybody cares. Or in any event, not everybody remembers that once it did. Can you recall when, as a child, you found everything amazing and thought everything had—and had to have—an answer? Even if you happened not to know what that answer was, someone a lot bigger than you probably would.

The answer definitely mattered to my small son Alex. He had not been speaking too many months when he asked me, out of the blue, "Mom, where did everything come from?" A bit unprepared, I asked him why he wanted to know, but he just shrugged: grown-ups and their questions! He just . . . did. I could have made it up, or like a proper suburban mother jump on the chance to encourage him to take up science and engineering, but instead I just told him that, actually, I didn't know. Without even blinking, he asked next, "You mean you weren't there?" Though long past thirty, I didn't take it personally: his question was perfectly sensible. I obviously had been around before *his* beginning; how was he to know for exactly *how long* before? He was just a little guy. I tried to explain that I wasn't the only one who didn't know, but stopped short of telling him that actually no one knew because the question itself defied definitive answer. Or to put it differently, that an answer would have to come in something other than a date on the calendar.

We read in the Bible that God had launched the universe by will, pure and simple: "In the beginning God created heaven and earth— the earth being unformed and void, with darkness over the surface of the deep and a wind from God sweeping over the water." But another translation has it that God created the universe by speaking, so to speak: "In the beginning . . . God *said*, 'Let there be light'; and there was light" (Italics added). Either way, first there was God and, before anything else, The Spoken Word.[8] That is to say, even before it was written down, The Word *WAS*.

But since God is already Everything, we are back to the first question: was there anything *before* God—which is to say, before everything? It should not surprise that among the most commonly heard answers is that God is infinite and infinity is forever (again, so to speak). But surely such words turn into mere sound and impression, trepidation or hope or dream, for how can we ever hope to understand them? The mind fails in the attempt. The heart has to take over and intuit with the certainty of faith or instinct or transcendent conviction that in the Beginning there was Being, Fire, Energy, Light, Beauty, Power. And, most of all, miraculously, at some apocalyptic point, there was Life. But what that means must forever elude us. For, in the words of *über*-astronomer Stephen Hawking, "the ultimate triumph of human reason" would be to "know the mind of God."[9] No such luck.

Unless such knowledge comes not by reason but is miraculously kindled within each soul. Enter: religion.

In the place we now call Egypt, one can imagine people thousands of years ago watching in awe, as each night would slowly dissolve over the desert while a mere promise of light would stealthily grow into a heart-stopping sunrise—the faithful return of the nourishing sphere of Fire. Why, they must have asked themselves, would the incandescent Spirit keep returning, with unflappable precision, to render everything visible and give it life anew, unless The Spirit had a reason? And how could that reason not be the inherent goodness of the world, since its beauty was incontestable, for all to behold. It was perfectly logical to infer that all creative force originated from the Sun god. Named by some Egyptians Atum, around the middle of the third millennium BC, they called their capital Heliopolis, which in Greek means "city of the sun." Writes Karen Armstrong in *A History of God*, "The idea of a holy city, where men and women felt they were closely in touch with sacred power, the source of all being and efficacy, would be important in all three of the monotheistic religions of our own God."[10]

Atum was the first being to emerge from the waters ("Nun") at the time of creation, having previously been a serpent, a form to which he will presumably return at the end of time. Often depicted in art as a man wearing the Double Crown of Upper and Lower Egypt, he is the first living human god (specifically, bi-sexual) conceived of by the ancient Egyptians. Since his semen contained all that was necessary to create new life and deities, the Egyptians called Atum, appropriately, "Great He-She"; the name also happened to mean "the complete one."

Elsewhere along the fertile valley of the Nile, the no less fertile imagination of its lucky inhabitants gave rise to many other fantastic primal scenarios, each more wonder-filled than the next. Sometime in the latter part of the second millennium BC, people from an Egyptian sect called the Memphites attributed the creation of everything not to the Sun but to something far more intangible: the Mind of the Universe, whom they called Ptah.

Ptah was the author of heaven and earth as well as everything that we can see around us—even other gods were his children. He was a creator god who brought all things into existence by thinking of them with his mind and saying their names with his tongue—not unlike the God of the Israelites, He "spoke" the world into being. Ptah's modus operandi was intellectual rather than physical: he was not a craftsman but a thinker. Nevertheless, he was the patron god of skilled craftsmen and architects. This may be due to the excellent sources of limestone near his temple in Memphis. As a craftsman, Ptah was said to have carved the divine bodies of the royalty.

According to the priests of Memphis, everything is the work of Ptah's heart and tongue: from him gods are born, towns are founded, and order is maintained. This beautiful prayer addresses Ptah as follows: "O Hidden One whose eternal form is unknown, Lord of the Years, giver of life at will."[11] The divine giver-of-life-at-will could not be imagined; yet since it had been his desire to will life that accounted for everything, for that he was thanked and loved. Ptah's ethereal nature would come closer to Judeo–Christian–Islamic monotheism than had any other deity up to that time.

Another Egyptian god from the cities of Elephantine and Philae Khnum, sometimes identified with the Sun god and other times with Ptah, was, like all the others, "Maker of heaven and earth and the underworld." Finally, one of the best known and most popular of the Egyptian gods, Osiris (the Greek corruption of the Egyptian name Asar or Usar), originally a minor god of Middle Egypt known mainly as the God of the Dead, eventually became identified with the Sun, thus eclipsing (no pun intended) earlier rivals.

But whatever His name, the various facsimiles of the main Egyptian deity "all had behind them, notwithstanding the inconsistencies, the conception of divine creative activity manifest in the sun, the wind, the earth and the heavens, making and fashioning all things according to predetermined designs and purposes. This was achieved either by sexual processes of procreation on the part of the Creator-god, or by the projection of thought given expression in divine utterance."[12]

When it came to the act of human creation itself, however, the Egyptians did not delude themselves about the place of mankind in the larger scheme of things: compared to the rest of God's magnificent creation, they concluded, mankind was no big deal. The Egyptian Sun god reigned over everything; mankind was simply another one of His artifacts. According to one story, the First Maker produced mankind out of clay on a potter's wheel. As the Supreme Deity, the Creator-god was known as "the Begetter" who brought people into being, along with everything else. It was no great feat for the Master of the World to count pottery among His talents—and man was merely a more sophisticated clay vase.

While the Hebrew authors of the several texts compiled into what we now call *Genesis* were unquestionably familiar with the rich and widespread culture of the people who lived along the Nile, the narratives that appear to have contributed most to the biblical stories actually originated in Mesopotamia, later known as Babylon. From that lovely land inhabited by imaginative, inspired people, the first biblical scribes inherited a vision of a world divinely rescued from a dark, primordial ocean. Some scholars are fond of noting that the Hebrew word for ocean, *Tehom*, meaning "deep," evolved from the Babylonian *Tiamat*, which meant "chaos." We must not make too much of that, but why not wonder . . . .

How else could man have imagined the world before creation if not as a dark, slimy, ocean—the womb of all reality? And how else could the world have been willed into being if not by design, with purpose, by a mind endowed with energy, light, and infinite reason? Had it continued unreasoning, chaos would have reigned as before.

This is, then, how Mesopotamians, at least as far back as 2000 BCE,[13] described the beginning of the world:

When in the height heaven was not named,
And the earth beneath did not yet bear a name,
And the primeval Apsu, who begat them,
And chaos, Tiamat, the mother of them both
Their waters were mingled together,
And no field was formed, no marsh was to be seen;
When of the gods none had been called into being,
And none bore a name, and no destinies were ordained;
Then were created the gods in the midst of heaven,
Lahmu and Lahamu were called into being.[14]

So the primal female waters of chaos and the primal male, Apsu, begat both earth and heaven though neither had yet been named. The actual gods, by contrast, were not simply begotten but were *called into being*. The power of *the word* was of another order altogether than anything concrete: *the word* implies reason or purpose, a thing beyond substance and matter, beyond the visible and the perishable. We could call it "spirit."

The gods themselves, who were evidently spirits, were thus *called into being* in the midst of heaven. Again, the source of holiness came from the intangible, infinite expanse that is rekindled every morning by the sphere of fiery hope—the Sun-spirit, the opposite of nothingness and night. What the Babylonian myth does not explain, however, is *why* anything at all could have existed. To which one answer is simply that . . . there is no answer. The mind will not travel that far; it cannot, so it does not. We are, after all, only human.

But that's no consolation and does not stifle the query. What we very much do need to know is why *us*? And no less important, if we have been given life, why were we also given the *knowledge* that we were given life? It is that knowledge that renders us at once the most fortunate and the most tortured of all the creatures in the universe. For we soon realize that we too decay and die, like every other being; yet we alone can picture, feel, and abhor chaos, while at the same time yearning for an Infinite we both cannot fathom and cannot help seeking for ourselves.

Whoever called us into being must have known that it was *good*: we believe that or anyway are eminently prepared to believe it. Our Author had to, simply *had to*, make it possible for us to understand what this meant. But is knowledge, more specifically self-knowledge, a good thing? A benevolent Creator could have wished nothing less. But what *did* our Author wish for us? That question would linger on throughout human history.

Our pre-Judaic ancestors, whether they hailed from Mesopotamia, Egypt, or Greece, certainly wished for, but did not harbor grandiose illusions about, the closeness of their gods' connection to humanity. Even the Egyptians, who were perhaps the most optimistic of the ancient people, did not kid themselves. They considered men to be of little consequence to their immortal creators—with the notable exception of the Pharaoh, who was assumed to be godlike. Despite their belief in postmortem resurrection, the Egyptians assumed there was no intimacy between mankind and the gods. Yet the Egyptians must be credited with initiating an enormous step toward the idea of a closer relationship between the deities and their human subjects: they fervently believed in the existence of a cosmic order and the human ability to grasp it.

The fertility and beauty of the Nile undoubtedly contributed to that belief: the cosmic order was thought to be mediated by the Pharaoh on behalf of the entire nation, whose well-being he was supposed to seek and protect. We will never know, of course, to what extent the human beings who were told how lucky they were to serve the god-like Pharaoh, the messenger of the eternal deities who looked after his subjects with wisdom, really did believe that all their kings actually governed in conformity with the rhythm of the universe, by observing law, justice, and truth. But this much is certain: the ancient Egyptians had a conception of such a rhythm as well as the sense that their Creator cared about them.

Some Mesopotamian stories, on the other hand, reveal a far more jaundiced view of the divine motivation for man's creation—to be outdone only by the cynical ancient Greeks, about which more later. That view, in brief, assumed that gods brought man into being simply in order to be served. In other words, we had been manufactured to be the gods' slaves. Unlike the gods themselves, who had been miraculously "called into being," the creation of humanity is described in the most celebrated of Mesopotamian narratives, the *Enuma Elish,* as basically little more than . . . a clever afterthought!

The god Marduk is said to have overheard the gods complaining that there were no shrines built in their honor, upon which he "devised a cunning plan."[15] That plan was—you guessed it—*us.* In addition to clay, like his Egyptians counterparts, Marduk is said to have used blood—indeed, divine blood. This explains, according to the ancient Babylonians, the human claim to special spiritual status.

These wonderful stories painstakingly deciphered by scholars from precious Babylonian tablets that are infuriatingly incomplete, broken, often inscrutable, their cuneiform script finally unscrambled a mere century ago, enchant like the most magical fairy tales. I catch myself reading on page after translated page of Babylonian mythology, directing the imaginary movie track, chuckling over the plots and intrigues of gods who cavort with their sisters and re-assemble their brothers and/or mates who hail from far-away lands. These ingenious fantasies rival top Hollywood hits.

Which, alas, obviously poses quite a challenge for our postmodern generation: for how can we expect these myths to be taken seriously by the jaded, overaccessorized self-described consumer, whose technological savvy is virtually guaranteed to render him (and, no less, her) immune to earnest faith? Compared to the entertainment value of the ancient religions, derisively called "primitive," the relevance of myth to the existential questions of our—postmodern—times seems negligible.

But maybe, just maybe, we can figure out how to read those precious scripts more carefully. I submit that what really lies hidden behind the cuneiform texts discovered on broken pieces of time-faded stone chips is even more elusive than the electrifying translations by brilliant, erudite archeologists: it is nothing less than humanity's self-image in an era that is long gone yet still a living part of our own heritage and, hence, ourselves.

Once upon a time, it had mattered how God had created man. It should again. The wisdom of our spiritual tradition, which constitutes the foundation of Judaism, Christianity, Islam, and their many branches, offshoots, and relatives, is generous and liberating. And nowhere is its moral import distilled more profoundly, its modern relevance more manifest and urgent, than in that deceptively simple, apocalyptic phrase, "God created man in His own image."

Male and Female in His Image

Then God said, "Let us make man [adam] in our image, after our like-
ness; and let them have dominion . . ." And God created him [adam]
in His own image, in the image of God created He him; male and
female He created them.
Genesis 1:26–27

The implication that male and female *adam* were *both* created in God's image seems incontestable. Would this mean that God is humanoid in various ways but nevertheless sexless? Even admitting that nothing about God is easy to understand,[16] this is hard to fathom. The predominantly male character of God's voice throughout most of the Judeo-Christian Bible would argue for primary likeness between Himself and the male human, with the female resembling the deity, shall we say, . . . a little less. Somehow, neither interpretation—God as (a) sexless or (b) a man—seems appropriate. In fact, of course, most scholars steeped in archeology and arcane textual analysis prefer the latter option: the Abrahamic God is assumed to be male.[17]

For a person brought up with Western iconography, a common way of visualizing God is Michelangelo's Sistine Chapel version: white-bearded and magnificent, His finger touching that of a languidly reclining yet no less Olympian young Adam. Indeed, throughout its history, Christian religious art—both painting and sculpture—depicts God as an older, powerful, large bearded man. It was not long before all traces of goddesses (the traditional symbols of fertility), some dating as far back as the Paleolithic era, around 22,000 BCE, would disappear altogether as monotheism turned patriarchal with a vengeance.

But whether any kind of anthropomorphic imagery with regard to the Creator is legitimate at all in the biblical tradition is very much an open question. Admittedly, most languages personify, and some even assign gender (though, as it happens, not English), and this certainly goes for Hebrew: thus when God is mentioned in the Torah, it is usually *He*, not *She*.[18] God is the *Father*, not the Mother. And yet . . . doesn't the biblical narrative also insist that God has no real image, that "He" has no face and no body? In *Deuteronomy* 4:15–16, Moses is said to have been reminded: "For your own sake, be most careful—since you saw no shape when the Lord God spoke to you at Horeb out of the fire—not to act wickedly and make for yourselves a sculptured image in any likeness whatever: the form of a man or a woman . . ." or of anything else for that matter, in the strictest interpretation of that Commandment.

God may "speak" and even "walk" with Adam and Eve in some sense but has no form as such. The Commandment to worship no other gods and shun all idols has been strictly interpreted by most Jews—and even more by Muslims, but also by some Christians—to imply that all pictures allegedly representing the Creator are absolutely prohibited.[19] To idolize is—no pun intended—no idle sin.

Fortunately, there are other possible readings of "image" and "likeness." Some early rabbis, for example, interpreted man's dual creation to mean that the very *unity* of man and woman blessed by God was *itself* the image of God. In her splendid book *God and the Rhetoric of Sexuality*, Phyllis Trible explains the passage most deftly and clearly: "'[M]ale and female' is the vehicle of a metaphor whose tenor is 'the image of God . . . .'" In other words, it is the *relationship* between the two that reflects the Divine image. Writes biblical scholar Maryanne Cline Horowitz, "The idea that a human being needs a spouse *to fulfill the image of God* was a theme running through Jewish tradition, which frowned on celibacy."[20] [It] is the finger pointing to the 'image of God.'"[21] It is interesting that both Martin Luther and John Calvin similarly rejected celibacy, although both stopped short of agreeing with Jews who do not call a man *adam* until he has a wife.[22] Calvin actually went so far as to say that the male is fully half of human nature and that only together with the female does he finally become complete. Amazingly, he does not even claim that the male is "the better" half.

The second account of mankind's creation that is found in *Genesis* 2 and 3 clarifies what it means to emulate God's image. The poetic narrative relates that shortly after having created the male by "breathing the breath of life into him" (*Genesis* 2:7), God observed that "it is not good for man to be alone." Accordingly, God set out to "make a fitting helper for him" (*Genesis* 2:18). All the animals were formed out of earth (or dust), each duly named by the diligent newborn human, but alas, "for man no fitting helper was found." A "helper" makes it possible to achieve your ideals. An animal—or a machine, for that matter—can be extremely helpful in tilling the soil, but only a *spiritual helper* can share your dreams. This means that such a "fitting helper" for a god-like creature would have to be equipped with a unique set of qualities: it must know . . . how to dream.

Whereupon the Lord cast a deep sleep upon the man, excised a rib, from which we are told that God manufactured that helper, and so was woman born. God then presented her to man, who immediately "recognized" her without any prompting, for it was self-evident: "This one at last is bone of my bones and flesh of my flesh." What Adam meant has long been debated: he may or may not have known that no other living thing had ever been fashioned from anything but dust before. In all likelihood, the comment was at least in part, if not primarily, allegorical. Here, for him to behold and cherish, was his *ideal* helper: although he could not have been expected to utter the word itself, he must have understood that she was his *soulmate*.

One thing that having been created in God's "image" seems to mean is *"being capable of having a soulmate."* Adam himself had been God's "soulmate" in the sense that he could name things and learn, "rule" the animals and the earth with purpose and benevolence, and "see"—as had God—that the world was *good*. But Adam was not fully human until he could feel love, in some way—however imperfect—similar to God's love for him. In order for this to happen, however, he had to be joined by a soulmate who—in addition to bearing his offspring (a feat that animals too perform for one another)—could help him *fittingly*, who would be capable of *sharing* and *understanding* his spiritual essence, which was the same as hers, and through this sharing feel (ideally) selfless, absolute affection. Phyllis Trible, again, explains that in describing woman as "bone of my bones and flesh of my flesh," "the man does not depict himself as either prior to or superior to the woman. His sexual identity depends upon her even as hers depends upon him. For both of them sexuality originates in the one flesh of humanity."[23]

Man would thus be destined to join his life to another's. In order to be with his woman, continues the story of *Genesis*, "man leaves his father and mother and clings to his wife, so that they become one flesh" (*Genesis* 2:24). The meaning here is clearly not merely sexual, since he need not "leave" his parents to copulate; rather, it is unequivocally and gloriously metaphorical. It symbolizes the strength of the bond that is both stronger than and independent of genetic ties.

When man and woman become one "flesh," the couple's being, their lives, their souls, intertwine—they merge and thus become *one*. The ability to feel as another, to be completely with—within, through, and for—another, is a pale facsimile of God's empathy for mankind. The spiritual connection between two people epitomizes the truest sense of emulating His spirit: God's love is reflected in that very connection, for His image, however faint, appears to us through human love.

I–Thou is a oneness: it has no shape.

The Quranic Account

And it is for women to act as they (the husbands) act by them, in all fairness.
Sura 2:229

But whose doth the things that are right, whether male or female, and he or she is a believer, these shall enter Paradise.
Sura 4:122

Mohammed considered the religion he founded to be the latest and most accurate account of God's actions and will on earth, presuming the Bible to be essentially correct; nothing indicates that he thought it inaccurate. The Quranic account of human creation is thus essentially consistent with *Genesis*. Since the Muslim Holy Book is not organized in historic or linear fashion, with relevant passages scattered throughout, the story of Creation is not placed in the beginning. What emerges from bits and pieces scattered throughout this literary masterpiece is a beautiful account of the first couple's reciprocal, fulfilling love that is altogether consistent with the vision of its Hebrew scribes. Not only does the Quran reiterate the mutuality and spiritual relationship of our human parents so eloquently described in the Old Testament, it actually reinforces the importance of that bond more decisively.

In the first place, unlike the much-debated second account of human creation in Books 2 and 3 of *Genesis*, the Quran does not insist that the male human being came first—thus eliminating one possible excuse for considering women subordinate *qua* subsequent. Equally important, humanity is said to have been created by God "*from a single soul.*" Here is the moving verse: "O people! Fear your Lord, who hath created you of one soul [*nafs*], and of him created his wife, and from these twain hath spread abroad so many men and women" (*Sura* 4:1).[24] The Quran specifically states that men and women have no preeminence in birth and their work is appreciated equally. To those who beseech God to be merciful, "their Lord answereth them: "I will not suffer the work of him among you that worketh, whether male or female, to be lost. The one of you is the issue of the other" (*Sura* 3: 195).[25]

Another passage from *Sura* 7:189 repeats the single spiritual origin of mankind: "He it is who did create you from a single soul, and from him brought forth his wife that he might dwell with her."[26]

The "bringing forth" of woman could well have been simultaneous. Nor does this imply that the woman is designed for man's rest and comfort: on the contrary, the first couple who thus emerged were meant to be *a comfort to one another*. Later in the Quran, we are told quite explicitly: "He created for you *helpmates* from yourselves that ye might find rest in them, and He ordained between you *love and mercy*" (*Sura* 30:21).[27]

This Divine gift—the feeling of love and mercy between man and woman—is, again, the spiritual "breath" God had breathed into His children that allows human beings to catch a glimpse of God's unique connection to us all. *Love and mercy* constitute the essence of the "I–Thou" relationship. It forms the moral basis of monotheism and is what unites us, the so-called people of the Book. The words of the Quran, as well as Mohammed's deeply intimate, respectful personal relationship to his first beloved wife, his spiritual and physical "helper" in every sense, who fully reciprocated his affections, supporting him when others doubted him, which we explore in chapter 9, amply testify to his full endorsement of this enormously powerful idea that lies at the very core of human civilization.

This usually astonishes Westerners, and with good reason. The celebrated Egyptian-American, now Harvard professor, Leila Ahmed captures the point perfectly: "The unmistakable presence of an ethical egalitarianism [in the Quran] explains why Muslim women frequently insist, often inexplicably to non-Muslims, that Islam is not sexist. They [the former] hear and read in its sacred text, justly and legitimately, a different message from that heard by the makers and enforcers of orthodox, androcentric Islam."[28] In fact, this is true not only of Islam but every religion: external factors, as defined by geography, economics, cultural, and other considerations, affect the way any sacred text is implemented.

Leila Ahmed indicates that it was "[t]he political, religious, and legal authorities of the Abbassid period [750–1258 A.D.] in particular, whose interpretative and legal legacy has defined Islam ever since, heard only the androcentric voice of Islam, and they interpreted the religion as intending to institute androcentric laws and an androcentric vision in all Muslim societies throughout time."[29] Mohammed himself had favored a far more egalitarian approach, which as it happens he experienced directly during his own lifetime, and the Quran reflects that attitude. In his very last sermon before his unexpected death in

632 CE, Mohammed reiterated that women had rights over men just as men had rights over women; indeed, among Muslims no one stands higher or lower than any other except in virtue.[30]

This is highly significant, since the Quran enjoys a unique place in Islam that sets it apart from its Abrahamic predecessors. Unlike Judaism and Christianity, the Muslim tradition cannot simply point to the historical and cultural factors that had to have influenced the interpretations of the Quran by its early scholars. While both the Old and the New Testaments were understood to have been human versions of an originally divine message, the Quran (which means oral "recitation," and came to imply "the text which is recited" rather than merely read silently to oneself) is assumed to be the actual, literal message of God, who spoke it in Arabic through his angel Gabriel, for Mohammed to record. While there is no evidence whether or not he used scribes during the early years while Mohammed lived in Mecca, later, at Medina, he appears to have had a group of them, each with a special responsibility for a part of the text.[31]

There is considerable disagreement among Muslims whether in addition to what is ordinarily known as the Quran itself—some five hundred pages revealed over a period of some twenty-three years—Mohammed's later alleged "sayings" should also be deemed to be God's literal words. Those sayings, known as *hadith* and recorded by others mostly after his death, are obviously less authoritative—which is one reason why Mohammed presumably ordered "whoever has written anything from me other than the Quran, let him erase it."[32] This provides an additional—theological, indeed "fundamentalist"—justification for relying primarily on Islam's holiest text for a faithful understanding of its original moral vision.

"Once upon a time . . ." Then, God created mankind in His own image—"man and woman He created them," having endowed them with the most precious gift of all: the ability to recognize along with the Lord Who created them as God's only mortal spiritual offspring, that the world is *good*. But mankind had to be free to choose which path to take—a fate that would not and could not be but fraught with great peril.

Notes

1. The text in Romanian is as follows: "A fost odata (*ah fohst oh-dahtah*)/Ca niciodata (*kah nichioh–dahtah*)/Ca daca n-ar fi (*kah dacha nahr-fee*)/Nu s-ar povesti *(nooh sahr poh-vay-stee)*."

2. Northrop Frye, *The Great Code: The Bible as Literature*, 32.
3. Ibid., 33.
4. Ibid.
5. Ibid., 37.
6. Ibid., 40.
7. Carl G. Jung, *Modern Man in Search of a Soul*, 65.
8. Writes Jaroslav Pelikan in *Whose Bible Is It? A History of the Scriptures through the Ages*: "'In the beginning the [spoken] Word already was.' On this, at least, Jews and Christians are in agreement, and so are their Bibles, that there was a Word of God before there was a written Bible of any kind, that the God of the Bible is the God who speaks," 9.
9. Stephen W. Hawking, *A Brief History of Time*, 175.
10. Karen Armstrong, *A History of God*, 9.
11. M. V. Seton-Williams, *Egyptian Legends and Stories*, 17.
12. E. O. James, *The Ancient Gods*, 207.
13. Leonard William King, *The Seven Tablets of Creation*, Introduction, lxxx.
14. Ibid., L. W. King, translation.
15. *Enuma Elish, Sixth Tablet. Line 2.*
16. Despite the common depiction of God as male in Christian paintings and icons, there is no basis for it in the Bible. Writes John M. Frame in "Men and Women in the Image of God": "Any limitation of the image of God based on sexuality would also contradict the thrust of Genesis 9:6 and James 3:9; such limitation would imply that only males are protected against murder and slander because only they are in God's image. Re-creation in God's image also applies without sexual distinction," *Recovering Biblical Manhood and Womanhood*, ch. 12, 227.
17 J. Maxwell Miller, "In the 'Image' and 'Likeness' of God."
18. The fascinating study documenting the persistence of the Goddess in the Jewish tradition, Raphael Patai's *The Hebrew Goddess*, will be discussed in a later chapter.
20. Maryanne Cline Horowitz, "The Image of God in Man—Is Woman Included?" 187.
21. Trible, *God and the Rhetoric of Sexuality*, 20.
22. Horowitz. ibid.
23. Trible, *God and the Rhetoric of Sexuality*, 99.
24. *The Koran*, 49
25. Ibid., 48. Rodwell comments that "these words were occasioned by one of the Prophet's wives having told him that God often praised the men, but not the women, who had fled their country for the faith," ibid., 440.
26. Ibid., 111.
27. I used the translation by Thomas Cleary, *The Essential Koran: The Heart of Islam*, 86. See also Rodwell, ibid., 269. Though Rodwell chooses to translate this as God having created "wives for you of your own species," the next phrase indicates that He "hath put love and tenderness between you"—which is an unmistakable indication of complete mutuality.
28. Leila Ahmed, *Women and Gender in Islam*, 66.
29. Ibid., 67

30. See Tamim Ansary, *Destiny Disrupted*, 30. See also the copious publications of Ahmed Mansour, notably "The Right of Women to Rule an Islamic State," on his Web site, www.ahl-alquran.com.
31. *The Koran*, Introduction, xix–xx.
32. Muhammad Abdel Haleem, *Understanding the Quran: Themes and Style*, 3.

2

Why Mankind?

When the Lord God made earth and heaven—when no shrub of the field was yet on earth and no grasses of the field had yet sprouted, because the Lord God had not sent rain upon the earth and there was no man to till the soil, but a flow would well up from the ground and water the whole surface of the earth—the Lord God formed man from the dust of the earth.
Genesis 2:4–7

How better to explain the ultimate question—*why does anything exist?*—than through a story, relating that the Lord our God did not send rain upon the earth in the absence of a human being who, in turn, would be able to make use of the earth's bounty. There had to be a *reason* for rain, a reason for something existing rather than nothing. It speaks to man's need to understand *why*: Why earth and heaven? Why the rain? Why grasses in the field? Why, indeed, mankind?

We already agreed that such questions require us to indulge in metaphor. At its best, a metaphor is able to inspire, to create a mood, as it were to place us in another world—even (or, rather, especially) if that world is inside ourselves, where language usually applied to objective reality works mainly by analogy. The right analogy will feel right: it will seem to capture an inner truth which, however subjective, can still be called "truth." We know that the "purpose" of a knife, for example, is to cut and that of soap is to wash because these are instruments whose use is defined by their user. The "purpose" of a flower, by analogy, is to render the heart awash with gladness.

Treating metaphor with condescension as wannabe fact, or truth in drag, is unwarranted: that word originally meant, quite simply, "transfer." A metaphor is nothing more complicated than imagining an "as-if" picture—superposing or "transferring" one image on another. For example, to say that a child is the apple of his mother's eye is merely to liken the little creature to a wonderful fruit, while

New York is called "the Big Apple" for its outsized seductiveness. As George Lakoff and Mark Johnson write in *Metaphors We Live By*, while "most people think they can get along perfectly well without metaphor [w]e have found, on the contrary, that metaphor is pervasive in everyday life, not just in language but in thought and action. *Our ordinary conceptual system, in terms of which we both think and act, is fundamentally metaphorical in nature.*"[1]

The beautiful biblical refrain that reappears after God creates each new aspect of the world—"And He saw that it was good"—is not literal, in the way "and he saw a chair" is literal. Instead, it is a ritual, an incantation, whose repetition underscores The Author's satisfaction with the universe that had emanated from His love. The world is a source of intense divine *joy* (or its unimaginably infinite equivalent). Therefore, God's cup runneth over, so to speak, as He wishes to share this satisfaction with another *spiritual* being no less capable than the Creator of *value judgment*. In brief, God desires a suitable companion.

Companion, in ordinary parlance, refers to a friend with whom one may share sustenance, literal or emotional: *com* is Latin for "with," while *panis* means "bread." Who does not yearn for companionship? Even the celibate monk who sees no one, the saintly hermit, consorts with a spirit beyond himself—convinced that God is listening. Far from being a weakness, the desire to share is a sublime virtue. What is anything worth if it is not appreciated and—this is the crux—*shared*?

To feel nothing for anything or anyone is difficult to even imagine, so deeply is sociability entrenched within the human psyche. True, the ancient Greek philosophers considered passion to be proof of want, which was then, as now, roughly synonymous with lack, and hence inapplicable to a perfect deity. The First Mover of the great Greek philosophers Plato and Aristotle was moved by nothing, either literally or figuratively. The God of the Abrahamic Bible, by contrast, is a merciful Creator who loves the world and rejoices in our shared rejoicing.

The biblical narrative thus proceeds: "And [so] God said, 'Let us make man in our image, after our likeness. They [humans] shall rule the fish of the sea, the birds of the sky, the cattle the whole earth, and all the things that creep on earth'" (*Genesis* 1:26).

Rule everything that moves? Whatever the Original Author may have had in mind by decreeing this, it was not that humans could tell birds when and where to fly, nor fish where and how to swim. It also could not mean that humans were the strongest of all the animals. Notwithstanding all our technological advances, we cannot be said even to be able to fully rule ourselves, as human self-annihilation is more plausible now than ever and weapons of inconceivable power are becoming more accessible to irresponsible actors. It is mastery of another sort that God had in mind.

The Hebrew original, as it happens, allows for several possible interpretations of "rule over" the various creatures of the world: it could refer to mankind "descending among" them, "take stewardship over" them, or "take charge of" them in the sense of assuming responsibility for them.[2] God intended for mankind to revere and rejoice in beholding the world, giving thanks to its—and everyone's—benevolent Maker. Mankind's purpose was to see that God's creation was, above all, *a work of infinite, unfathomable goodness.*

"And He saw that it was good."

A Living Soul He Created Thee

[H]e formed thee, Adam, thee, O Man,
Dust of the ground, and in thy nostrils breathed
The breath of life; in his own image he
Created thee, in the image of God
Express, and thou became'st a living soul.
Male he created thee, but thy consort
Female, for race . . .
    Milton, *Paradise Lost*, Book VII: 525–30

But could mankind, created from dust and destined to toil the earth (*adamah*[3] —"ground or "earth" in Hebrew; it is also related to *adom* "red," *admoni*, "ruddy," and *dam*, "blood" in Hebrew[4]) into which God breathed the wind (or breath) of life, really be said to bear God's very own image? Physical image was out of the question, since the God of the Torah had no face or body: the Abrahamic deity was not merely a super-being, albeit omnipotent, omniscient, and immortal. Although the Hebrew word for "image" found in *Genesis* is *tselem*, which was admittedly often used to refer to a representation or a likeness in a literal sense, in this context it was obviously intended figuratively or metaphorically. The question therefore remains: in what way was mankind supposed to be "like" God from the outset?

A clue may be found in *Adam*'s first action: "And the man gave names to all the cattle and to the birds of the sky and to all the wild beasts . . ." (*Genesis* 2:21) By immediately proceeding to name the other creatures, *Adam* evidently "took charge" of them in a new and immensely powerful way—by means of his mind–soul. Mankind inaugurated language, but speech is not only the instrument of thought, its main purpose is not merely contemplative, it is also practical. To think is to behold consciously, to understand, to categorize, and to predict: all prerequisites for truly effective rule and wise oversight.

Strength may change the world, but only intelligence can do so with purpose. An earthquake or a tsunami may be enormously devastating but is mindless and thus futile; the sun and rain are both indispensable for growth, herbs may feed and heal, but only knowledge—acquired and transmitted through language—can alter outcomes toward a consciously desired end. Speech lies at the heart of deliberate, human understanding, as reason partakes of the divine. To name is to think, thereby making it possible to rule wisely.

But while *Adam* could exercise his reason, he was still woefully incomplete. The verse cited above from *Genesis* 2:21 ends thus: "but for Adam no fitting helper was found." It should be noted that at this stage, *Adam* technically lacks a proper name, because there is no account of anyone having named him, and he seems to have neglected naming himself. A fitting helper obviously did not refer merely to a sexual mate—surely God could have created male and female versions of this species as with every other, but evidently did not do so from the outset, so to speak, for a reason. Rather, what *Adam* needed was clearly something qualitatively, radically different than just a biological counterpart. All animals, with the exception of self-replicating organisms, have reproductive partners; only *Adam* could have a *spiritual* helper who would truly be considered "fitting." Humans are unique: only to human creatures does God speak in the first person; though animals are divided into species, none is referred to as "male or female"; and the woman's uniqueness is supreme, for she alone, of all creatures, is made of a spiritual being, thus constituting the very zenith of creation.

It may be worth noting here that biblical scholarship attributes authorship of the second account of creation, in *Genesis* 2 and 3, which has God fashioning first the male and only subsequently the female, to a source or sources as early as the ninth or tenth century BCE hailing from Judah (hence known as J), which is nearly half a millennium earlier than the creation story we read in *Genesis* 1, which is generally assigned to a priestly source (sometimes known as P).[5] That said, we must not think of these sources as early ghostwriters or prehistoric freelance authors. On the contrary, not unlike Homer, these are highly skilled cultural archivists who, in the words of biblical scholar Robert Davidson, "inherit, and are the servants of, their people's religious and historical traditions."[6] Though undoubtedly creative and even original, these authors are Judaism's unsung prophets: "some of Israel's greatest thinkers; no less great because they are anonymous."[7]

This historical data is not without exegetic significance; it helps us make better sense of the seeming inconsistency. For as book 1 of *Genesis* came long after books 2 and 3, its author (P) could be seen as embracing and incorporating the latter, indeed reinforcing its message. Again, writes Davidson, "The appeal of *Genesis* 1 is to the imagination: it is poetic, a hymn written by faith for faith"—just as later—"the essential need of male and female for each other is underlined. Together they form the full unity which is human life."[8] The full unity, however, does not imply the loss of individuality; it simply reiterates the mutual need and harmony of purpose.

What the first book underscores is the unity of man and woman as "mankind," even as books 2 and 3 elaborate on the metaphorical fact that woman is of the same "flesh" as her male counterpart, his fitting partner and helper, that is to say, a *fellow soul*.

Unlike a conventional aide or assistant, whose function is to accomplish some particular task, the human couple are no ordinary helpers to the divine Creator. The relationship of a master to his slave, or employer and employee, involves two individuals who are essentially antithetical despite the commonality of purpose, their interests sometimes, perhaps often, conflicting. Even team members who compete together for a title, or soldiers who must defend one another, are in an important sense also competitors against one another: a better player will shine over a lesser, and in war, sometimes a soldier can save his own life only if he fails to save that of another.

The contrary is meant to be true of woman, who is her mate's God-given fitting helper/soulmate. For her, Adam will willingly leave his father and mother, and cling to her "so that they may become one flesh." As we will see later, she is in an important sense his very complement, as the Soul (Psyche) was wedded to Love (Eros) in ancient Greek mythology: their union is inescapable, spiritually Siamese.

Upon finding this "fitting helpmate" beside him, the ecstatic Adam resorts to poetry:

This one at last
Is bone of my bones
And flesh of my flesh.

This one shall be called Woman ['ishshah],
For from man ['ish] was she taken.
(Genesis 2:23–24)

Adam's reference to himself as *'ish* and to his partner as *'ishhah*, in a manner reminiscent of the English "woman" as a composite for "wife of man," though somewhat deceptive (for in fact, the terms derive from different roots[9]), underscores again Adam's recognition of their metaphorical and spiritual complementarity.

Later, after their expulsion from Eden, he will name his woman and friend, his wife and soulmate, with a proper name—Eve (*Hawwah or Chavvah*)—to indicate that she would be mother of all the living (in Hebrew, the word for "living" is "*hai'n*").[10] This would represent the first time a creature had been singled out with a proper, capitalized (rather than a lower-case, generic) name. For unlike every other thing her husband had ever labeled before, Eve is unique: she is an individual, herself and no other. Their children (Cain, Abel, Seth, and so on) would receive proper names as well.

But we must return briefly to the lovely expression "becoming one flesh." By now degenerated into a mere cliché, its origins are steeped in magic. Indeed, many an ancient myth of creation envisages the original humanoid to be a hermaphrodite (the word itself is a composite of *Hermes*, the Greek god of war, and his sister *Aphrodite*, the goddess of love and beauty), meaning both male and female, or androgynous (from the Latin *andro*, male, and *gyny*, female)—meaning either male or female (thus an androgynous haircut, such as mine, would suit either men or women).

In what is probably the best known Platonic dialogue, the sometimes bawdy yet profound *Symposium*, Socrates listens to two of his companions, Eryximachus and Aristophanes, telling burlesque versions of the story of Love as consisting of (literally) two complementary halves yearning to return to their original wholeness. Discussed in greater detail in chapter 4, its main purpose in Plato's dialogue appears to be a mixture of entertainment and ridicule designed to induce hilarity while describing love among two individuals as a universal value referring to the search for completeness.

Socrates is duly amused by the story, but addresses the subject with the seriousness he feels it deserves, and retorts with his own story, told to him by his beloved mentor Diotima, a woman of great wisdom "who was versed in this and many other fields of knowledge." He tells the assembled wine-imbibing but still alert audience how Diotima acknowledged "it ha[ving] been suggested . . . that lovers are people who are looking for their other halves" like two halves of a circle, but that she rescued the concept from absurdity by elevating it to an abstract level. "[A]s I see it, Socrates," Diotima is quoted to have opined, "Love never longs for either the half or the whole of anything except the good. For men will even have their hands and feet cut off if they are once convinced that those members are bad for them. Indeed I think we only prize our own belongings in so far as we say that the good belongs to us, and the bad to someone else, for what we love is the good and nothing but the good."[11]

When Socrates, whose peculiar modesty is famously captured by the claim that he knows nothing, confesses to be still confused about the nature of Love among men and women, Diotima reportedly tries a slightly different approach. "Conception, as we know, takes place when man and woman come together, but there's a divinity in human procreation, an immortal something in the midst of man's mortality which is incompatible with any kind of discord."[12] So Love is not exactly a "longing for the beautiful itself, but for the conception and generation that the beautiful effects."[13] In other words, what Love really longs for is not just another person, but *The Good* which that person embodies. *The divinity, the "immortal something," is what is truly loved; particular human beings are a mere conduit to that spiritual experience of love.*

The picture of two human beings literally becoming one is not as strange as it might seem to the modern reader. In fact, primitive religions embraced the idea, not in the literal sense satirized in the *Symposium* but in a metaphorical, highly sophisticated fashion. In his highly original study of hermaphrodite mythology, *The Myth of Reintegration*, Romanian-born novelist and historian of religions Mircea Eliade, who joined the University of Chicago after his emigration to the United States in 1956, warned against understanding mythological bisexuality in a concrete (or "profane") sense. The same goes for "woman," which "in myth or ritual, is never just woman: it includes the cosmological principle woman embodies." Eliade adds, "And the divine androgyny which we find in so many myths and beliefs has its own theoretical metaphysical significance. The real point of the formula is to express— in biological terms—the coexistence of contraries, of cosmological principles (male and female) within the heart of the divinity."[14]

Eliade points out that virtually all primitive religions conceive the divinities of cosmic fertility as either hermaphrodite, androgynous, or else successively male and female (say, male one year and female the next). The primal god who creates the world is believed to be androgynous not only in primitive Australian religions but also in much more advanced India. Similarly, several of the most ancient Egyptian gods were bisexual; almost all the major gods in Scandinavian mythology preserved traces of androgyny; the Iranian counterpart of the Greek god of time, Chronos, was androgynous; even the Chinese had a hermaphrodite Supreme Divinity, the god of darkness and light.[15] The next step was the original state of "mankind," which Eliade interprets as the image of "a state of perfect humanity in which the sexes exist side by side as they coexist with all other qualities, and all other attributes, in the Divinity."[16] In some ways, Eden could be thought as such a state, before the "Fall."

The metaphor of love as a longing for completeness, for Beauty and for Good, is much more than the residue of a pagan mythological story. Without resorting to dialectic, the Bible recounts that when God breathed life into dust to create Adam "in His likeness," He first made sure that Adam appreciated what he lacked before the partner of his spiritual being, namely woman, had been created to complete him. God saw to it that Adam did not merely name her as he would a sheep or a monkey but would understand who she was in relation to himself: she was a "part" of him that he would yearn to re-embrace as literally as possible so they would be "one" again. As Diotima observed, we often only miss something once it is gone, so Adam "missed" his metaphorical rib that had been metamorphosed into his lover. He would yearn to *have* her back, to merge with her.

It is through love that man can "become one" with his beloved. Again, writes Eliade, "we may even talk of the 'androgynization' of man through love, for in love each sex attains, conquers the 'characteristics' of the opposite sex (as with the grace, submission, and devotion achieved by a man when he is in love, and so on)."[17] It is precisely in that spirit that the Bible intends for man to appreciate what it is to be "one" with another in the deepest and most meaningful way possible: God first made man *lonely*. No other creature could be *Adam's* "helper" except another spirit that could relieve him of that loneliness, of a need to share his soul, and that could understand what it is to really *see* creation, to appreciate it. Such a helper would have to be "like himself" just as humans were in turn both "like" their common Author.

This interpretation is consistent with that of the Jewish mystical Kabbalist tradition—which dates from the fifteenth to the nineteenth centuries, although not accepted as a legitimate part of mainstream Judaism until after the Holocaust—as illustrated in its most important literary work, the *Zohar: The Book of Splendor*[18]:

Male and female God created them
To make known the Glory on high
From here we learn:
Any image that does not embrace male and female
Is not a high and true image.[19]

The masculine and feminine attributes of perfection are certainly symbolic of complementarity, more generally, of a *ying* and *yang* dialectic that we find everywhere in nature. Mankind's original sexual bipolarity is reflected in the original Hebrew: since *afar*/dust is masculine, while *adamah*/earth is feminine, one could say that a potter has to take both male dust and female earth to insure that his vessel will be sturdy.[20] God is the Great Potter.

After fashioning mankind, God was finished at last, and thoroughly approved of the final product. Referring to all creation, including— indeed *especially*—man and woman, God found it all to be "very good." (*Genesis* 1:31) Yet in that "good" were there not also the seeds of evil? Over the course of human history, monotheism has struggled to understand how tragedy and injustice, cruelty and ignorance, indeed torture and genocide, could have been created by a perfect Deity, a God who is all merciful and all powerful. How could God have failed to establish the preeminence of human compassion and respect from the very beginning? Wasn't the creation of the first humans' example enough?

And in turn, how could the first parents fail to inculcate the concept of compassion and brotherly love into their own offspring, their firstborn?

My Brother's—and Sister's—Keeper

[While] the text clearly says that Cain brought an offering "unto the Lord" (Yahweh) . . . *[t]he careful reader will notice that this represents a change from "Lord God"* (Yahwey 'elohim), *the name used for God in the story of the Garden of Eden. This change is in keeping with the view that Cain is sacrificing to the name of he-knows-not-what, and not to the God who had dealt with his parents in Eden. . . . [A]s the story amply shows, he has no good idea of who God is or, more important, what would truly please Him."*
Leon Kass, The Beginning of Wisdom

Animals kill—for food, sex, fear, and protection—but animals do not murder. Only man is capable of killing in cold blood, out of envy or contempt. Only man is capable of killing his own brother who had done him no harm out of sheer spite. What kind of wisdom could the first parents have possibly gained that would not go even as far as to prevent their very first child from killing the younger? Evidently, ingesting the sacred fruit from the Tree of Knowledge was not enough for man's progeny to become sufficiently godlike. What was still missing (besides, of course, immortality)?

Whatever wisdom had been literally or spiritually digested by the first parents, they seem to have imparted but a woefully diluted version to their firstborn, Cain. A tiller of the ground, Cain envied his younger brother Abel, a shepherd, on the ground that God invariably seemed to prefer Abel's hearty offerings while ignoring Cain's more modest gifts. Eventually it proved too much for the older son, who set upon the innocent Abel and killed him, manifestly ignorant of the respect due to a fellow human being, let alone a blood brother. Cain's blasphemously impertinent rhetorical question to his outraged Maker—"Am I my brother's keeper?"—earned him a punishment almost as dire as death: God declared that tilling the soil "shall no longer yield its strength" to him. Cain was thus destined to become "a ceaseless wanderer on earth" (*Genesis* 4:12). When Cain protested that such a punishment is "too great to bear," God took pity on him and marked Cain protectively, "lest anyone should kill him" (*Genesis* 4:15). It seems that God had considerable patience with mankind; still the lesson was clear: yes, indeed you are your brother's keeper. *You may not kill someone who has done you no deliberate harm.* This is the core of all civilized behavior.

In subsequent millennia, the wisdom of the Old Testament would be invoked again and again, to assist the morally challenged, insufficiently Godlike creature who lacked the will, even as he had presumably inherited the knowledge, to obey the most basic principle of morality: *You are not to kill the innocent.* Thus, not unlike older religions and mythologies, monotheism would record many instances of mankind's near self-annihilation. We are staring at its possibility once again now, in the twenty-first century.

Invariably the cause is sin and corruption, evil in its many guises. Floods and other calamities were reportedly sent by the Creator more than once in ire and disgust at His children's outrageous behavior, their cruelty and faithlessness. The God who had declared Himself fully satisfied by all His works in the immediate aftermath of their original creation would soon become disappointed by the inability of human beings to opt for the good despite their biblically documented potential to discern it from evil.

In an effort to tame man's cruel instincts that flow from envy and other noxious passions, most religions have appealed to the lure of that other sacred Tree of paradise, which had been left untouched: the Tree of Life. Through a realization of his own mortality, it was reasoned, mankind might come to realize the futility of murderous hatred. Sundry narratives promising immortality, however posthumous, have succeeded in varying degrees to entice humans into respecting others, and even show compassion. But not always; throughout man's bloody history, every religion has been interpreted at one time or another by some to justify unimaginable forms of torture and murder inflicted upon innocent human beings merely on the basis of their beliefs, physiognomy and skin color, or habits and language, to say nothing of gender. Of all intraspecies atrocities, man's cruelty to his fellow woman has been, if not the worst, surely the most perplexing.

What had ever happened to the original picture of the unity of all mankind, the symbolic (at times reinforced by the concrete) fusion of man and woman, the intimacy between God and the one creature He fashioned in His own Likeness, indeed the unity and harmony of all nature? Is it possible to hope, that at this point in our sorry history, the narrative of *Genesis*, which had been meant to inspire mankind in primitive times, might reinvigorate morality more than five millennia later?

Can we take to heart the idea that we are all one family?

We

> *This new creature with the long hair is a good deal in the way. It is always hanging around and following me about. I don't like this; I am not used to company. I wish it would stay with the other animals. . . . Cloudy today, wind in the east, think we shall have rain . . . We? Where did I get that word?—I remember now—the new creature uses it.*
> *Mark Twain,* Diaries of Adam and Eve

You can name the animals, and you can name the plants, but where does "we" come from? When is it used correctly, and who decides? When and where does "we" stop and "they" begin? How can "we" feel as warm as a woolen wrap yet suddenly morph into a rope that strangles as surely as a hangman's noose? Why is it that some people yearn for it, while others dread it? Why are some fellow humans excluded from being part of "us" merely to satisfy a visceral need for a "them"? (I am reminded of the old story about a rich curmudgeon who bought an island for his own use and had it all built up—including, strangely enough, two synagogues. When asked by a visitor why he needed two, he answered, "Well, in this one, I pray. The other one—I wouldn't set foot in.") Not in the least funny are the massacres that mark human history, which render any claim to superiority over lesser creatures laughable were it not so profoundly tragic. No wonder some question whether God even exists, or at least whether Nietzsche's infamous obituary, proclaiming that God is dead, does not contain a kernel of plausibility.

Sometimes "we" is little more than a sinister camouflage, cynically used to destroy some people for the vaunted good of others. It is the "we" that brands some human beings as dispensable, to be purged or eliminated—the metaphor of moral excrement. My parents barely survived that "we" during the Second World War in Nazi-allied Romania. Their few possessions packed in a couple of bags, they had been ready to travel on short notice and follow other family members to the terminal "labor" camps at Auschwitz and other crematoria. A few years later, our little family escaped the "we" of totalitarian communism, which ultimately spares no one, as even I surmised merely from strict censorship and the indigestible diet of Big Lies. To be sure, there are crimes committed in the name of "I." But no matter how heinous, those pale by comparison with the mass atrocities that invoke "us."

Fortunately, most often the "we" is justifiably comforting, when lovingly applied to family, community, and even all of humanity. It then can and usually does envelop each of us with the pleasure of sharing and mutual learning, lessening our sorrows and magnifying our joys. "We" is still the best word for human camaraderie and fellowship, for alleviating the loneliness to which each one of us is sentenced, guilty or not. Above all, it captures the mutuality that marriage can offer (ideally, at any rate).

It comes as no surprise that all three major Abrahamic religions have turned to the semimythical couples who were the first practitioners of each sect—Abraham and Sarah, Joseph and Mary, Mohammed and Khadija—as quintessential examples of soulmates who were completely devoted to one another, as discussed in chapter 9, "The First

Wives." No meaning is more important than the hardest "we" of all, the rarest and most difficult: also called "intimacy;" it is the ultimate gift, the blessing without which "I" is little more than an empty shell. We are all in search of soulmates and personal meaning, as discussed in chapter 10. The experience of complete empathy, of human reciprocity, is what Martin Buber called "I–Thou." That expression is not self-evident, but I can think of none better.

While true that in English "thou" is now virtually obsolete—the dictionary quaintly calls its usage "archaic"—it can still play a unique role, compensating for the deficiencies of its victorious successor, the democratic "you." "Thou" is most often applied to the Almighty, to spare the supplicant from having to resort to the overly democratic "you," which does not even preserve the common French distinction between the informal *toi* and the formal, polite *vous*. Since "you," even if capitalized, cannot hope to capture the category leap to the Higher Sphere, the lovely word "Thou" deserves rehabilitation as a colloquial vocabulary member in full standing.

But archaic or not, it serves as an important reminder that the relationship between a believer and the Author he presumes to invoke for solace has an extraordinarily special and unique texture, which must be emulated in our attitude toward other human beings. The *I–Thou* relationship with God is unlike any human connection, as God is assumed to already know what we are saying and feeling; moreover, God loves each one of us with the most profound love imaginable. The believer should know that each of us shares in the Divine Spirit: since we are made in God's image, He treats us with absolute compassion and respect. The corresponding relationship among human beings, therefore, should emulate that relationship at least in the sense that another soul is to be treated with absolute respect. Conversely, whenever we treat one another in any other way than as God treats each of us—as spiritual beings equally loved by God—we transform another into an object, or a means, which is to say, an "it."

When used with lower caps, as in "thou," the word may refer to a relationship precisely similar to the human–divine connection. Hence the expression "I–thou" may resemble "I–Thou" in that both involve a spiritual bond, utterly incompatible with an un-reciprocal relationship that exists among morally unequal individuals. Martin Luther King Jr. explained this idea with crystaline clarity in his classic "Letter from a Birmingham Jail": "Any law that uplifts human personality is just. Any law that degrades human personality is unjust. All segregation statutes are unjust because segregation distorts the soul and damages the personality . . . Segregation, to use the terminology of the Jewish philosopher Martin Buber, substitutes an 'I–it' relationship for an 'I–thou' relationship and ends up relegating persons to the status of things."[21]

Buber's language, unfortunately, is not as easily accessible: academic, arcane, and excessively cerebral, it belies the profoundly emotional undertone of his message. We will explore his work in greater detail in chapter 11. But the fundamental problem, I am afraid, is the medium itself: the language of rational thought, which engages the wrong part of the brain, or at least not enough of it. For besides reason, we also need heart and soul to penetrate the mystery of intimacy. A far more promising venue is allegory, symbol, story, and legend: in brief, the language of myth. It is for this reason that in the end we can appreciate in a whole new way the magnificent story of creation.

No ordinary prose can match the image of God resting after having created the world: The Author of our universe beheld His handiwork and saw that it was *good*. How could God not wish to share that joy? A celestial pause and then, with the simplicity of plainsong, proceeds the beginning of history: "And God created man in His image, in the image of God He created him; male and female, He created them. God blessed them. . . ." (*Genesis* 1: 27–28). And when He was finally finished, on the sixth day, "God saw all that He had made, and found it very good" (*Genesis* 1: 31). Male and female are blessed as the Creator's *soulmates,* for they were made in God's image as not mere living things but souls in the highest sense. At the same time, they are *soulmates* to each other, spiritual helpmates who alone of all God's creatures can also truly *see* the world's goodness. Unfortunately, with the advent of science, modern man has been finding it increasingly difficult to understand the idea of a soulmate.

Respect

The true community does not arise through people having feelings for one another (though indeed not without it), but first, through their taking their stand in living mutual relation with a living Center, and second, their being in living mutual relation with one another.
Martin Buber, I and Thou

The fear and love of God combined give man his true autonomy in the world. . . . Buber has a strong sense of the paradox involved in the

> *divine power of grace. Grace is free and uncontrolled—"He bestows his grace and mercy on whom he will"—and yet man's deeds count. Without grace there is nothing, and yet man must make the "beginning."*
> *Will Herbert,* The Writings of Martin Buber

Perhaps the main distinguishing feature of Western civilization is the importance placed upon the sanctity of the individual as against group-based or collectivist ideologies. A critical characteristic of contemporary American culture, it nevertheless needs to be qualified. Individualism at its most crass is little more than egoism that, reduced to solipsism, can become pathological. The form of individualism truly conducive to morality and creativity is necessarily reciprocal, presupposing mutual respect among sovereign human beings. Its celebrated expression is the Golden Rule: *Do not do onto others as you would have them not do onto you.*[22]

This—negative—formulation of the Golden Rule is in many ways the essence of the Abrahamic creed. One of its most eloquent expressions is credited to Rabbi Hillel the Elder, born in Babylon about a century BCE. In response to a heathen who, wishing to become a Jew, asked him for a summary of the Jewish religion in the most concise terms, Rabbi Hillel allegedly said, "What is hateful to thee, do not unto thy fellow man: this is the whole Law; the rest is mere commentary."[23]

A more complex but still fairly straightforward statement of the same principle was articulated by the German philosopher Immanuel Kant at the dawn of the nineteenth century. Known as the categorical imperative, the Kantian commandment states, *Treat another always as an end, never as a means.* Or, to quote Buber again—and Martin Luther King—always consider another as a "thou," never as an "it." As will also be seen in chapter 11, Kant had taken the story of creation very seriously in defining the relationship of respect among human beings. Indeed, all three—Kant, Buber, and King—promoted the same original idea that lies at the root of the Abrahamic tradition and hence of Western civilization, indeed at the root of every civilization: human beings must treat one another with due respect.

Who belongs to Western civilization and who does not is not merely a question of geography, or even of theology. Emphatically, it does—or at least can—include Islam. For the Quran says,

> Verily, they who believe [Muslims], and they who follow the Jewish religion, and the Christians, and the Sabeites—whoever of these

believeth in God and the last day, and doeth that which is right, shall have their reward with their Lord; fear shall not come upon them, neither shall they be grieved. (*Sura* 2:59)[24]

Nor does this refer only to men. The Quran addresses us all:

O people! Fear your Lord, who hath created you of one soul [*nafs*], and of him created his wife, and from these twain hath spread abroad so many men and women. (*Sura* 4:1)[25]

Malaysian Muslim scholar Amina Wadud-Muhsin explains that according to the Quran, "the final step in the creation of humankind is that step which elevates them above the rest of creation: the breathing of the Spirit of Allah (*nafkhat al-ruh*) into each human—male or female."[26] That Spirit is in everyone who does no harm and hence should, in turn, be left unharmed. She reinforces the opinion of the much-loved nineteenth-century Egyptian scholar Sir (yes, he had been knighted) Sayyid Ahmad Khan (1817–1898), who had stated unequivocally that "in truth, in no religion and in no nation's law have women and men been considered as equal as in the religion of Islam"[27]—by which he meant, specifically, the creed of the Quran alone, absent subsequent additions and distortions.

Every religion is born in hope and compassion; this is certainly true of all the monotheistic Abrahamic religions. Yet no one religion has stayed absolutely true to its original benevolent intent, and no religion or sect has been spared distortion or failed to be manipulated, sometimes unwittingly but often cynically, by misguided individuals who have taken advantage of the poetry and metaphor that permeates all sacred texts to incite others to commit acts of cruelty, at times of monstrous proportions. Unfortunately, absent miraculous intervention (whose improbability has disappointed many a pious gambler), the chances that humans will choose brotherly love over unbrotherly strife are scanty at best.

Not everyone longs equally for love, brotherly or otherwise. An orphan raised on the street who has never known the warmth of a parent's hug may lack any conception of it, and in its hurt, his soul may be filled with nothing but desperate anger. If all there was to a sexual encounter in someone's experience was rape, amounting to a physical struggle followed by disgust, small wonder that "soulmate" does not capture anything remotely familiar. But if there is any hope for civilization, for an uplifting, ennobling, and worthwhile human community to emerge out of the current cacophony of strife, debasement, nihilism, and fanaticism, I believe we must start by revisiting the original vision of our two fore-parents. And that means we must start with resurrecting Eve.

It was no accident that the mother of life was willing to take risks, even very dangerous ones. She was the first who wanted *to know, to feel, to fully be*—at almost any price.

Notes

1. George Lakoff and Mark Johnson, *Metaphors We Live By*, 3 (italics added).

2. See Shira Halevi's *Adam and Havah: A Targum of Genesis 1:26–5:5*, 61–63. Citing the eleventh-century biblical commentator Rabbi Shlomo Isaac, she notes that *v-yirdu* is actually a "weak" verb in Hebrew, because it loses one of its three consonants during conjugation—meaning that it carries the possibility of more than one root word, which could be either "go down" or "descend" or "rule/dominate" and "take charge of."

3. Throughout this section, I italicize *Adam* to capture the ambiguity of the concept, which refers to both mankind (*adam*, uncapitalized) and a particular individual (Adam), who is, however, not specifically so named by God or, indeed, his own spouse Eve, in the beginning. Trible, in *God and the Rhetoric of Sexuality*, 100, explains how male and female became sexually differentiated after the metaphorical excision of Eve from her helpmate's body.

4. Citing the *Talmud Bavli*, Sotah 5a, Halevi notes that the name for human (*Adam*) indicates dust and blood. Other Talmudic commentators emphasize that the dust is collected from the four corners of the earth, added by God to breathe from the four winds of the world, as well as the waters of the world, creating humankind red, black, and white. Ibid., 37–38.

5. A thorough discussion is available in *The Making of the Old Testament*, p. 60–72, though an overview is found in Robert Davidson, *The Cambridge Bible Commentary, Genesis 1–11*, 5–7.

6. Davidson, ibid., 7.

7. Ibid.

8. Ibid., 18 and 26.

9. Ibid., 37: "The words *'ishshah* and *'ish* come from two different roots in Hebrew, just as female and male do in English. It is one example among many in the Old Testament of a popular play on words, based on similarity of sound."

10. Davidson notes that many scholars have claimed that *hawwah* should be linked with the Aramaic word for snake (*hiwya*). Ibid., 47. Even so, the context implies that Eve's name is meant to indicate hope and procreation.

11. Plato, *Symposium* 201 d.

12. 206 c–d.

13. 206 e.

14. Mircea Eliade, *Patterns in Comparative Religion*, 421.

15. Ibid.

16. Ibid., 424.
17. Ibid., 425.
18. See Gershom G. Scholem's brief yet authoritative Introduction to *Zohar: The Book of Splendor*.
19. Halevi, *Adam and Havah: A Targum of Genesis*, 55—59.
20. Halevi cites *Bereshith Rabbah* XIV.7, ibid., 38.
21. Martin Luther King Jr., "Letter from a Birmingham Jail," paragraph 16.
22. A seemingly equivalent corollary—*Do onto others as you would have them do onto you*—while somewhat simpler, is not quite synonymous with the former. The former mandates a negative, the latter a positive.
23. Babylonian Talmud, tractate Shabbat 31a. http://www.jewishencyclopedia.com/view.jsp?artid=730&letter=H#ixzz0wDTSeWDc
24. *The Koran*, 8.
25. Ibid., 49.
26. Amina Wadud-Muhsin, *Qur'an and Woman*, 17. She adds in a footnote: "This is the closest that the Quranic version of creation comes to the biblical version of man in God's image" (27).
27. "Rights of Women," in *Modernist and Fundamentalist Debates in Islam*, ed. Moaddel and Talattof, 159.

3

To Know or Not to Know—
Is That the Question?

Now that the man has become like one of us, knowing good and bad,
what if he should stretch out his hand and take also from the tree of
life and eat, and live forever!
Genesis 3:22

What if, indeed! Humans would then become immortal? *Not* an option. In Greek mythology, any human who had the *hubris* (*chutzpa,* i.e., gall) to steal the gods' ambrosia or even contemplate immortality would pay for it with eternal torture.

What an extraordinary passage this is: God has just acknowledged that, after tasting the fruit from the Tree of Knowledge, by suddenly gaining the capacity of knowing good and bad, mankind has come perilously close to its Creator. No longer merely fashioned in God's image, humans were now *like* the gods! And as such, they could be expected to desire—and even achieve?—immortality. It was this eventuality perhaps even more than the original transgression that precipitated their expulsion from Eden. But what does that tell us about being human?

Let's look more closely at the logical sequence of events. After humans were created in God's image—let's call this phase one—came a second phase, when they became like the gods by knowing good and bad; this was to be followed, at least in principle, by a third phase, in case they were to have tasted the fruit from the Tree of Life—in God's estimation, a very real possibility, had they been allowed to stay in Eden. Interestingly, the only real difference between phases two and three seems to be that in the former, humans are mortal, while in the latter, after tasting from the most truly coveted Tree, they would no longer die. Thus it would seem that humans who know good and bad are far closer to the Divinity than they are to animals despite their

45

common earthly origin. Both humans and animals had been fashioned by God from dust. (Well, except for Eve, who was fashioned from a human being . . . but never mind.) Clearly, the special knowledge of good and bad evidently made (almost) all the difference. After gaining that knowledge, humans became more godlike than ever before.

But what, exactly, accounted for that enormous difference? What special faculty, or insight, or quality, did humans suddenly came to possess after eating from the Tree of Knowledge?

Humans are smarter than animals, of course, but intelligence is simply a matter of degree. We now know that many animals—even plants!—are capable of communication that may well be described as quasi-linguistic. Any dog or cat owner knows that it is possible to converse with their furry friends, even (well, at least in the case of dogs) fairly successfully. Hence language is not enough of a divider; there has to be something else involved.

That something else is the genius for *evaluation*. What no other species but *Homo sapiens* possesses is the ability to know good from bad and also, for that matter, beautiful from ugly. More to the point, knowing what good and bad (or beautiful and ugly) *mean* is a feat no other species is capable of attaining. Animals obviously have preferences, but they do not discriminate on either moral or aesthetic grounds. If they seem to punish another animal by killing or wounding it, the cause is not moral outrage but either hunger or self-defense. Nor can mere beasts reward righteousness, no matter how affectionate they may be—often more than most humans. While animals may be lovingly devoted to the point of unflinching self-sacrifice, what they do *not* do is render value judgments. Their approval or disapproval seems simply reflexive.

How, then, did mankind become catapulted so perilously close to the highest echelon of being, simply through the ability to know good and evil? The original creation of mankind in God's image had already secured humanity's place far beyond the other, lesser species, by partaking in spiritual affinity and Divine love, which are God's essential infinite attributes. Through language and thought, mankind was able to analyze and reason; mankind could immediately correctly *name*— and hence understand, and in that sense rule over—the animals. But it took still one more leap forward for human beings to realize that they could also grasp the difference between good and bad, or right and wrong. Humans could suddenly grasp the fact that they could choose, whether well or ill. They could evaluate: they could tell that something—like, say, the world—was *good*.

And . . . . wasn't that the reason God had created them in the first place?

After venturing to taste the sacred fruit against which they had been duly warned, humans instantly realized the overwhelming, frightening fact that they could suddenly reflect upon their own behavior and judge it. They could be conscious and self-conscious. They could also then think of themselves as being and *not being*—as living or dead. They could contemplate their *own* mortality and—unlike any other breathing organism—deplore and dread it.

But once Adam and Eve became aware that they would die, once they pondered, comprehended, and absorbed what it meant, what could possibly prevent them from yearning for immortality? And since, therefore, man would understand death as no animal can, what would happen if he should stretch out his hand and take also from the Tree of Life and then eat and live forever? God had every reason to worry.

It is true that knowing good and bad can mean many things, and scholars have long speculated what the biblical writers might have intended by those words. In light of similar biblical passages, for example, E. A. Speiser concludes that its usage in *Genesis* is intended to indicate that Adam and Eve were "in full possession of mental and physical powers"—as contrasted to the eighty-year-old Samuel, whose "capacity for physical and aesthetic pleasures is no longer what it used to be [and hence] . . . has lost his ability to appreciate good and bad."[1] Such knowledge, then, is a form of active appreciation, neither general theoretical understanding nor mere scientific information. Other biblical scholars believe the expression is shorthand for omniscience (i.e., knowing everything "from A to Z").

The authors of *The Bible and the Ancient Near East* are typical in lamenting that the expression is "a much misunderstood phrase. The antonyms 'good and evil' mean 'everything' here (see also *Genesis* 24:50, *Zephaniah* 1:12, and *Proverbs* 15:3). The same expression in inverted order occurs in Egyptian, where 'evil–good' means 'everything.' . . . [Rather,] man obtained universal knowledge, and to that extent shares with God a faculty that had been a divine prerogative."[2] This last sentence, however, slithers inexcusably from *obtaining* universal knowledge to *having the faculty for* obtaining such knowledge—two concepts as different as buying a ticket is from winning the lottery: one may possess the *means* to attaining complete knowledge (the faculty) yet not actually possess the prize itself (the knowledge).

It seems best to turn to the biblical context itself, where good and bad come across as referring to values, not facts. The immediate consequence of eating the forbidden fruit is a kind of knowledge that does not admit of truth or falsehood: after their transgression, when Adam's and Eve's eyes truly open for the first time, the two are astonished to discover that . . . they are *naked.* But it is certainly not as if they suddenly put on glasses to see the fine print; they do not gain new information, previously unavailable. What they acquire is not, so to speak, rocket science: rather, they suddenly understand the potential effect of nakedness on other human beings, the allure of sexuality, and the meaning of modesty.

It is generally assumed that eating the forbidden fruit, a sin committed by Eve first, followed by Adam, presumably at her urging, positively infuriated God. Apparently incensed, God expelled mankind from Eden, condemning the two upstarts forever to tragic exile and sentencing them both to death. But important nuances are lost in version of the seminal event. Without doubt, God's response upon learning of the transgression does look a lot like anger:

Cursed be the ground because of you;
By toil shall you eat of it
All the days of your life . . .
Until you return to the ground—
For from it you were taken.
For dust you are
And to dust you shall return.
(*Genesis* 3:17)

So mankind is indeed punished—fated to become mere dust once again, after a difficult life. Are we to infer, perhaps, that had it not been for disobeying God's admonition against eating the fruit of the Tree of Knowledge, mankind would have lived happily in Eden, literally ever after? Boston University professor Roger Shattuck adopts this, commonly held, assumption: "After forming Adam, the Lord God plants two particular named trees and imposes an interdict on the Tree of the Knowledge of Good and Evil. No such restriction applies to the Tree of Life, presumably because Adam is created immortal and does not need it—not yet."[3] This ambiguity is misleading: surely it is not that no such restriction applies to the latter. God simply says nothing about that Tree. Maybe the Creator simply didn't want to take a chance. As any parent knows, and the admonition against the Tree of Knowledge confirmed, an explicit ban is often the surest guarantee of its disobedience.[4]

It should give us pause, however, to believe too readily that an all-powerful, all-loving God would react with such seemingly disproportionate cruelty. The two humans had certainly defied God's unequivocal commandment, but the ultimate death sentence—abolishing forever the Edenic (perhaps even endless) life—simply for eating a piece of fruit? To be sure, the fruit of the Tree of Knowledge was altogether extraordinary, but that would almost provide an additional argument for leniency. After all, the fruit did not cause sloth or stupor; on the contrary, by God's own assessment, it would render mankind *more godlike*!

One might have even expected God to have outright urged mankind to taste a worthy fruit whose immediate aftereffect is the recognition of nakedness—welcome testimony to a newly acquired sense of modesty, leading to the felicitous acquisition of clothing. One might have thought that God might have been pleased to watch them as "they sewed fig leaves together and made themselves girdles." Rather than baring themselves in wanton lasciviousness, man and woman were suddenly no longer comfortable naked, like oblivious children: one could say that they had . . . grown up.

The acquisition of clothing has been traditionally seen as positive signs of civilization, as many commentators have observed—notably Leon Kass in *The Beginning of Wisdom: Reading Genesis*: "Sexual shame becomes the mother of invention, art, and new modes of cooperative sociality; note well, it is not the woman alone who sews."[5] Besides, why would an infinitely good God want humans to obey blindly when they were obviously—and mercifully—created to be knowledge-seeking? Could God want them *not* to know good and evil? Should they be moral morons?

In his exquisitely researched book, informed by personal wisdom, Leon Kass expresses my own, I suspect not uncommon, reaction to Eve's desire for knowledge: "The woman's dialogue with the serpent shows that it is she, not the man, who is open to conversation, who imagines new possibilities, who reaches for improvement . . . Her aspirations, however diffuse in direction and ambiguous in result, are the first specifically human longings."[6] Surely God would not wish to smother such a noble impulse. The lady has gumption—or, shall we say, *chutzpa*.

It is hard to accept that God was testing our innocent ancestors by presenting *"To know or not to know"* as the Edenic equivalent of

Shakespeare's "*To be or not to be.*" It seems so utterly ungodlike. "*To know and not be, or not to know and be*" is a dilemma to which no loving deity would subject its spiritual progeny. On the contrary, a benevolent God would wish us to know and choose wisely, no matter if our stay on this earth were brief and ephemeral or somewhat indefinite, even if not infinite. After creating a world full of wonder and beauty, seeing how very good this world truly was, God would naturally wish that the human children created in their Author's own image should see the same, to share the joy. Again, wasn't that the whole point of creating us?

This seems evident to me, and fortunately, there is additional solid textual evidence to support it. Properly understood, God's benevolence toward *adam* is actually reflected in the divine desire to create a being capable of free choice—which was impossible without impressing upon human creatures the enormous consequences of personal responsibility. It is the profound spiritual insight into the human condition that renders the biblical narrative so truly revolutionary: the fact that mankind is capable of value judgment, accompanied by the inevitable awareness of personal mortality.

Contrary to the generally accepted narrative of the Original Sin, the divine challenge posed to mankind by God may be understood rather as a gift than a curse. Faced with the dilemma *To know and not be, or not to know and be*, mankind simply chose knowledge, no matter what the price: rather than a failure, this looks more like an awakening, even a triumph. Writes Roger Shattuck:

> Despite its familiarity, the creation story from *Genesis* is as invisible to many of us as air, as our own personality. It surrounds us too closely. We cannot stand back in order to see it better. The Bible nowhere uses the word *fall* to designate what happened to Adam and Eve.[7]

If the so-called Fall is understood instead as the Divine initiation to freedom, it follows that the very consciousness of *choice* is itself the lesson, even before the fateful step is taken transgressing against God's Word. As Eve evaluates the pros and cons in dialogue with the guileful serpent, there is recognition of options, consideration of costs and benefits, and eventually a verdict. Adam then chooses to follow her advice, having the additional benefit of her example. The chosen act turns out to cause unintended consequences for them both.

So while seeming to treat Adam and Eve like children who are expected to obey on pure authority, by warning them against eating the Fruit of Knowledge, God deliberately *requires* them to realize that they both have the choice *not* to obey. "*To obey or not to obey*" is a live dilemma, a sharp, mutually exclusive dichotomy. As Adam and Eve must grasp the concept of facing a real, viable alternative, they cannot but realize that choice implies opting for one over another set of consequences.

God thus offers the first humans a practical lesson in understanding the essence of spiritual existence by illustrating the true nature of *freedom*. And for mankind to choose is to value, to select that which is—or appears to be—*better* than the alternative. In other words, it is to opt for good over evil.

Freedom implies future responsibility: if the choice is good, the result is positive; a bad choice, by contrast, is regrettable. What is truly (as opposed to just seemingly) good or bad is partly a matter of experience, partly unknowable insofar as unforeseen circumstances may occur, sooner or later, to contradict an earlier judgment, but *that* a difference exists is a prerequisite to understanding choice as such. Choice, in turn, is required by morality.

This is, therefore, the human predicament, to which there is no alternative: for mankind, "*To choose or not to choose*" is not a viable option. Once a human being chooses, the Godlike verdict is delivered: this, my choice, is good—or not. Like God, humans have the ability— indeed privilege—to behold the world and see whether and how it is good (or in some respects bad), and if so, why. We choose what seems good to us and must accept the consequences. Though manifestly dangerous, it is also an awesome privilege—no small reward for being sentenced to mortality.

Eve gives it a try first, by deciding to risk a bite, then Adam follows suit at her urging but also by seeing her example. *Eve's thought process of weighing consequences, pros and cons, had constituted the prototypal exercise in moral deliberation.*

Eve's principal concern seems to have been whether or not the punishment for insubordination would be death, which the serpent dismissed as unlikely, and she chose to either believe him or run the risk—although it is far from clear whether at that point she could even understand the meaning of personal death. Indeed, God's concern that subsequent to their transgression (though presumably not before) the two humans would want to seek immortality seems to underscore that mankind neither possessed immortality at the time nor realized the fact. That realization would inevitably come later, with shame and the consciousness of harm, the dangers of otherness, and the eventual despair of finality, which would lead to the quest for some kind of personal salvation.

Freedom is hard, as is self-consciousness. To know that acts may have good or bad consequences yet not to possess infinite knowledge, as does God, implies the possibility—in fact, probability—of error and evil, for which the retribution may be exceptionally painful. Mankind's existence carried a hefty price: by choosing to disobey, the first woman and man chose above all *choice* itself. An omniscient God had to know that eating the forbidden fruit was the necessary, even indispensable, prelude to being truly, consciously, human: that seminal act would be fated to provide a lesson in the meaning of *personal responsibility*.

An especially insightful analysis of this celebrated episode, the misnamed Fall, is once again carried out by Leon Kass:

> The "punishment" for trying to rise above childishness and animality is to be forced to live like a human being. The so-called punishment seems to fit the so-called crime, in at least two ways. If the crime of transgression represents the human aspiration to self-sufficiency and godliness (free choice necessarily implying humanly grounded knowledge of good and bad), the so-called punishment thwarts that aspiration by opposition: human beings instead of self-sufficiency receive estrangement, dependence, division, and rule. Second, and more profound, the so-called punishment fits the crime simply by making clear the unanticipated meaning of the choice and desire implicit in the transgression itself. . . . He learns, through the revealing conversation with God, that his choice for humanization, wisdom, knowledge of good and bad, or autonomy really means at the same time also estrangement from the world, self-division, division of labor, toil, fearful knowledge of death, and the institution of inequality, rule, and subservience.[8]

And it is true that, according to the biblical text, God does not curse either the woman or the man, exactly, but *the earth*—which will thenceforth be tilled, so humans may use its yield. "Far from being incensed," writes Kass, "God was especially pleased to find, following the discovery of mankind's transgression, that neither man nor woman denied responsibility." Yes, they both made excuses for themselves, but this was a welcome concession that they had done something which needed to be excused. "Judgmental self-consciousness gives birth to conscience," writes Kass. "Conscience, in turn, can face the music, to learn and live with the consequences of one's wrongful choice and deed,"[9] if wrongful they turn out to be. There is no other way of becoming human.

The inference is that the other crucial dilemma—*To know or not to know*—is, similarly, neither a question nor an option: to be human is *to have to know*. Some knowledge will be dangerous, painful, even devastating. Few would deny that there are many things we would sooner keep from those we love, to avoid hurting them.

For example, I will never forget when, having tried hard to prevent my dying mother from learning how rapidly her brain was being invaded by a malignant tumor, one of her attending doctors inadvertently blurted it all out. Admittedly, after the initial horror had turned her face whiter than chalk, she smiled at me with a serenity that has sustained me ever since. But I still could not help harboring homicidal thoughts against the inconsiderate doctor.

Many things, too, should not be known until we are ready for it. Sex education is inappropriate in kindergarten (with allowances for *tactful* advice to toddlers on both avoiding pedophiles and seeking help), but indispensable later during adolescence, preferably delivered in a discrete, family setting. In fact, sexual knowledge would seem to be indispensable for all adults, since procreation in a safe and loving environment is so essential to growing up healthy.

This brings us back to the immediate aftereffect of Adam and Eve's infamous meal: their eyes were opened to see their nakedness for the first time, indicating their new awareness of sexual expression— implying consciousness of having to cover something up, preventing it from being seen. But "shame," writes Kass, "presupposes a concern for self-esteem and the presence of pride; only a being concerned with self-esteem could have his pride wounded and experience shame."[10]

Certainly, sexual awakening is also accompanied by the awareness of lust, which garments, especially alluring ones, may transform into civilized, enhanced admiration. Adam and Eve's newly sewn loincloths, therefore, played a dual role: in addition to coverage and protection, they presaged art. The needle is actually the first human invention (language, another potential candidate, is considered by many to be an endowed capacity—as, of course, does *Genesis*, since Adam started naming things immediately after "birth"). "By taking up the needle, the human beings," continues Kass, "whether they know it or not, are declaring the inadequacy of the Garden of Eden. By becoming artisans, they are voting for their expulsion from the garden; they are choosing civilization." Protection, adornment, beautification, as well as the use of reason, "therefore provide[s] the space for the imagination to grow, transforming human lust into love and allowing room for courtship and intimacy."[11]

In other words, eating the infamous fruit was indispensable for the relationship between man and woman to become not merely physical but spiritual—and in that sense, truly human. This is the precise opposite of the far more common interpretation of the so-called Fall as a euphemism for the deplorable, sinful first sexual act, and by implication, sexuality itself. Though common, however, that interpretation seems implausible on the face of it: how could God be upset by the human couple engaging in what they had been urged to do upon being blessed at the outset of their life's journey, namely, to be fertile and multiply? It comes as no surprise that the first thing reported about Adam and Eve's earthly sojourn is the conception of a son, whose very existence Eve attributes to God's help. (*Genesis* 4:1)

There is no indication that Adam and Eve thought themselves banished for their promiscuity. On the contrary, Adam and Eve start their post-Edenic career by acknowledging God's good will and love. God's gifts to them had been immeasurably generous: having first given them one another, they were next blessed with a child, followed by a second, and many more later. They both lived for a very long time—presumably, each nearly a millennium (although the Bible does not indicate when Eve died) as one another's companion. According to *Genesis*, not only were Adam and Eve always soulmates but also, to one another, *sole* mates.

Prometheus and Pandora

Prometheus: *"I found them [humans] witless, and gave them the use*
of their wits and made them masters of their minds."
Aeschylus, Prometheus Unbound

The story of Prometheus, originally recorded in the eighth century BCE by the poet Hesiod,[12] is actually the oldest source for the story of human creation. Hesiod's account was later adapted by the playwright Aeschylus (525–456 BCE) and by the philosopher Plato (427?–347 BCE). The latter's account, in the dialogue *Protagoras*, has the gods starting the job of creating men and other assorted living creatures from a mixture of clay and fire, but soon, rather casually, giving up in midstream.[13] In the manner of pampered children bored with a game and uninterested in its final outcome, the gods task the two Titan brothers Epimetheus and Prometheus to finish up. After the unwise of the two, Epimetheus, distributes all the gifts of nature among the animals, leaving men naked and unprotected, his brother comes to the rescue of the hapless humans. Prometheus steals some of the fire of creative power from the gods and gives it to mankind, thereby becoming humans' first benefactor and friend. The crime, however, enrages Zeus, who proceeds to punish the brazen Titan with a form of torture exceptional even by Olympian standards. Notwithstanding some minor differences, all the Greek accounts of the Prometheus story agree on the nature of his punishment: tied to a rock, a vulture was to help himself to Prometheus's liver, whose daily regeneration would insure that visits from the hungry beast need never end. But Zeus doesn't stop there.

The King of Olympus also decides to have a woman fashioned by one of the Gods, the handy Hephaistos, to compensate for man's undeserved—certainly unauthorized—gift. Named Pandora (meaning, "all the gifts") by the god Hermes, who is told "to put in her in a shameless mind and a deceitful nature" and also give her a jar, which she was forbidden to open, filled with misery, she is then sent to seduce Prometheus and Epimetheus, whereupon a series of events would occur that would spell tragedy for mankind. Prometheus (whose name means "foresight") immediately warns Epimetheus (meaning—what else?—"hindsight") against falling for the winsome airhead, but to no avail. Following her marriage to gullible Mr. Hindsight, Pandora obviously ignores her warning and opens the mysterious jar, thus releasing toil, sickness, and death to the unsuspecting humans. By the time she manages to close it, allegedly all that is left at the bottom is, of all things, hope. Talk about a curse!

To summarize, then, Pandora, the first woman sent to earth, unwittingly proceeds to bring man only grief, by way of punishment for a transgression against the gods committed by someone else, while she herself flaunts—as planned, mind you—divine orders. How better to reinforce the message that gods are *not* to be disobeyed, no matter what? Whether well-intentioned toward mankind as was Prometheus, or irresponsibly vain like Pandora, it mattered not at all to the gods of ancient Greece: they obviously did not much care about human well-being.

Admittedly, there are other interpretations of the Pandora story. Besides the question whether she was indeed supposed to have been the first woman,[14] she may have been viewed more positively in versions other than Hesiod's. For example, excavations that are believed to represent Pandora portray her as the goddess Gaia, who was also known as the Giver of All Gifts—thereby belying the assumption that her jar contained only calamities. Also, in *The Birds*, a comedy by the witty Aristophanes, a contemporary of Socrates and Plato in fifth century BCE, there is a reference to sacrificing a lamb to Pandora, who is identified as the Earth "because she bestows all things necessary to life." Actually, even Hesiod concedes that mankind needs to experience suffering and hard work, which throws a rather different light on the moral of the narrative: pain is not all evil but an intrinsic part of life. In any event, in all the versions, it seems clear that if anyone is to be blamed for the entire sorry episode, it is neither Prometheus nor Pandora but Zeus himself, whose capricious behavior is here on full display.

Let's take a closer look at the gift that Prometheus gives mankind, which is usually assumed to be ordinary fire. Aeschylus, in his play *Prometheus Unbound*, however, has the brave Titan describe a gift of a far more precious kind of flame: he claims to have given humans the fire of reason and wisdom. Not only does Hesiod mention nothing but fire, he actually blames Prometheus for helping mankind if the price is committing the sin of insubordination. Hesiod evidently represented a common Greek belief that disobeying the all-powerful, fickle gods, is the greatest transgression, far outweighing the virtues of courage and benevolence that earned Prometheus his reputation as mankind's first and foremost ally and friend. Such was Hesiod's fear of the gods that it eclipsed his gratitude to the great Titan.

A few centuries later, the Romans adopted the Greek religion and recast the story of human creation though still denying them any credit for our birth. Among the best known accounts is by Ovid (43 BCE–17? CE), who in the opening to his famous *Metamorphoses* credits the Titan Prometheus alone with shaping humans from clay and water, in the image of gods but absent any divine assistance. The implication seems to be that humans might never even have existed, for all that the gods cared. While Greek mythology is full of stories illustrating divine intervention on behalf of humans—to say nothing of infatuations galore—the distinct message is that gods generally cannot be counted upon to help us. Such help, when bestowed upon lucky mortals, is merely a fortunate fluke. But one thing is certain: disobeying the gods, whether by man or anyone else, would be invariably punished, if only out of sheer caprice. With such role models, no wonder that the Greeks turned away from Olympus altogether and found better guidance in Reason, Beauty, and Love.

Love, indeed. It is in fact the story of Psyche and Eros that best captures (foreshadows?) some of the key insights of the biblical story of man's creation—and specifically the punishment incurred by a woman who dares to disobey a god, her curiosity getting the better of her. The great humanist philosopher Erasmus may have actually confused Pandora with Psyche, on the basis that both had "succumbed to temptation," according to art historians Dora and Erwin Panofsky. They speculate that Erasmus confounded the two myths, that of the first woman's creation and the myth about the origin of the soul, because of their uncanny resemblance to the story of Eve.[15]

Eros and Psyche

> *Oh! yet too dearly loved! Lost Psyche! Why*
> *With cruel fate wouldst thou unite thy power,*
> *And force me thus thine arms adored to fly?*
> *Yet cheer thy drooping soul, some happier hour*
> *Thy banished steps may lead back to thy lover's bower.*
> Mary Tighe, Psyche; or, The Legend of Love *(1805)*

The most ancient extant version of this splendid story dates from the second century, as told by Lucius Apuleius (b. 125?) in *The Golden Ass*, although the original is likely to have been much older.[16] Since no other ancient myth before the Bible reveals as sophisticated a conception of the human soul, and the importance of knowledge as expressed through intimacy, it deserves at least a brief summary at this stage, with more to come in the next chapter that zeroes in on the inseparability of love and self.

I had always wondered why the men who had authored that ancient myth should have felt that the inner being, the essence of the human psyche, is most aptly symbolized by a woman. Apparently, the ache of awareness, the burden of self-consciousness, seemed most aptly feminine; control, meanwhile, would remain the domain of the male. The fact that the mythical Soul was imagined to have been even more beautiful than Beauty Herself—the proud goddess Aphrodite (Venus, to the Romans)—is testimony to the infatuation with man's prize possession, what he believes to be most irresistibly tempting: his inner nature. The gods were bound to punish us for our Soul's splendor. The wound that Psyche was to receive had been intended never to heal.

Fiercely jealous, the clever goddess of beauty was cruel enough to spare Psyche's life: at first, Aphrodite/Venus decided that the exquisite mortal should live crippled by a spell, destined for loneliness. Much as she would yearn to offer herself, Aphrodite made sure that no one would want Psyche's libation. Shunned, her treasures would become irrelevant; her cry, mute. All her enviable attributes were no better than undeliverable parcels. And since she could not give, she had nothing.

Admittedly, giving is a presumptuous conceit; we all have only what we borrow from the world, except for our life, which we received as an ephemeral gift to begin with, and so is ours only elusively. We attempt to give by extending a wish, a greeting, with hope. We are immeasurably lucky if the gift is ever embraced. (That is, rather than merely accepted, which makes it merely a notice of interest.) And to share completely, to share another's soul, is better than sharing merely another's body. Beautiful Psyche understood that well.

Psyche's loveliness could have been neither prevented nor obliterated by the Goddess of Beauty, yet the formidable Aphrodite was not without insidious tools of vengeance and obedient accomplices. The goddess's next chosen instrument would be delivered by her mischievous son Eros, who complacently complied with the wishes of his jealous and cunning mother queen. Yet Aphrodite, overly confident in her son's Oedipal attachment, had failed to predict the effect of young Psyche's power even upon so undaunted and ruthless a spirit as the winged archer.

Coming upon the stunning mortal, Eros stumbles, intimidated, uncomfortably altered as never before. His heart pierced, he emerges for the first time enslaved by the same passion he had so heedlessly been inflicting upon his victims up to now. No arrow had pierced him before, nor would one ever do so again. He too had evidently found his *sole* as well as, literally, *soul* mate.

Psyche herself, innocently asleep, had done nothing to lure him. His love embraces her instantly: once having seen her, he needs no more words, enchanted on the spot. The encounter fuses them, as they are wedded after merely a look from him. The moment she awakens, however, all is dark. Eros tells her that it must stay that way.

Eros returns night after night, as Psyche waits for him with trepidation and expectation—the passionate fear. But when she tries to light a candle to catch a glimpse of him, he stops her with terror and asks that she promise never again to try to see him. Grateful and mesmerized, she respects his categorical admonition as the price of their marriage. She obeys as if in a trance. Yet it makes no sense to her: Why the secrecy? All too human, Psyche longs intensely—how could she not?—to know the identity of her husband.

Fretting over the mystery, it later occurs to her that at least she is not prohibited from asking those around her whether they have any clue as to who her elusive lover really is—at least, what he looks like. Whereupon one of her sisters, jealous and not a little malicious, decides to tell her that the strange man can only be a dangerous monster, a kind of snake perhaps. (Archetypal shades of Eden?) Psyche dismisses the suggestion as preposterous, but the sister insists, undaunted, urging her to find out for herself the next time Eros visits her.

At first, Psyche is afraid to break the conjugal promise and rejects the suggestion, but her curiosity, enhanced at once by fear and fearlessness, prevails in the end. Upon her husband's next descent into her chamber, she is especially sweet and soothing. Charmed and content, Eros soon falls asleep next to her, quite at peace. Once she has assured herself that he is not likely to awaken, although unable to stop the trembling of her hands, Psyche lights the fateful candle. Mortified yet too curious, she musters enough courage to bring the flame close to his face. At which moment, far from horrified, she is stunned by his beauty and utters an involuntary cry of joyful surprise. Her winged lover is, literally, divine.

As if branded with hot irons, Eros jumps to his feet, furious to have been discovered. Thundering, he informs her that she must now be alone—he can no longer return, ever again. And promptly vanishes.

Candle in hand, Psyche is left speechless and devastated. She is as incapable of understanding the rationale for her punishment as she was bound to fall for the comely immortal youth whom she had not been permitted to behold. Does she regret having seen him? She needed to know him, and yet . . . . was this punishment worth it?

Undone, she recoils at the injustice: Why did the price have to be so unspeakably high? What could possibly explain his peculiar need for secrecy? Eros had seen her, and the vision had prompted his infatuation. But she, on the other hand, had been required to stay in the dark. Her marital duty would thus amount to nothing more than allowing herself to be loved passively—in truth, raped; unfairly, she was being denied the intimacy that is enhanced by sight.

She couldn't stop speculating: Was he perhaps afraid that once she saw him she might not reciprocate? An absurd suggestion—for he was dazzlingly handsome. No one could think otherwise. So what did this all mean? Could it now be really over—so suddenly? The story has a remarkably happy ending: despite the initial punishment, Psyche is eventually reunited with her husband. More than that, she is literally resurrected, as the gods permit her to join Olympus as . . . a goddess!

A fascinating modern version of the Psyche myth is found in the novel *Till We Have Faces,* by the late Oxford professor of medieval literature and Christian thought, the inimitable C. S. Lewis. Surprisingly little known, considering the popularity of the author's other writings, the novel's insights into biblical wisdom are also evidence of Lewis's profound understanding of the power of stories to convey spiritual truths. Dedicated to his young American wife Joy Davidson, *Till We Have Faces* is about faith and love that render all our faces beautiful. Rather than condemning curiosity, the impulse to know, the novel contrasts faith with empirical knowledge without, in any way, condemning the latter.

The novel is written from the point of view of Psyche's sister named Orual by Lewis, who according to legend had persuaded Psyche (here named Redival) to see her lover so as to make sure he is indeed a god and not a monster. In Lewis's version, Orual is afraid that her innocent Redival may be deluding herself and threatens to kill herself if her sweet little sister fails to verify who her husband really is. After Redival's demise, which inevitably follows her insubordination, Orual—who happened to be exceptionally ugly, though unlike Psyche's sisters, in no way jealous—is disconsolate and rages against the gods with these words, appealing to her audience:

> Now, you who read, judge between the gods and me. They gave me nothing in the world to love but Psyche and then took her from me. But that was not enough. They then brought me to her at such a place and time that it hung on my word whether she should continue in bliss or be cast out into misery. They would not tell me whether she was the bride of a god, or mad, or a brute's or villain's spoil. They would give no clear sign, though I begged for it. I had to guess. And because I guessed wrong they punished me—what's worse, punished me through her.[17]

Orual blasphemes readily, brazenly fearless:

> I say the gods deal very unrightly with us. For they will neither (which would be best of all) go away and leave us to live our own short days to ourselves, nor will they show themselves openly and tell us what they would have us do. For that too would be endurable . . . . I say, therefore, that there is no creature (toad, scorpion, or serpent) so noxious to man as the gods.[18]

After she becomes queen, following the death of their father, the Orual decides to hide her hideous face. With experience and with time, over the years, she gains some perspective on what had happened. Then finally, at the end of this unique novel, Lewis has her meeting Psyche/Redival again, at which point Orual finally understands all. She finally experiences faith; she finds herself "silenced by joy," in a manner similar to Lewis's own revelation detailed in his highly acclaimed autobiography, appropriately titled *Surprised by Joy.*[19]

Orual describes her feeling, standing next to Psyche/Redival, as follows:

> Each breath I drew let into me new terror, joy, overpowering sweetness. I was pierced through and through with the arrows of it. I was being unmade. I was no one. But that's little to say; rather, Psyche herself was, in a manner, no one. I loved her as I would once have thought it impossible to love, would have died any death for her. And yet, it was not, not now, she that really counted. Or if she counted (and oh, gloriously she did) it was for another's sake. The earth and stars and sun, all that was or will be, existed for his sake . . . . "You are also Psyche," came a great voice. I looked up then, and it's strange that I dared. But I saw no god, no pillared court. I was in the palace gardens, my foolish book in my hand. The vision to the eye had, I think, faded one moment before the oracle to the ear. For the words were still sounding.[20]

Her last words are simply, "I ended my first book with the words no answer. I know now, Lord, why you utter no answer. You are yourself the answer. Before your face questions die away. What other answer would suffice? Only words, words; to be led out to battle against other words."[21] And words will not do. What the story illustrates is beyond words.

Lewis confesses having felt free to take Apuleius's version of the story, since the Roman storyteller was merely its "transmitter, not its inventor," but remained faithful to the principal dilemma of the Psyche narrative that revolves around the concepts of faith and human curiosity. That is indeed what caused the Fall to become the symbol of the human propensity to know more than it should. Roger Shattuck describes that dangerous quality astutely when he observes that "the desire to know the world and other beings as well as ourselves belongs to our highest aspirations, celebrated by Homer and Dante and all the great authors, and to our basest concupiscence in wanting to reach beyond our *portee*"[22]—beyond what we should be entitled to know.

While the Psyche–Eros story, at least as compared to the major events of Olympian mythological history, is relatively insignificant, it cannot fail to reflect a very deeply held belief about the inextricable relationship between the human soul, as symbolized by Psyche, and divine love, through Eros. For that reason, I find it rather mystifying that more has not been written about its influence on Western culture,[23] and the few studies, particularly by Jungian psychologists, which offer superb insights deserve to be much better known.

Psyche and Eve: The Curious Feminine

Among the most brilliant is Erich Neumann's imaginative and intriguing *Amor and Psyche: The Psychic Development of the Feminine*, first published in German in 1952. While Neumann's commentary is not meant to be historically accurate, it is highly original and reveals a deep concern with grasping the conceptual basis of the emotional vocabulary that we all share, reflecting psychic scenarios that help define meaningful human existence.

Neumann notes, for example, that Psyche's refusal to obey Eros's command—whose rationale Eros fails to provide—forbidding her to see what he looks like, far from deserving punishment, is highly commendable. Writes Neumann, "the coming of light makes Eros 'visible,' it manifests the phenomenon of psychic love, hence of all human love, as the human and higher form of the archetype of relatedness."[24] Her disobedience is testimony to her courage, and "through Eros, through her love for him, Psyche develops not only toward him, but toward herself."[25]

This is highly relevant to a deeper understanding of Eve, whose similarity to Psyche is profound and multi-faceted: like Psyche, Eve disobeys a god; like Psyche, she is a conduit to a radical redefinition of the relationship between man and woman that focuses on *seeing* the other seriously and self-consciously; and, also like Psyche, Eve has to pay for her transgression. The fact that, in the end, Psyche is resurrected to the status of goddess—in Greek mythology, a unique privilege for a mere human—is comparable to the apparently contrary fate that awaits Eve who must leave Eden along with her husband, who both must die.

Yet Eve's inevitably mortal nature, by contrast to Psyche who is eventually promoted to deity, requires a rather different perspective in order to properly evaluate the divergent *denouements* of these narratives. The marriage of the god Eros with the goddess-to-be Psyche, however anthropomorphic, is altogether symbolic. Eve and Adam, on the other hand, are supposed to be *human beings*, however prototypal, whose love is fundamentally different from that of Psyche and Eros insofar as the human couple's principal shared burden is the expectation of a temporary existence. Still the similarity lies in the fact that both couples are defined by their mutual relatedness: in the end, they both find their respective soulmates' love indispensable.

Neumann points out that Psyche, like Eve, succeeds in attaining a higher feminine consciousness "only by breaking the taboo that Eros has imposed . . . [and her coming] into conflict with Eros . . . is the foundation of her own development. As in the Biblical episode, the heeding of the serpent leads to expulsion from paradise and *to a higher consciousness*."[26] Neumann is to be commended for his superb analysis of Apuleius's rendition of that underestimated myth, whose earlier popularity had undeservedly waned—its recent revival, albeit modest, long overdue.

Another celebrated psychologist, Bruno Bettelheim, whose study of fairy tales and other symbolic narratives was equally motivated by reverence for man's imaginative life as an essential component of psychic development highlights some of the same issues in his analysis of Apuleius's Psyche–Eros story. Though better known than previous versions,[27] Bettelheim notes that it belongs to a rich Western tradition of animal-groom stories (among the best known being "The Frog King," about a frog who turns into a king after being kissed by a lovely princess), all of which explore the transformation brought about by love as a by-product of a revulsion that arouses the deepest feelings.[28]

In that context, Bettelheim interprets the Psyche episode as follows:

> Naive sexual enjoyment is very different from mature love based on knowledge, experience, even suffering. Wisdom, the story tells, is not won by a life of easy pleasure. Psyche tries to reach for knowledge when—contrary to the warning she was given—she lets light fall on Eros. . . . In desiring mature consciousness, one puts one's life on the

63

line, as Psyche does when she tries to kill herself in desperation. The incredible hardships Psyche has to endure suggest the difficulties man encounters when the highest psychic qualities (Psyche) are to be wedded to sexuality (Eros). Not physical man, but spiritual man must be reborn to become ready for the marriage of sexuality with wisdom.[29]

In contrast with (the male) Eros, who, it is not difficult to conclude wishes to keep his sex life separated from all else he is doing, (the female) Psyche is unwilling to accept the separation and isolation of the purely sexual aspects of life from the rest of her existence. She tries to force their unification, and in the process, she achieves the spiritual merging of soul and love, as well as that of male and female.

What Bettelheim says about Psyche, therefore, could as well be said about Eve and all other similar symbols before and since:

> Despite all warnings about the dire consequences if she tries to find out, woman is not satisfied with remaining ignorant about sex and life. Comfortable as an existence in relative naivete may be, it is an empty life which must not be accepted. Notwithstanding all the hardships woman has to suffer to be reborn to full consciousness and humanity, the stories leave no doubt that this is what she must do. Otherwise there would be no story: no fairly story worth telling, no worthwhile story to her life.[30]

To go even further, there would be no worthwhile story to *our* life. As the Romanian fairy tale has it, "for if it wasn't so, it wouldn't be told" (*"ca daca n'ar fi, nu s'ar povesti"*). To be reborn to full consciousness and humanity is the point not only of the biblical story but of life itself. To be is to feel with another, for another, through another.

C. S. Lewis's entire magnificent opus, ranging from the esoteric and breathtakingly erudite to allegorical fairy tales that enchant all ages, has done an immeasurable service to Christianity by rekindling its immediacy for ordinary believers in the twentieth and, now, the twenty-first century. His joyous, sometimes even whimsical, approach to Christianity has provided a much-needed antidote to the morbid conflation of lust (also contemptuously known as concupiscence) with intellectual curiosity, which constitutes surely one of the most deplorable misunderstandings of *Genesis*.

No one contributed more to that error, which has plagued the Christian church for centuries, than did Saint Augustine, bishop of Hippo (354–430). In his *Confessions*, Augustine actually identifies intellectual curiosity by the explicitly sexual phrase *libido sciaendi*—literally, lust for knowledge—fully aware of the negative reactions it would inevitably invite. Augustine deliberately conflates the two, licentiousness and its alleged intellectual counterpart, with a contempt that vaguely foreshadows the murderous fury of the Inquisition:

> There is also present in the soul, by means of these bodily senses, a kind of empty longing and curiosity, which aims not at taking pleasure in the flesh but at acquiring experience through the flesh, and this empty curiosity is dignified by the names of learning and science. Since this is in the appetite for knowing, and since the eyes are the chief of our senses for acquiring knowledge, it is called in the divine language *the lust of the eyes*.[31]

Luckily for human civilization, the Western world eventually rejected this visceral distaste for empirical investigation.[32]

Science aside, *Genesis* does not seem to condemn sexuality as such. It is silent about the specific manner in which man and woman would come to, well, know each other. What is more, God explicitly not only condones but mandates reproduction: humans are meant to be fruitful and multiply. Needless to say, since sexuality constitutes a form of knowledge, like all knowledge it can be used for ill or good. Curiosity as such is simply the human impulse to learn about our world created by an all-merciful God. That world is dangerous, and humans are prone to error. This does not, however, imply retreating from it, despising it, and rejecting it. On the contrary, as God rejoiced in His created world, so should human beings. Once again, this is the basic truth that suffuses the entire Abrahamic tradition.

Islam is supposed to be no exception. Unfortunately, almost from the outset, a wide variety of social, political, and economic factors have derailed the Quranic tradition beyond recognition.

Sexuality and Knowledge in Islamic Law

> *[Yasmina] noted that many of the things people enjoyed doing most in life, like walking around, discovering the world, singing, dancing, and expressing an opinion, often turned up in the strictly forbidden category. In fact, the* qa'ida, *the Invisible rule, often was much worse than walls and gates. With walls and gates you at least knew what was expected from you. . . . [But] then what did* hurriya, *or freedom, mean?*
> Fatima Mernissi, Dreams of Trespass

The exquisite poetry of the Quran renders it ideal as an inspirational, spiritual torch to warm the believer's heart with the rays of heaven. It fits less comfortably to the legalities of the courtroom, the hairsplitting that is the barrister's stock and trade. Beauty is often born of mystery and the haze of ambiguity, allowing emotions to soar along wings of dream, free to escape the straightjacket of mundane literalness. But ambiguity is a double-edged sword: in the wrong hands, it can be wielded to the bearer's advantage against a victim both unsuspecting and powerless. And since Quranic commentators, like their other Abrahamic kin, were invariably male, the predictable result was not good news for the weaker sex.

Thus the literary beauty of the Quran, unfortunately, gives rise to its own peculiar problems. Quranic precepts are essentially general propositions of an ethical nature rather than specific decrees; accordingly, the individuals who are empowered to interpret and apply those precepts in a concrete environment are influenced by particular circumstances—social, political, and economic—which can and do vary widely.

One important example is polygamy: the Quran allows a man up to a maximum of four wives; at the same time, however, husbands are enjoined to treat all wives "equally." If they cannot do so, they must not marry more than one wife. But since obviously no man can ever treat multiple wives with scrupulous equality—each wife, for example, feels jealous of her rival(s)—it is possible to interpret this to imply a subtle but unmistakable argument supporting monogamy. According to Hanafi Muslims, for example, the Quran may allow some flexibility in order to accommodate particular circumstances, most notably a paucity of males as a result of warfare or other calamities, but they believe that their Holy Book essentially endorses monogamy. The Hanafi even go so far as to "allow an adult woman to arrange her own marriage, on condition that she chooses a man of her own rank and fixes an adequate dowry."[33] But this has been very much a minority view in an overwhelmingly patriarchal culture.

Mohammed's death left the responsibility for interpreting the Quran to the caliph (literally, "successor"), whose selection was notoriously fraught with difficulties from the outset, there being absolutely no procedural guidelines. Adding to the problem was the rapid expansion of the Arab world: by the middle of the eighth century, the Umayyad empire, whose capital was based in Damascus in modern-day Syria, confronted suddenly with a large, multiethnic territory that had to be administered somehow, ended up adopting the Byzantine machinery it had just replaced. The new government-appointed judges understandably tended to come up with a composite of their personal interpretations of the Quran and—what else?—local laws. This obviously led to wide regional disparities and infiltration of foreign, non-Islamic elements into the legal system. As a result, "the Quranic elements within it were largely submerged."[34]

Yet this does not seem to have prevented the rapidly expanding Muslim jurisprudence by the end of the tenth century to become formally recognized as final and definitive. According to legal scholar Noel J. Coulson, although the great bulk of the law had originated in customary practice, traditional Islamic belief came to hold that the law as articulated in this motley tradition was sacrosanct: "The elaboration of the law is seen by Islamic orthodoxy as a process of scholastic endeavor completely independent of historical or sociological influences."[35] As a result, "the Quranic provisions concerning women's status and position in the family were largely lost."[36]

Yet even in that Eve-hostile tradition, there were widely divergent practices related to the relationship between men and women. The Hanafi school mentioned above, which allowed women to obtain a divorce in oppressive situations, though certainly an anomaly, suffices to prove the point. Leila Ahmed is fully justified to conclude that "a reading by a less androgenic and less misogynist society [than was usually the norm in Muslim societies] one that gave greater ear to the ethical voice of the Quran, could have resulted in—could someday result in—the elaboration of laws that dealt equitably with women."[37] It may indeed, we must hope.

The overwhelmingly male perspective of Islamic juridical rulings did lead to a minor yet not irrelevant positive outcome for women, as sexual services—seen as wifely duties—were given precedence over childbearing, which meant that women did not automatically have to become procreative machines. The deeper rationale is not hard to find: in a system that permitted polygamy and concubines, it was not in a man's interest to have too many children, at least not beyond a certain point.

In the larger picture, however, this represented a very minor consolation indeed, for a woman was still seen primarily as a tool, a sex object—a very far cry from the equal status implicit in the Quran. Most Muslim countries throughout history have treated their female population virtually like a subhuman species. Sir Sayyid Ahmad Khan, writing in the late 1880s, had deplored this development in the Muslim world, concluding from his observations of the British and other Western countries that the Islamic peoples were far behind; they had all but squandered their egalitarian legacy:

> Despite the fact that the laws of the developed nations regarding women were extremely defective and miserable, those nations have elevated the position of their women to an extremely high level while Muslims, despite the fact that the laws of the rest of the world are less generous, on accord of being uncivilized have treated women so badly that all the nations laugh at the condition of Muslim women.[38]

Throughout the Muslim world, the idea that women could be as thirsty for knowledge, as eager for freedom, and neither more nor less entitled to sexual satisfaction as were men was given no legal protection.

Yet eager they were indeed. Fatima Mernissi captures the feeling in her wonderful autobiography, *Dreams of Trespass: Tales of a Harem Girlhood*, as a child growing up inside the walls of a Tunisian harem:

> Roaming freely in the streets was every woman's dream. Aunt Habiba's most popular tale, which she narrated on special occasions only, was about "The Woman with Wings," who could fly away from the courtyard whenever she wanted to. Every time Aunt Habiba told that story, the women in the courtyard would tuck their caftans into their belts, and dance away with their arms spread wide as if they were about to fly. Cousin Chama, who was seventeen, had me confused for years, because she managed to convince me that all women had invisible wings, and that mine would develop too, when I was older.[39]

She would eventually grow those wings, though they were not made of feathers but of courage. Like Psyche, who is traditionally portrayed with wings, like her lover Eros, the Muslim woman would come to read the Holy Book on her own if she lived in a culture that did not deny her that opportunity. Like Psyche, she would soar and finally join her equally winged partner beyond the narrow horizons of simpleminded, bigoted men.

Notes

1. E. A. Speiser, *The Anchor Bible: Genesis,* 26
2. Cyrus H. Gordon and Gary A. Rendsburg, *The Bible and the Ancient Near East,* 36–37.
3. *Forbidden Knowledge: From Prometheus to Pornography,* 51.
4. The celebrated scholar Mircea Eliade, in his superb study *Patterns in Comparative Religion,* while acknowledging that some scholars (notably Paul Humbert) take the Tree of Knowledge and the Tree of Life to be one and the same, he is inclined to disagree, suggesting that the latter is meant to be hidden, "only to become identifiable and therefore accessible at the moment when Adam should snatch at the knowledge of good and evil, or, in other words, of wisdom," 287.
5. *The Beginning of Wisdom: Reading Genesis,* 109.
6. Ibid., 106.
7. *Forbidden Knowledge,* 50.
8. Ibid., 94–95.
9. Ibid.
10. Ibid., 89–90.
11. Ibid.
12. Hesiod, *Theogony, Works and Days.*
13. *Protagoras,* 320d–323a.
14. Patricia A. Marquardt, "Hesiod's Ambiguous View of Woman."
15. See Anne Baring and Jules Cashford, *The Myth of the Goddess: Evolution of an Image,* 518.
16. Robert Graves, in the introduction to his translation of *The Transformations of Lucius, Otherwise Known as The Golden Ass,* writes that Apuleius "probably invented none of his stories, though it is clear that he improved them" (xix).
17. *Till We Have Faces,* 249.
18. Ibid
19. C. S. Lewis, *Surprised by Joy.*
20. Lewis, *When We Had Faces,* 308.
21. Ibid.
22. *Forbidden Knowledge,* 47.
23. Among the more notable are Carl C. Schlam's *Cupid and Psyche, Apuleius and the Monuments,* and James Gollnick's *Love and the Soul: Psychological Interpretations of the Eros and Psyche Myth.* There are also a number of studies that concentrate on representations of this myth in paintings and sculptures.
24. Erich Neumann, *Amor and Psyche: The Psychic Development of the Feminine,* 109.
25. Ibid., 110
26. Ibid., 74 (emphasis added).
27. Bettelheim cites Ernst Tegethoff, *Studien zum Marchentypus von Amor und Psyche* (Bonn, Schroeder, 1922) as a reliable source, 322.
28. Bruno Bettelheim, *The Uses of Enchantment: The Meaning and Importance of Fairy Tales,* 291
29. Ibid., 293.
30. Ibid., 295

31. Saint Augustine, *Confessions*, Ch. 35, 242.
32. For a compelling account of the compatibility between natural science and biblical monotheism (specifically, though not exclusively, Christianity) see *The Language of God: A Scientist Presents Evidence for Belief* by the biochemist Francis S. Collins, leader of the Human Genome Project during the mid-1990s.
33. Wiebke Walther, *Women in Islam: From Medieval to Modern Times*, 55.
34. Leila Ahmed, *Women and Gender in Islam*, 89.
35. Noel J. Coulson, *History of Islamic Law*, 85. Cited in Ahmed, *Women and Gender in Islam*, 90.
36. Noel J. Coulson and Doreen Hinchcliffe, "Women and Law Reform in Contemporary Islam," in *Women in the Muslim World*, ed. Lois Beck and Nikki Keddie, 38. Cited in Ahmed, *Women and Gender in Islam*, 91.
37. Ibid., 91.
38. Syyid Ahmad Khan, in Moaddel and Talattof, *Modernist and Fundamentalist Debates in Islam: A Reader*, 161.
39. Fatima Mernissi, *Dreams of Trespass: Tales of a Harem Girlhood*, 22.

4

Love and the Soul

*At last she [the soul] does behold him [beauty], and lets the flood
pour upon her, releasing the imprisoned waters; then has she refresh-
ment and respite from her stings and sufferings . . . .*
Plato, Phaedrus

Love and Beauty

O most beautiful soul, how blessed is he who beholds you.
Dante, Vita Nuova

Though Dante had been instantly enchanted by the lovely Beatrice
in the flesh when they first met as children, their passion was never
consummated. When he saw her again, she was already married. But
the reference to her beautiful soul in the quote above alludes to their
encounter in heaven, where he would finally behold her disembodied
soul, after her very untimely, tragic death.

Dante's exquisite poetry would epitomize the medieval tradition
of courtly love. That genre, popularized in contemporary America
through the various movie versions of *Camelot*, centers on a knight's
love (Lancelot) for a beautiful woman (Guinevere). The lady was quite
out of reach since, for one thing, she was (as was typical) married;
and for another, her husband (in this case King Arthur) was the very
Lord whom the knight was sworn to serve.

Non-consummation of the relationship resulted in the desired female becoming elevated to the status of a quasi-goddess. But courtly
love, though seeming to wed love and the soul, does it in a highly
artificial, unrealistic manner: sublimated sexuality, which leads to
idolizing the beloved almost beyond mortal recognition, is quite different from the lifelong affection between two real, three-dimensional,
imperfect human beings. The beauty of an unattainable sexual object
is a kind of illusion: Beatrice, for one, is forever beautiful in heaven
because she is both young and, well . . . , dead.

Human beings have traditionally been justifiably ambivalent about beauty, particularly in a woman: on the one hand, it is coveted; on the other hand, it is feared. The ancient Greeks for example, as the myth of Pandora amply demonstrates, had a largely jaundiced view of female allure. Writes Bruce Thornton, "The details of Pandora's creation reveal what is so troubling about her to men: her sexual power, both attractive and duplicitous, but also necessary to humanity in order to reproduce and have the children who will protect them from what Hesiod calls 'deadly old age.' . . . Continually in Greek literature women, like Pandora, are linked to the procreative yet volatile forces of nature."[1] That literature was undoubtedly influential far beyond the confines of the Greek city–states and was probably known to the authors of the Hebrew bible.

Scholars of rabbinic literature, it turns out, have documented a number of *Midrashic*[2] versions of the Adam and Eve story that are strikingly similar to the Pandora myth.[3] More to the point, the story that seems to have especially influenced the idea of Eve— notwithstanding that she was female—appears to have been Pandora's allegorical double, that of Prometheus. Like Prometheus, Eve acts upon her own initiative, transforms human existence, and then ends up paying for it dearly.[4] But like Pandora, Eve is seductive; her actions moreover, however unwittingly, bring about great pain and sorrow. Conceptually, Greek mythology seems to have set the stage for Eve through a composite that consists of Pandora and Prometheus in a curiously transgendered allegorical mixture.[5]

This reading is not as far-fetched as it might seem. For difficult as this may be to believe, an often repeated Talmudic explanation for the single formation of man and woman by God entailed that *adam* was bisexual or even hermaphroditic—both man *and* woman.[6] Among the best known Christian scholars who rejected this interpretation, probably gained through an oral tradition, was Saint Augustine, who dismissed the Hebrew speculation of an original hermaphrodite. Much later, Martin Luther mentions the theory, but only as evidence of "the malice of the devil, who suggests such absurd ideas to human beings." Absurd perhaps, certainly if taken too literally. It so happens, however, that such an image would not have seemed so preposterous to the ancient Greeks.

But let's now return to Plato's *Symposium*, mentioned in chapter 2, as Socrates and his merry friends speculate about the nature and origin of Love. We hear Eryximachus, perhaps after a tad too much wine, suggest that in the beginning, the human race was divided into three groups: besides male (descended from the Sun) and female (descended from the Earth), a third (descended from the Moon), by far the most numerous, "partook of the nature of both." Endowed with four limbs, two faces, etc. and considerable strength, these last were quasi-Siamese except for having a "globular" shape. To make matters even worse, the repulsive creatures, far from feeling dejected, seemed equally deficient in self-reflection and humility. Furious, yet reluctant to destroy the whole lot of them and deprive the gods of so many useful servants, Zeus came up with a plan: split the unsightly hybrids in two. As a result, for the rest of their miserable existence, each would be fated to seek their other half, yearning to become whole again. (This seemed to have implied that a minority would be destined for homosexuality, both male and female, having originated from an initial mono-sexual sphere.[7])

The allegory is considerably less grotesque when viewed—as so much of Greek mythology must be—metaphorically. Describing love as a search for one's other half is not uncommon in the poetry and romance of most cultures, even past adolescence. The soul seeks its romantic counterpart, which explains the resonance and ongoing appeal of the Greek myth about the origin of human love: the saga of Psyche and Eros, discussed in the last chapter.

The nagging question at the heart of that story persists: Why did Eros leave the beautiful Psyche, whom he supposedly loved so much, just because she disobeyed his order not to look at him? Was the god's wrath at her disobedience greater than his affection for her? If so, what sort of love was it, anyway? Why shouldn't she wish to not only feel his presence but see it, connect to her lover/husband by actually *knowing* who he was? What was the point of Psyche eventually, vanquishing the ire of his mother Aphrodite, the goddess of love and beauty, with Eros's help, though not until the very end? Did it mean that Eros was so afraid to confront his mother that he would leave his wife?

These are all fascinating questions, but what matters here is that Greek mythology was evidently wrestling with the idea of the soul as encompassing empathy, friendship, and love. This complementary aspect of love and soul, the Psyche–Eros fusion, was also critical to the Abrahamic conception of the first human helpmates/soulmates. It also required the differentiation of the human soul from that of the one God. Our souls and God's Spirit are related yet distinct, and the love among ourselves is similar to God's love for us, even if only as a pale image.

Primitive religions traditionally embraced an *animistic* worldview, which assumed that all nature is literally alive with spirit. (*Animus* is roughly the Latin equivalent of the English *soul*, which derives from the Gothic *saiwala*, about which more later.) This is hardly bizarre. Much like a motionless "inanimate" object, a person or animal can awaken from sound sleep, seemingly spontaneously, and turn ferocious. So why couldn't a chair or a stone not suddenly come to life as well? Trees seem to die in the winter, yet they bloom again in the spring. To be sure, the bodies of animals and humans who lose their breath or whose blood drains out eventually deteriorate, indicating perhaps that something essential and vital has abandoned them.

But what is that something, if we cannot even see it? For centuries, mankind has sought to imagine the invisible soul through ingenious metaphors ranging from the early Egyptian winged creatures, such as birds, butterflies, or bees, to later ghosts, breath, and increasingly ethereal, unsubstantial entities.[8]

It is hard to resist wondering what really gives impetus, or causes motion, in the absence of any obvious external assistance. A seemingly self-propelled object may appear mysterious and awe-inspiring to the primitive or innocent observer when in fact it is simply activated by a mundane motor. But we don't always know whether we are confronted with an automaton or a living thing. Just as an animal cannot always figure out whether something that moves is animal, mineral, or paper, a baby does not realize that squeezing a paw, unlike a rubber duck, can cause an unwelcome scratch.

And if differentiating between physical motion and purposive behavior were not hard enough, imagining the psychic reality of another soul is virtually impossible: philosophers have long wrestled with the so-called problem of other minds. That problem, in short, is to explain how we may be said to know that other people think as we do, that they are like us at all. At bottom, the challenge is to refute the solipsist, the person who believes that only he or she, the subject, the I, truly exists, because it is experienced firsthand. A strict solipsist believes that any knowledge regarding the existence and content of other minds is at bottom indirect, inferred, and therefore fundamentally unknowable.

For people who suffer from severe neurological disorders such as autism, this is no mere academic hairsplitting. Recent research has revealed the extent to which these individuals are unable to fathom that others can experience what they do. The expression "I know how you feel" is particularly meaningless to them, even more than to the rest of us.

You really don't need to take a college course in Philosophy of Mind to recognize that no one truly knows what is in another person's heart; the best we can do is presume that others react more or less like we do, in roughly similar circumstances. But if we have trouble imagining what other human minds are like, how much more difficult is it to understand how we are different from the lesser animal species? How are we to understand what it is to be not only alive but uniquely *human*?

We are the apogee of creation, yet other species surpass us in countless ways. We cannot fly or live indefinitely under water. For all our supposed intelligence, a computer can out-calculate and beat most of us easily at chess. While humans are capable of speaking, reading, and writing, having created different languages and other highly sophisticated forms of communication, a complex machine can do it too. But we are something more than the most elaborate intelligence of any breathing species: we are creative machines and more. We believe ourselves to be uniquely self-aware, and with good reason. In the end, most of us would say that what sets us apart is being endowed with a conscious *soul.* Defining it and explaining what it means, however, is difficult. Seeking its origin in languages and cultures that precede ours by hundreds or even thousands of years may help us in that task.

The English word *soul* is but one among a bewildering variety of concepts to which the hapless translator has to find the closest equivalent, depending on context.[9] The scholarly literature distinguishes several different words in Hebrew, Assyrian, Greek, Akkadian, Ugaritic,[10] and other ancient languages, each highlighting a particular aspect of this highly abstract idea as it appears to have been conceptualized thousands of years ago. The biblical message, in its simplest terms, is that God's creation of our first parents in God's own image reflects God's divine love, while they, in turn, would love each other and procreate, and naturally love the One who gave them life. It would seem obvious, therefore, that the human soul is inexorably linked to the idea of love—and specifically that human love is a representation of divine love. The truly revolutionary import of the compassionate wisdom underlying the story of *Genesis* is best understood in historic context, through the key words used to describe the myth of human creation.

The most frequently used Hebrew equivalents for soul in the Bible are *ruah* and *nephesh* (or *nepes*). The latter is the seat of pleasure and of life, in general, and applies also to animals (*Genesis* 1:30). Originally, what we might call the soul was most often connected with blood, and later also with breath.[11] Sometimes the Hebrew word for "heart" (*leb*) is used in a somewhat related fashion to refer to mental or spiritual activities, though *leb*, unlike *nepes*, is virtually never applied to animals in the Old Testament but only to humans.[12] Also arguably related to *nepes* is *panim*, which in Hebrew literally means "face." In the Old Testament, *panim* is used to refer to various attitudes and sentiments as indicated in facial expressions.[13]

Ruah sometimes also refers to "breath" in a manner not unlike what we ordinarily mean by "soul" today. For while animals may also be said to have *ruah* to mean generally the force directing an organism's life, in the human context a distinction is made between "good" and "bad" *ruah*. The good *ruah* is given for the purpose of understanding, for becoming capable of being stirred by God when God wishes mankind to act in a certain way. By contrast, a person who experiences something painful is said to feel a bad or bitter *ruah*. Thus *ruah* is applied in connection with appreciating, evaluating, approving or disapproving, and judging love and hate. In some contexts, *ruah* is understood as an intangible force through which God miraculously works.

The idea that a soul would need a *partner* for its fulfillment is a radically new notion in the history of religion. Heretofore, humans had provided merely sacrifices, gifts, sexual favors, and other services; the idea of a need to share divine love is novel in the Abrahamic tradition. The biblical God, after fashioning the entire universe, wished to share it with a creature made in "His own image," prompted by generosity and infinite love that linked God to mankind as never before. The idea of a force that can only be expressed through a connection, comparable to an electrical current, presupposes a duality, like negative and positive charges that together—and only together—produce energy. Far from defining "need" as somehow a negative quality, a lack, or an imperfection, in this context the reciprocity of love is as much a part of the soul's essence as bipolarity is to electricity. That reciprocity exists on both the human and the divine level.

The celebration of love's reciprocity is thus intrinsic to the biblical idea of spiritual communion. God can and does love all humans; mankind experiences spiritual communion through love of fellow spiritual, albeit mortal, beings. Anyone who is totally incapable of loving another cannot possibly love God. The inability to engage in or even desire companionship is a fatal flaw and was understood as such from the earliest times. This does not mean that human beings cannot and should not differentiate between divine and human love, but it does mean that the two are intimately interconnected.

Not that the biblical concept of spiritual love sprung spontaneously into the minds of the ancient Hebrews, by any means. Thanks to the extraordinary work of archeologists and students of the ancient world, we have learned a great deal about the mix of cultural and religious traditions prior to our own. We now know, for example, that the biblical authors were familiar with the epic saga of Gilgamesh—the oldest and most highly celebrated written religious text.

While the most commonly cited similarity between *Genesis* and *Gilgamesh* is the episode relating to a devastating flood that destroyed the entire human race except for one man and his wife—the story of Noah, who is named Uta-napishti in *Gilgamesh*—there are many others. Notable among them are two intertwined narratives: that of the two friends Gilgamesh and Enkidu, alongside Enkidu's romance with Shamhat. These two intimately connected relationships foreshadow the Adam—Eve episode, underscoring the biblical story's exceptionally rich psychological complexity.

After a brief overview of *Gilgamesh*, we will then turn to another saga: that of Odysseus, the hero of Homer's monumental epic *The Odyssey*, better known by his Roman name, Ulysses. Since at bottom what we are seeking to grasp is the nature of love binding human beings, which both mirrors and facilitates the love between mankind and God, all these wonderful precursor stories reveal surprising, invaluable insights that help us appreciate even more profoundly the genius of the Abrahamic metaphor of human creation.

Soul and Friendship: Gilgamesh, Enkidu, and Shamhat

'My son, the axe you saw is a friend,
Like a wife you'll love him, caress and embrace him,
And I, Ninsun, I shall make him your equal.
A mighty comrade will come to you, and be his friend's saviour,
Mightiest in the land, strength he possesses,
His strength is as mighty as a rock from the sky.'

Said Gilgamesh to her, to his mother,
"May it befall me, O mother, by Counselor Enlil's command!
Let me acquire a friend to counsel me,
A friend to counsel me I will acquire!"
"[So did Gilgamesh] see his dreams."
[After] Shamhat had told Enkidu the dreams of Gilgamesh,
[T]he two of them together [began making] love.
  Gilgamesh Epic—He Who Saw the Dee [Tablet I, I 288–97]

The myth of Gilgamesh, one of the first known religious master-pieces without which civilization would be absolutely inconceivable, explored the spiritual struggles of mankind as had no previous mytho-logical narrative. It represents the dawning of a new self-awareness and search for personal meaning. The story is only indirectly about man's relationship to God; its main theme is the connection among human beings, and coming to grips with our own mortality. It is about accepting our limits, about what matters most in life, and why. In other words, Gilgamesh is a remarkably modern masterpiece of sacred literature.

The narrative features the near-demigod Gilgamesh, who makes up in *chutzpa* what he lacks in judgment. Arrogantly self-sufficient, he is said to have dared to reject even the advances of the beautiful goddess Ishtar, risking, and incurring, her predictable fury. Only after his exasperated subjects, at their wits' end, finally begged the gods to commission the creation of a companion, to somehow calm him down, did his mother, the goddess Ninsun, fashion him a friend whose name was Enkidu. The story of the ensuing intimacy between these two semidivine men who were both directly manufactured by the gods, albeit not of a sexual nature (ambiguous language to the contrary notwithstanding), is perhaps the earliest version of an *I–Thou* human–spiritual connection.

As may be expected of a story that was widely circulated orally not only before but long after having been committed to writing, there is no unique version of the *Gilgamesh* epic. The so-called stan-dard version reflects the principal elements of the epic, but ongoing archeological discoveries, evolving scholarship on ancient religions and cultures and reinterpretations of extant texts, continue to expand our understanding of this rich, important narrative. The oldest extant tablets, which refer to "Bilgames," written in Sumerian, the language first spoken in Mesopotamia, differed from the Akkadian tablets that are some one thousand years more recent, dating from the eighteenth century BCE. The political, economic, and cultural power of the region, the widespread use of Akkadian (traces have been found as far as Armenia and Palestine), and the story's translation into many of the ancient languages throughout the Near East[14] are responsible for its enormous impact. The chances that it was not known to the authors of *Genesis* seem slim.

The revolutionary impact of *Gilgamesh* cannot be overstated: the story represented a wholly unique and novel way of understanding what it is to be a human being. According to Assyriologist William L. Moran, unlike typical religious narratives this should be seen as nothing less than "a document of ancient humanism,"[15] concerned more with what it is to be a man than what it is to serve the gods. And while the epic contains many stories that may be described as "myths" in the sense of allegorical religious narratives, from the most ancient times Gilgamesh was admired and loved for its universal wisdom and practical relevance.

Reflecting on the meaning and function of myth in ancient cultures generally, G. S. Kirk singles out the Babylonian narrative:

> Above all [this epic] retains, in spite of its long and literate history, an unmistakable aura of the mythical—of that kind of emotional exploration of the permanent meaning of life, by the release of fantasy about the distant past that Greek myths, at least as we experience them, so often fail to exemplify in their own right.[16]

The two opinions do not conflict; rather, they complement each other. For it is true that there are unmistakable mythological components in this epic that resemble the profound emotional exploration that makes religious narratives such as the Fall, the Creation, the Burning Bush, and others, such important components of the collective psyche. But it is also true that *Gilgamesh* anticipates the biblical narratives, breaking away from other ancient mythologies (including many Greek myths, although, with all due respect to Prof. Kirk, decidedly not all) whose principal practical function was to appease the all-powerful, often capricious, gods through libations and sundry rituals.

Finally, the sentiments of friendship and love as intrinsic to true intimacy, of the *I–Thou* relationship, are explored in the Babylonian epic by means of a highly singular device: the tripartite connection that involves the demigod though mortal Gilgamesh, the divinely created but equally mortal Enkidu whose express function is to serve as Gilgamesh's friend, and the quite human woman Shamhat who is sent to civilize Enkidu by becoming his lover—a task she performs lovingly and devotedly, however temporarily. This last point is not surprising, given the gender ideology of the times. Observes Tikva Frymer-Kensky in her 1992 book *In The Wake of the Goddesses: Women, Culture, and the Biblical Transformation of Pagan Myth*:

> The true companion for Gilgamesh is not a woman to occupy his attention, but a male to be his close companion. The gods' solution to Gilgamesh's arrogance indicates a cultural sense that the truest bonding possible is between two members of the same gender. The true equality that leads to great bonding is between male and male . . . . [Meanwhile,] in a similar situation, the God of the Bible creates a woman."[17]

Yet woman is an indispensable, key player in the Babylonian narrative: for without Enkidu's lover Shamhat helping to tame him away from the animals, he would have remained wild and unapproachable, unable to befriend Gilgamesh.[18] Not only do Enkidu and Shamhat have a passionate relationship, but Shamhat offers him wise advice, which he duly follows. By contrast, Gilgamesh rapes as many women as he can find, behaving little better than a brute without reason or capacity for affection or empathy. We will return to the ambivalence toward the female figure evident in this epic in due course.

The evolution of an all-powerful king from bully to humble hero is the principal theme of the Gilgamesh epic, yet its real subject is Everyman. Gilgamesh starts out as feared and invincible, arrogant and alone. He ends up seemingly defeated—weak, old, and exhausted— but at last wise, having loved and lost, able to understand and even accept the inevitability of death. The all-powerful superhero with the emotional maturity of a steer had to first experience suffering in order to acquire the more precious qualities of humanity and compassion.

The dramatic metamorphosis turns Gilgamesh into the first tragic hero of Western civilization. His apparent fall becomes, in truth, his rise: at the end of his journey, he has gained moral insight. He may have lost both youth and strength, but his newly acquired wisdom is far more precious, more sublime, than mere omnipotence. If the fruit of immortality must forever elude him, in spiritual terms, his noble acceptance of temporality is immeasurably greater.

But let's adjust the camera for a close-up of this extraordinary tale. First, the context: ancient Babylonian tradition—not unlike the later European vision of the "noble savage" canonized by Jean-Jacques Rousseau in the eighteenth century—assumed the first humans to have been wild, albeit quite devoid of nobility. A text dating from around the middle or late first millennium BCE, though its contents are presumed to be much older, describes the circumstances of a related divine creation: that of a king, whom the gods endow with the tools necessary for the task.

The curtain rises:

Ea opened [H]is mouth to speak, saying a word to the Lady of the Gods:
"You are Belet-ili, the sister of the great gods,
you have created man the human,
fashion now the king, the counselor-man!
Gird the whole of his figure sweet,
make perfect his countenance and well formed his body!"
The Lady of the Gods fashioned the king, the counselor-man!
They gave to the king the task of doing battle for the "great" gods.
Anu gave him his crown, Enlil gave him his throne,
Nergal gave him his weapons, Ninurta gave him his corona of splendor;
The lady of the Gods gave him his features [of majesty],
Nuska commissioned counselors, stood them before him.[19]

The well-endowed king was certainly not placed on earth merely for the sake of his uncouth fellow humans: he was to fight the gods' battles. As the Babylonians' sovereign, his job description was to oversee the maintenance of the temples, making sure they are well stocked with food and treasure. Yet he is also to listen to his counselors and act the shepherd to his flock, ruling justly. Given his tyrannical personality, the uncommonly (even for a king) aggressive Gilgamesh happened to be especially in need of wise counsel.

At the beginning of the epic, we are introduced to the misery caused by this belligerent tyrant who also happened to be oversexed: his long list of horrors includes a systematic practice of "the right of the first night." The exasperated narrator reports how "Gilgamesh will couple with the wife-to-be, he first of all, the bridegroom after." (To be sure, one version of the narrative concedes that the practice had been—inexplicably—sanctioned "by divine consent;" but even so, Gilgamesh was abusing it with impunity and without mercy.)

The last straw, however, was the devastating effect of the king's superhuman energy, exacerbated by his callous disregard for others. Incapable of sympathy for those whose testosterone levels were closer to average than his own, he amused himself by coercing his young male subjects in Uruk to engage in interminable exhausting games. In desperation, the people implored the gods to create someone of comparable physical stamina who would not only take on the job of keeping up with the king and give his benighted subjects a much-needed break, but who might also prove to be a fitting soul-companion to their self-absorbed sovereign, and who could perhaps even awaken in him some feelings of empathy.

Enter Enkidu. Fashioned by the mother goddess and endowed with great strength, he is not exactly the picture of perfection at first: coated in hair "like the god of the animals," he roams among the beasts, reportedly grazing with the herd and blithely joining them in drinking at their water hole. When Gilgamesh gets wind of Enkidu's enviable physical endowments, the feisty king is eager to engage him, but recognizes that this potential fighting partner could use some initial taming. He thus suggests summoning the beautiful Shamhat, a skilled practitioner of the oldest profession, to be sent to Enkidu's water hole, where she is to discard her clothes and perform her . . . magic.

The ruse works. Actually, it works all too well—the potency of her charms lasting for no less than six days and seven continuous nights (presumably nonstop). So, no wonder:

Enkidu was weakened, could not run as before,
but now he had reason, and wide understanding.
He came back and sat at the feet of the harlot,
Watching the harlot, observing her features.
Then to the harlot's words he listened, intently,
[as Shamhat] talked to him, to Enkidu:
'You are handsome, Enkidu, you are just like a god!
Why with the beasts do you wander the wild"
Come, I will take you to Uruk-the-Sheepfold,
To the sacred temple, home of Anu and Ishtar,
Where Gilgamesh is perfect in strength,
Like a wild bull lording it over the menfolk.'
So she spoke to him and her word found favor,
He knew by instinct, he should seek a friend.
(I 201–14)

How utterly remarkable! After his experience with Shamhat, though somewhat drained, Enkidu actually improves spiritually: he *gains reason and wide understanding*! What is more, Shamhat tells him he is "just like a god," and he realizes the wisdom of her admonition against wandering with beasts. And lastly, he recognizes his own need for genuine companionship. Not that she brainwashes him: *he knew by instinct,* as soon as he reflects upon her advice, that he should travel to the sacred temple in Uruk where *he should seek a friend.*

One might observe that Shamhat herself, after all, is already a friend, for she counsels him wisely, with no personal agenda. Yet she disappears after her job is complete; evidently, she is not deemed his equal. The express mention of her profession as a lady of pleasure seems to insure that no reader would mistake her for a worthy potential mate. Shamhat has performed as she was bid: "she did for the man the work of a woman" (I 192). The wording implicitly conveys as well that Shamhat is the *archetypal* woman. In addition to performing her sexual task, she has also tamed Enkidu, civilizing and ennobling him.

The newly humanized Enkidu is thus finally ready to meet Gilgamesh. Having been "born in the wild and [having] no brother" (II 177), Enkidu is certainly open to intimate fellowship. The two semigods become friends instantly and soon join together in a battle against the fierce enemy Humbaba. Gilgamesh says to Enkidu, "[Let him who] goes first be on guard for himself and bring his comrade to safety!" [IV 257]. Yes, this is friendship. But it would not last long: in retaliation for Gilgamesh's rejection of the propositions by the goddess Ishtar, as mentioned earlier, Enkidu's life is taken away.

Upon his deathbed, Enkidu delivers another fascinating monologue, in which he curses none other than Shamhat for having been the source of all his calamities—"because [she had made him] weak, who was undefiled!" (VII 131–32). The god Shamash who hears Enkidu responds immediately, chastising him sternly:

Straight away from the sky there cried out a voice:
'O Enkidu, why curse Shamhat the harlot,
who fed you bread that was fit for a god,
and poured you ale that was fit for a king,
who clothed you in a splendid garment,
and gave you as companion the handsome Gilgamesh?
And now Gilgamesh, your friend and your brother,
[will] lay you out on a magnificent bed.
[On] a bed of honor he will lay you out,
[he] will place you on his left, on a seat of repose;
[the] rulers of the underworld will all kiss your feet.
(VII 134–46)

Calmed, Enkidu repents and apologizes to Shamhat, blessing her with all the goods he can conjure up, including a heartfelt wish that she should enjoy the love of governors and noblemen, the respect of men far and wide who upon seeing her should "slap their thighs" and "shake out their hair," showering her with the most expensive gifts and fine jewelry. But as if this weren't enough, Enkidu does one better: he hopes Ishtar herself, "the ablest of gods," will help Shamhat find the richest and most established man who will desert his own wife, "though the mother of seven"—indicating that Enkidu still had a great deal left to learn about love and morality. (VII 151-161) Whether the young woman was impressed or insulted the record is silent. The list does, at least, convince the reader that Enkidu has come to his senses with regard to her fortuitous role in his own life.

The god Shamash reminded Enkidu of the most precious gifts that Shamhat had made possible: the deep, abiding friendship of Gilgamesh. The affection between these two mythical creatures is the first recorded example of soul-transforming, deeply reciprocated human empathy. As Enkidu lies dead, Gilgamesh tries to come to grips with what has happened to his friend:

Now what is this sleep that has seized [you]?
You've become unconscious, you do not [hear me!]"
But he, he lifted not [his head.]
He felt his heart, but it beat no longer.
He covered, like a bride, the face of his friend,
Like an eagle he circled around him.
Like a lioness, deprived of her cubs,
He paced to and fro, this way and that.
(VIII 55–62)

Gilgamesh recoils, inconsolable after losing the companion he had "loved so dear." He refuses to believe that Enkidu is truly gone and will not bury him "until a maggot dropped from his nostril." At that point, admits Gilgamesh, "I grew fearful of death, and so wander the wild. What became of my friend was too much too bear" (X 62). Now that he has finally realized the monumental import and inevitability of his own demise, he embarks upon a long journey to seek the one man who is said to have attained immortality: Uta-napishti, the precursor of Noah.

The rest of the story tells of Gilgamesh's journey to the underworld where he eventually meets Uta-napishti, whom he asks:

O Uta-napishti, what should I do and where should I go?
A thief has taken hold of my [flesh!]
For there in my bed-chamber Death does abide,
And wherever [I] turn, there too will be death.
(Tablet XI 242–46)

Uta-napishti takes pity on him and tells him where he might find a plant that will make him forever young, but Gilgamesh later ends up dropping it in the water, thereby losing it forever. He finally realizes that he will never be able to attain immortality. Devastated at first, he slowly comes to terms with his fate and at last attains true peace.

As the boatman takes him back home, the two break bread along the way, stopping for the night. Upon arriving at last, Gilgamesh lovingly beholds his home, Uruk. At the end of his difficult journey, he could look upon his world and see—as Adam was meant to do, for so too did God Himself—that it is good. This knowledge would sustain the old, now wise, king for however brief a time he still has left on this earth.

The Babylonian story illustrates the double-faceted meaning of human intimacy that consists of friendship accompanied by love. Both Enkidu and Shamhat (the latter indirectly, through Enkidu) help Gilgamesh escape his self-absorption and, ultimately, his loneliness. The intimacy that blossoms between the two couples—Shamhat and Enkidu first, then subsequently Enkidu and Gilgamesh—prepares Gilgamesh to appreciate what he loses upon the death of Enkidu. In a sense, the spirit of Enkidu lives on, through the love of his royal friend, ensuring that Gilgamesh would never revert to his previous narcissism.

Love and Marriage: Odysseus and Penelope

The archetypal wife in ancient Greek literature is Penelope from the
Odyssey. In her character we see all the ideal qualities of a wife, and
in her marriage with Odysseus all the characteristics of a good
marriage.

Bruce Thornton, Greek Ways: How the Greeks Created Western
Civilization

At first blush, it may not seem as if Gilgamesh has much in common with the hero of the *Odyssey*, though some scholars find it "necessary to conclude either that the author of the Odyssey knew the Gilgamesh epic, or at least, and perhaps more probably, that the two poems had a common cultural denominator."[20] Immortalized by the greatest poet of Greek civilization, the wily and deceptive Odysseus is the quintes- sential seeker of fortune who survives by his wits and defies the odds set against him by furies and gods whom he cannot help antagonizing while on a quest for experience, for worldly knowledge. Unlike the crass warrior Gilgamesh, Odysseus is cunning: he wins with his brain rather than his brawn. But consider the similarities: both Odysseus and Gilgamesh travel to the ends of the world and find themselves at the conclusion of their respective journey at last able to appreciate the true meaning of life, which is at once very far from where they had originally started and astonishingly close. Both find that what ultimately matters is not winning, whatever that may be, but finding peace and beholding the beauty of the world—an appreciation that is ultimately made possible only by another mortal companion.

Just as Gilgamesh at last accepts his fate and returns home, so too does Odysseus come back after a long trip (whence our word "odyssey" to refer to a series of wonderings). In his case, however, the journey had been prolonged against his will. Odysseus, moreover, had been tempted with immortality by a seductive goddess named Circe whom he explicitly and categorically rejected, preferring to return home to his faithful wife Penelope. For unlike Gilgamesh, who had sought eternity and at last died without a soulmate—his male friend having preceded him in death, never to be replaced by anyone else—Odysseus ends his days in the comfort of love, having voluntarily chosen mortality.

At the end of the Odyssey, Homer describes the tenderness of the old couple:

> [After they] had taken their fill of sweet love, they had delight in the tales, which they told one to the other. The fair lady spoke of all that she had endured in the halls at the sight of the ruinous throng of wooers, who for her sake slew many cattle, kind and goodly sheep; and many a cask of wine was broached. And in turn, Odysseus, of the seed of Zeus, recounted all the griefs [sic] he had wrought on men, and all his own travail and sorrow and she was delighted with the story, and sweet sleep fell not upon her eyelids till the tale was ended.[21]

In the final episode, Odysseus's young son Telemachus beholds his father and utters the following words: "Father, surely one of the gods that are from everlasting hath made thee goodlier and greater to behold."[22]

This is in fact the principal—and critical—difference between *Genesis* and the *Odyssey*: Odysseus's final triumph could not have happened without the support of a strong marriage—and he knows it. During his exile, when he approaches the beautiful princess Nausicaa for help, he wishes her by way of exchange "a husband and a household, and noble like-mindedness. For nothing is more powerful or greater than this, when a husband and wife, being like-minded in their thoughts, hold the household."[23]

Bruce Thornton observes that indeed the best illustration of Penelope's and Odysseus's "'like-mindedness' . . is in the way they together bring about the destruction of the suitors [pretenders to his throne], even before Penelope knows Odysseus has returned. Penelope is no passive, immobile, helpless female awaiting rescue by her knight. Without her planning, Odysseus could never destroy the suitors, for the odds are against him. . . Sexual passion, contrary to our romantic expectations, results from 'like-mindedness,' the shared character and values that fortify the marriage, rather than preceding the strength and integrity of the bond."[24] Isn't this "like-mindedness" a perfect synonym for the shared spirituality, the connecting love, between Adam and Eve?

It seems clear that in many ways Odysseus played the role of Adam as the prototypal man, while Penelope, like Eve, became the ideal partner whose devotion is not only physical but psychological and spiritual. She is privy to Odysseus's full story: she is the first to hear it, and she absorbs it with alacrity, with her entire being. They exemplify the first, albeit allegorical, human soulmates.

To be sure, there had been various accounts of mythical "ideal" men and women before Odysseus —some, godlike in either virtue or sin, others wedded to gods, born to them, or in love with them. But Greek mythology, indeed all the ancient religions, basically considered mankind's creation by the gods as an afterthought, even a regrettable mistake. Men were used by gods, whether as lovers, usually to be discarded, or as sycophants. The pagan deities, jealous of their prerogatives, punished mortals mercilessly whenever any of them dared to aspire to divine qualities. Immortality was particularly *verboten,* but insubordination of any kind carried a higher than average risk of death and destruction.

Yet was immortality truly so, well, divine? Were the ancient gods not in so many ways inferior in character and virtue to courageous and generous humans? Odysseus is the first mythological human to consciously reject the gift of eternal life in exchange for companionship with his beloved soulmate—fully understanding the import of his seminal decision. Adam and Eve had not been given the option explicitly, though it seems likely that they would have done the same—a topic for additional exploration in chapter 10.

In brief, the Abrahamic tradition establishes an entirely new conception of mankind as, in many respects, superior even to the prebiblical deities. After all, unlike most of the immortals, Adam and Eve are capable of lifelong love and friendship. For that and many other reasons, the biblical vision of human beings surpasses that of the fickle, narcissistic inhabitants of Olympus. And the single God who made the world for us to behold, the soil destined to yield its fruit to us, and our fellow subhuman creatures for us to rule over with compassion, as their wise shepherds, emerges as absolutely worth praising and loving. Our one God is our Great Friend.

Love and Friendship

The holy passion of Friendship is of so sweet and steady and loyal and enduring a nature that it will last through a whole lifetime, if not asked to lend money.
Mark Twain, Pudd'nhead Wilson *(1894)*

No less cynical was Twain's French predecessor, the witty Voltaire, who defined "Friendship" in his *Philosophical Dictionary* of 1764 as "the marriage of the soul, and this marriage is liable to divorce." So, obviously, is a marriage of the flesh – and money is all too often at the root of it. Many a separated couple will list financial disagreements as the major (if never sole) obstacle to an otherwise perhaps tolerable cohabitation. Nor is sex a guarantee of happiness—the contrary is often the case. Why, then, hold up the heterosexual union as the ideal prototype of spiritual communion? Doesn't sex of any variety tend, if anything, to undermine rather than strengthen the bond of friendship? We may read in Shakespeare's *Much Ado About Nothing*, a well-known versions of the truism, that "friendship is constant in all other things/Save in the office and affairs of love." Every major branch of biblical monotheism denounces lust, that instrument of the devil, as constituting the principal threat to attaining virtuous marital bliss. But is lust—whether of a heterosexual or, indeed, homosexual nature—necessarily incompatible with friendship?

Some would say no, friendship is simply one kind of love while lust, or "eros," is another—both ennobling in their own way. In his wonderful book *The Four Loves*, C. S. Lewis describes two more—affection and charity—the latter considered quintessential by Michael Novak, as we shall see further in chapter 11. Theodore Zeldin, in his eclectic book *An Intimate History of Humanity* (a dazzling display of interdisciplinary scholarship) about the history of intimacy throughout the ages and across the globe, observes that "in parts of Africa, among the Bangwa in the Cameroons, for example, and among the Nzema in Ghana, men and women enter into close friendships which last a lifetime. When they are together, "the woman relaxes her usual demeanor of almost theatrical deference before any man and they are permitted to joke, talk frankly and even eat together"—and now comes the clincher—". . . a practice normally tabooed between men and women, particularly husband and wife"![25] While interesting, such a custom that explicitly prohibits spouses from enjoying the same degree of mutuality with one another as with total strangers is hardly the Abrahamic concept of equal helpmates.

Whatever its name, true love for another human being must contain the element of respect on an equal footing with one's own self. Charity, however commendable, is not genuine if it involves pity and an accompanying sense of superiority that leads to treating another, however unwittingly, as less than fully human. Nor is it possible to consider camaraderie based on group egocentrism, on elitism or even racism, as constituting love in any way. As C. S. Lewis rightly points out, friendship can easily turn into group coterie; a positive feeling can become a weapon against others, who are thought lesser or suspicious outsiders. Similarly, *eros* alone can be merely a form of selfishness masquerading as love. Yet he concedes that "the co-existence of Friendship and Eros may . . . help some moderns to realize that Friendship is [or, can be] in reality a love, and even as great a love as Eros."[26]

In the end, observes Lewis, friendship is "the instrument by which God reveals to each the beauties of all the others."[27] When Adam saw his helpmate beside him, he immediately recognized that she was beautiful for she was (metaphorically or literally, the distinction becomes irrelevant) his own flesh: that is to say, he loved her. *Genesis* does not use the word; it does not have to.

But this conceptual honeymoon of the first soulmates would soon be over. Adam's successors would soon follow the lead of their mythical father and deflect the blame for the expulsion of mankind from paradise on the other sex, known thereafter as "opposite." Before long, Eve would start to resemble Pandora far more than Prometheus.

It started with the Jews. Then, despite a promising beginning, the virus of misogyny found its way into Christianity. And finally, it overwhelmed Islam, not long after Mohammed, with lasting effects to this day. But its origins are ancient indeed, and persistent.

The sixteenth-century painter Jean Cousin the Elder of Sens, who created a picture entitled *Eva Prima Pandora* (Eve the First Pandora), could well have been inspired by Hesiod, the first Greek poet who had extrapolated from Pandora's story a lesson that many were later to draw from *Genesis*:

Do not let any sweet-talking woman beguile your good sense
With the fascination of her shape. It's your barn she's after.
Anyone who will trust a woman is trusting flatterers.[28]

That unflattering image of the first temptress would stigmatize women to this day. The soulmate Eve, benighted, is still awaiting resurrection.

Notes

1.   Bruce Thornton, *Greek Ways: How the Greeks Created Western Civilization*, 41.
2.   The *midrash* refers to rabbinical literature, usually referring to sermonic implications derived from the biblical text.
3.   Samuel Tobias Lachs, "The Pandora-Eve Motif in Rabbinic Literature."
4.   Tikva Frymer-Kensky, *In the Wake of the Goddesses*, 110.
5.   *You* could call it pseudohermaphroditic, if you were so inclined.
6.   Maryanne Cline Horowitz, "The Image of God in Man—Is Woman Included?" 184.
7.   Plato, *Symposium*, 189 c–192 a.
8.   A highly readable account is Rosalie Osmond's *Imagining the Soul: A History*.
9.   For a brilliant analysis of the enormous complexities of translating this concept across cultures, see Anna Wierzbicka's *Semantics, Culture, and Cognition: Universal Human Concepts in Culture-Specific Configurations*, specifically Ch. 1, "Soul, Mind, and Heart" (31–64).
10.   Some commentators, however, believe that tracing nephesh (or nepesh) to either Akkadian or Ugaritic is unhelpful at best, since in those languages seems to have meant "throat" or "neck." See the brilliant article by James Stambaugh, "'Life' According to the Bible, and the Scientific Evidence," 98–121.
11.   Staples, "The Soul in the Old Testament," 164, 174–75.
12.   Stambaugh, "'Life' According to the Bible, and the Scientific Evidence," 100.
13.   Ibid.
14.   Andrew George, "Introduction," *The Epic of Gilgamesh: The Babylonian Epic Poem and Other Texts in Akkadian and Sumerian*, xvi–xxx.
15.   William L. Moran, "The Epic of Gilgamesh: A Document of Ancient Humanism," *Bulletin, Canadian Society for Mesopotamian Studies* 22, 15–22.
16.   G. S. Kirk, *Myth: Its Meaning and Function in Ancient and Other Cultures*, Ch. IV.
17.   Tikva Frymer-Kensky, *In The Wake of the Goddesses: Women, Culture, and the Biblical Transformation of Pagan Myth*, 30.
18.   I was thrilled to find Morris Jastrow Jr., in his article "Adam and Eve in Babylonian Literature," also taking note of "another phase of the Adam and Eve story to which a Babylonian counterpart exists, but which, so far as I

can see, has escaped the attention of scholars." He was referring Enkidu and Shamhat, and the article appeared over a century ago, in 1899. A more recent excellent comparison is John A. Bailey's "Initiation and the Primal Woman in Gilgamesh and Genesis 2–3," in 1970.

19. Andrew George, *The Epic of Gilgamesh* , xli.
20. Michael Grant, *Myths of the Greeks and Romans*, 84.
21. Homer, *Odyssey*, Book xxiii, 363.
22. Ibid., xxiv, 371.
23. *Odyssey* 6.181–84.
24. Thornton, *Greek Ways*, 54–56.
25. Theodore Zeldin, *An Intimate History of Humanity*, 323.
26. C. S. Lewis, *The Four Loves*, 67.
27. Ibid., 89.
28. Hesiod, *Theogony, Works and Days*.

Part II

The Misogynist Turn

5

The First Temptress

From the woman came the beginning of sin, and by her we all die.
Ecclesiasticus 25: 33

What horror is captured in this brief sentence! Not from the snake, not from the first couple, but specifically *from woman* came sin. What terrible legacy these words would bestow upon half the human race, what agony was to follow! Not by God's original design of man from dust—to which he and everyone else was presumably fated to return—but *by her* we all die. What burden was every little female baby doomed to inherit from her mythological mother! The reverberations cannot be overestimated: they have resonated through the ages, and continue to do so, across the world. For Eve, the bell tolls. But through her, so it does for everyone.

This ominous passage represents one of the earliest post-Genesis associations of Eve with the entrance of sin and death into the world.[1] True, *Ecclesiasticus* does not appear in the official Jewish Bible, having been written too late (some two centuries BCE) for inclusion among the accepted scriptures.[2] Even so, the nasty worm of Eve-bashing and general female hatred did first crawl into monotheism through Judaism. But this was primarily through the writings of a renowned Jewish scholar Philo of Alexandria (20 BCE–50 CE), whose Hellenistic education heavily influenced his interpretation of the Bible.

Here is how Philo, in a book entitled *Questions and Answers on Genesis*, explains why woman touched the forbidden fruit first, while man ate it only afterward: "For it was fitting that man should rule over immortality and everything good, but woman over death and everything vile."[3] No mincing of words here. He also responds as follows to the question why the man and not the woman was mentioned first in *Genesis* 3:8 as having hid from the Lord after eating the forbidden fruit ("Adam and his wife hid themselves"): "It was the more imperfect and ignoble element, the female that made a beginning of transgression and lawlessness, while the male made the beginning of reverence and modesty and all good, since he was better and more perfect."[4] Once again, there is little room left for ambiguity. Adam, good; Eve, bad.

How could this radical inversion have happened? How could Eve, whose very name signifies "life-giver," be blamed for having brought *death* upon mankind?[5] Notwithstanding God's commandment in the very first book of *Genesis* for the first couple to be fertile and increase, a vast number of biblical commentators throughout history have interpreted the act of eating the fruit from the Tree of Knowledge as virtually synonymous with indulging in sexual intercourse which itself implicitly deserved the death sentence. Why else, so the thinking goes, would the shamed culprits have sought to cover their genitals in the immediate aftermath of the euphemistic ingestion? (One or two alternative explanations suggest themselves, but never mind.)

The logical next step from identifying sex and sin with death was blaming Eve for the calamity. (Maybe not so logical, but again, never mind.) Accordingly, if the most plausible interpretation of the biblical narrative is that woman is the instrument of Satan (unwittingly or not, it matters little), the idea that man and woman are one another's helpmates mirroring the Divine Spirit becomes not merely implausible but vaguely ludicrous.

It is tempting to explain this astonishing derailment of the *Genesis* story by appealing to garden-variety male prejudice, sexual pathology, especially among the clergy (in any or all of the religious sects), and prebiblical cultural traditions that influenced biblical commentators, whether consciously or not. Some or all of these motivations may well have been a factor, in addition to many others, including political considerations and myriad psychological motivations, but any further exploration is beyond the scope of this book. In fact, a definitive study of the subject, given the paucity of relevant data and the inscrutable nature of the human heart, would seem quite impossible. I will certainly refrain from pseudo-psychoanalytic assumptions about unconscious drives like womb envy or vaginophobia.[6] What is worth exploring, however, is the way in which several important biblical traditions have tried to come to grips with the *Genesis* text, which admittedly does consist of more than one version of woman's creation.

Without doubt, the overly literal interpretation of the Bible is the most widespread malady afflicting all the so-called People of the Book. The members of the Abrahamic tradition are, after all, defined by an adherence to a more or less common written text that is considered to be holy. It follows that any casual departure from The Word—meaning, literal, written word—is fraught with danger, even outright heretical. Given the apparent discrepancy concerning Eve's creation between the first and second accounts in *Genesis*, therefore, it is entirely understandable that speculations would ensue. For many interpreters, it was just not good enough to say that the two versions were roughly similar.

To recapitulate that discrepancy, chapter 1 of *Genesis* seems to imply that the first woman was created simultaneously with Adam, while chapter 2 relates that woman was created from Adam's rib. Logical questions arise: Was it the same woman, or was it . . . a second one? If a second woman was created, isn't it safe to assume that there was something wrong with the first? But was the first woman named Eve also, or was that only the name of the second? While some people actually speculated that there were indeed two Eves, the most popular conjecture reserved that name for the second and called the first one *Lilith*.

Lilith

When God created His world and created Adam, He saw that Adam was alone, and He immediately created a woman from earth, like him, for him, and named her Lilith. He brought her to Adam, and they immediately began to fight.
Alphabet of Ben Sira *(c. ninth century)*

Early rabbinic speculations about the nature of the first female range over the entire spectrum, from demonic to angelic. One obvious, if admittedly rather drastic, solution to rescuing the purity of Eve as the first mother of mankind, and hence presumably our true feminine role model, was to attribute everything negative to a prior woman who was emphatically *not* our mother. Enter the sinister Lilith. Though the origin of this specific name is unclear, the celebrated scholar Raphael Patai, in his highly influential work *The Hebrew Goddess*, traces her story to Sumerian culture, though adding that no she-demon has ever achieved as fantastic a career as the alleged biblical Lilith. He speculates that she could have been the "night hag" mentioned in *Isaiah* 34:14; but among the most credible predecessors are several nasty Mesopotamian demons. Though admittedly supernatural, their intimate interactions with men and women rendered them borderline enough to provide role model material for the symbolic first female.

According to the Sumerian king list that dates from around 2400 BCE, for example, the father of Gilgamesh was a Lillu-demon, one of four such creatures. Another one—Lilitu or Lilith—was a she-demon; a second was her handmaid, Ardat Lili, who was thought to visit men by night and bear them ghostly children; while the fourth and last, Irdu Lili, evidently her male counterpart, would visit women and beget children by them (a notably nonsexist narrative).[7] An assortment of other prebiblical stories, some harking to various and sundry goddesses, left their mark on early Judaism. In the end, a peculiar mixture of the rabbinic tradition of hypothetically two Eves, one consistent with *Genesis 1* and the other with *Genesis 2,* combined with the prebiblical story of the demon Lilith, resulted in the fantastic narrative tradition of Lilith in Judaism, which casts the drama of human creation in an eerie, on occasion even sinister, new light.[8]

Lilith's name appears only once in the Bible, in *Isaiah* 34:14, in a description of Yahweh's day of vengeance—a frightening spectacle: "Wildcats shall meet hyenas, Goat-demons shall greet each other; there too the lilith shall repose and find herself a resting place." In the Jewish bible, the *Tanakh*, "lilith" is not capitalized and is explained in a footnote simply as "a kind of demon."[9] But Raphael Patai notes that she was well known in Israel of the eighth century BCE. Who was this nefarious creature, anyway?

While Talmudic material about Lilith is limited, Aramaic incantations dating from about 600 CE have been found in Nippur, Iraq, on bowls that were inscribed and used by Jews, thus following the Talmud, which was compiled around 500 CE, by about a century. Writes Patai, "While the Talmud contains the views of the learned elite about Lilith, these bowls show what she meant for the simple people. It is surprising to see to what extent the sages and the quacks shared the fear of Lilith and the belief in her evil nature."[10] Among other devilish characteristics, Lilith was thought to be the ghostly lover of men and a danger to women on many occasions—notably during childbirth and menstruation. The incantations found on excavated bowls were supposed to protect against this she-devil's vengeful caprice.

As the story presumably goes, God had intended to create mankind, male and female, as entirely equal. But happiness and understanding was not to be their lot:

> When Adam wishes to lie with her, Lilith demurred: "Why should I lie beneath you," she asked, "when I am your equal, since both of us were created from dust?" When Lilith saw that Adam was determined to overpower her, she uttered the magic name of God, rose into the air, and flew away to the Red Sea, a place of ill-repute, full of lascivious demons. There, Lilith engaged in unbridled promiscuity and bore a demonic brood of more than a hundred a day.[11]

Does this imply that she rejected the missionary position? Hard as it may be to believe, the inference, though laughable if not outright ludicrous, is not implausible and was widely so interpreted.

The great medieval Talmud commentator Shlomo Yitzhaq, better known as Rashi (1040–1105), speculated that Lilith was supposed to have looked human, with wings, not unlike a Cherub. (As an interesting aside, portraying the human soul—often imagined as a butterfly—as winged was exceedingly common in the ancient world.) As late as the eighteenth and even the nineteenth century, her presence is detectable in Western religious consciousness. Comments Patai, "There can be little doubt that a she-demon who accompanied mankind—or at least a part of mankind—from earliest antiquity to the threshold of the Age of Enlightenment must be a projection, or objectification, of human fears and desires which, in a deeper sense, are identical with those of oft-mentioned 'plagues of mankind' said in Kabbalistic literature to be the offspring of Lilith, but recognized by us as her psychogenic progenitors."[12]

Although already well developed by the seventh century, it was Kabbalistic[13] Judaism that propagated the myth of Lilith most widely. The most famous Kabbalistic book, written in Aramaic in the nineteenth century by Moses De Leon (who actually claimed it had been written by a second-century rabbi, though there is much debate on the matter), was the *Zohar*. This highly influential mystical text goes so far as to claim that woman was actually created *before* man: the "living creature with whose swarms God filled the waters was interpreted to have been no other than Lilith."[14] Taking *Genesis* literally to the point of seeming to contradict it seems a bit far-fetched, but there you have it.

Another ancient Jewish story about Lilith has her created together with Adam from dust, but instead of using clean earth, God inexplicably used filth and impure sediments out of which He formed a female.[15] Still other, no less fantastic, versions of the first creation describe her as Adam's first female consort before the birth of Eve.

Differences aside, they all share one characteristic: Lilith is invariably evil and frightening. What is more, unlike Eve, who was famously mortal, Lilith was demonically immortal and much feared. Lilith was believed to hover at night, to sexually stalk men who travel alone and to threaten newborns and expectant mothers, and so on—the graphic list of horrors amounting to a compendium of male as well as female fears and insecurities to satisfy the most jaded Freudians.[16]

Clearly, splitting the female protagonist of *Genesis* into two separate women, allowing Eve to be the "good wife," is hardly a solution to the problem. In the end, Lilith would turn into little more than a pre-Eve, as a kind of evil inner twin. And while open misogyny, unabashed hatred of women, is generally considered fairly "rare" in early rabbinic writings,[17] there is ample reason for concern. One need not go as far as feminist scholar Leila Leah Bronner in characterizing Talmudic and *midrashic*[18] materials as outright biased "male discourses that depict Eve as the tempter of Adam" to conclude that their net effect has been to "concentrate on formulating guides to daily observance and conduct for women to follow in order to atone for Eve's sin and to achieve the modesty required for the fulfillment of their roles in marriage and matrimony."[19] The female sex would seem to continue to have to pay for the original transgression against God's commandment.

In sum, whether or not Lilith was differentiated from Eve, whether or not the stories and legends involving these two mythological creatures were merely imaginative fictional musings, there is little doubt that Lilith affected the way Eve—and with her, woman as such—was perceived within the Jewish tradition. The idea that Eve had been responsible for mankind's expulsion from the Garden of Eden was used by some religious Jews to justify making Jewish women subservient to their fathers and husbands. Louis H. Ginzberg explains the rationale: "because woman extinguished the light of man's soul, she is bidden to kindle the Sabbath light."[20] And since women were thought by some to be untrustworthy, just like their original mother, "woman covers her hair in token of Eve's having brought sin into the world; she tries to hide her shame; and women precede men in a funeral cortege, because it was woman who brought death into the world."[21] The effect of misogyny on Jewish and then on later monotheistic religions cannot be underestimated.

While the Jewish psychotherapist and biblical scholar Dr. Naomi Rosenblatt finds widespread evidence in the rabbinic tradition for feminine courage, initiative, and power in the great heroines of the Old Testament, she concedes that her foremost "mission and . . . passion is to extricate the women's voices from a male-centered narrative . . . never ignor[ing] the context of their day-to-day lives: a patriarchal and polygamous society, a short life span,"[22] and a nominally genderless Deity, Yaweh, whose literary persona was nevertheless unquestionably male. Her erudite book goes a long way to fulfill that mission.

But the story of Lilith is not only a result of too literal an attempt to reconcile two seemingly divergent chapters of *Genesis*, it also reflects a profound ethical dilemma about the nature of God the Creator. In the first place, how could the all-infinite, all-benevolent God create imperfect humans capable of disobeying their Maker? And second, how could God have banished His own children mercilessly from Eden, condemning them to die ostensibly just for having disobeyed their Creator? And if God was not to blame for the expulsion, who *was*? Satan? Eve and/or Lilith? Adam? All of the above?

The extensive literature about Lilith and her various permutations, as well as the plethora of painstaking attempts to come to grips with the implications of the creation story, testify to the intractability of the dilemma, which just wouldn't go away. Indeed, thirteenth-century Kabbalism further split Lilith *herself* into two, a younger and an older, each of whom is sometimes good and sometimes bad, sometimes fused with a male, sometimes even semidivine. Yet no amount of additional metaphysical and supernatural splicing succeeded in making the dilemma disappear. The notion that good and evil both emanate from God was and continues to be exceptionally problematic for all the biblical religions. At root the problem is monotheism itself: how can not only good but also evil result from *one* all-loving, absolutely good Creator?

Whether Lilith, or Satan, or Lilith-as-Eve, or Satan-through-Eve, or Eve-as-Satan, the symbolic feminine-as-evil became entrenched in the Abrahamic tradition. Since Judaism is not rigidly canonical—meaning that since one true interpretation of the Bible is not considered possible, conflicting interpretations are not only expected but encouraged[23]—the Jewish Eve enjoys greater latitude than do at least some of her Christian counterparts. It probably helps too that Judaism never adopted the concept of the Fall, or Original Sin, which is so manifestly central to Christianity.

In Christianity, Eve is pitted against the Virgin Mary, who is sometimes actually called "the second Eve." The two are practically mirror images, with Eve, so easily seduced by the evil serpent, seeming closer to the Antichrist than she does to Mary.

Early Christian Eve-Bashing

The woman taught once and for all, and upset everything. Therefore he [I Timothy] *says, "Let her not teach." Then does it mean something for the rest of womankind, that Eve suffered this judgment? It certainly does concern other women! For the female sex is weak and vain, and here this is said of the whole sex.*
John Chrysostom, Homily 9 on I Timothy *(c. 386 CE)*

We now return to the question of God's punishment of mankind after the first transgression in Eden, since Christianity is focused specifically on the evil of mortality. One version goes something like this: since a perfect God created our world, some explanation is necessary to account for sickness, degeneration, pain, and suffering. The well-known literary critic Northrop Frye noted that the principal difference between primitive Earth-mother, or sexual, types of creation-myths and the subsequent biblical monotheism lies in divergent approaches to the idea of death. Divine sexual creation, which is manifestly anthropomorphic, assumes that death is a part of life, intrinsic to the generation–growth–decay cycle of organic development. On the other hand, writes Frye, "an intelligent God, it is felt, can have made only a model world, a world he could see to be 'good' ([*Genesis*] 1:10, etc.), and consequently it could not have had any death or sin or misery originally in it. Such a myth therefore must have an alienation myth of a 'fall' to account for the contrast between the perfect world [that] God must have made with the world we live in now."[24]

This is by no means obvious—it certainly was not to most Jews. It is also not necessary in a more strictly logical sense; after all, perfection could be defined in such a way as to accommodate the changes that may seem bad or undesirable but are, in a more objective (or at least less anthropocentric) perspective, simply the normal unfolding of physical phenomena. We might not think that something is good, but then again, we have only our own interests in mind, and don't understand God's big plan.

In stark contrast to Judaism, the idea of man's Fall from the Garden of Paradise as defined by Original Sin is central to Christianity's concept of humanity's redemption through the sacrifice of Christ, the Son of God. Anne Baring and Jules Cashford observe that "Christ was to be the Second Adam, who removed, through his death and resurrection, the curse placed upon the first."[25] Thus we read in *I Corinthians* 15:22, "For as in Adam all die, even so in Christ all will be made to live." Adam had brought death upon mankind after listening to Eve, who in turn had fallen to the lures of the serpent—Satan.

Begging to differ, John Phillips points out in his book *Eve: The History of an Idea* that the teachings of Christ as described in the Gospels do *not* refer to Original Sin, nor do they equate sexuality with sinfulness. Phillips argues that the practice of demonizing Eve, nowhere to be found in the teaching of Jesus, is a clear departure from the New Testament. But his is decidedly a minority view; most Christian theologians argue that Jesus came to rescue us from the evil that befell upon mankind in the Garden of Eden, an evil for which Eve was principally to blame.

So common is the assumption that Eve's eating the forbidden fruit constitutes the essence of the Original Sin that most Christians simply take it as given, failing to take into consideration its relatively recent origin, let alone its virtual absence from the Jewish tradition. It is not a little ironic that the first and most important Christian figure to blame Eve for mankind's fall from grace should be none other than a Jewish convert—the venerated apostle Paul, whose original Hebrew name was Saul.

Although the so-called Pauline corpus of writings attributed to the great apostle indicate a genuine ambivalence toward women rather than uncompromising hostility, the deepest impression on posterity was made by the misogynous corpus, at least as handed down by the male scribes who may have "improved" upon the original.[26] In *I Timothy* 2:14, for example, Paul—at least, as he has come down to us—unequivocally declares that a moral abyss separated the two first humans. It was Eve, definitely *not* Adam, who was to blame for disobeying God: "Adam was not deceived, but the woman was deceived and was in sin."

This might be taken to mean that Adam was not less culpable than Eve but indeed more, since he couldn't—or anyway, didn't—claim to have been deceived. The fact is that Paul specifically singles out Eve, and not Adam, as being "in sin." He elaborates upon her inferiority elsewhere as well; the net result is to place the bulk of the responsibility on the most cataclysmic event in human creation, the loss of innocence and immortality, squarely on woman. Far from symbolizing universal fertility, generosity, and life, the first female was reduced to the devil's instrument of cupidity and death. What a reversal!

The Apostle Paul draws the following lesson for the Christian home in *Ephesians*, 5:24: "[J]ust as the Church is subject to Christ, so also let wives be to their husbands in all things." Lest there be any question of woman's inferior status, Paul writes in *I Corinthians* 14:34–35, in the section "Order Necessary": "Let women keep silence in the churches, for it is not permitted them to speak, but let them be submissive, as the law also says. But if they wish to learn anything let them ask their husbands at home, for it is unseemly for a woman to speak in church." Nor is this just his opinion, bidding his readers two verses later "to recognize that the things I am writing to you are the Lord's commandments."

Finally, Paul notes that a Christian woman is required to cover her head, just like Jewish women. A man "ought not to cover his head, because he is the image and glory of God. But woman is the glory of man. . . . For man was not created from woman, but woman from man" (*I Corinthians* 11:7, 11:9). If this statement seems inconsistent with verse 11—"yet neither is man independent of woman"—it is mitigated by the caveat in verse 12, to the effect that "all things are from God," implying that their mutual dependence is hardly more momentous than that of, say, cats and mice, fellow creatures but hardly chums. Gone, certainly, is the idea that man and woman were created as helpmates to one another, equal in every way, soulmates through life, to the end.

Worse was yet to come. The most learned and prolific of the early Christian Fathers, Origenes Adamantius, better known as Origen (c. 185–254 CE), and his contemporary Quintus Septimius Florens Tertullianus (Tertullian for short), a Christian theologian from North Africa, further degrade Eve to the level of her pagan predecessor, the evil Pandora. Tertullian explains the conflation, "If ever there was a certain Pandora, whom Hesiod cites as the first woman, hers was the first head to be crowned by the graces with a diadem; for she received gifts from all and was hence called 'Pandora'; to us, however, Moses . . . describes the first woman, Eve, as being more conveniently encircled with leaves about the middle than with flowers about the temple."[27]

In other words, the graces were wrong to crown such a despicable creature; it was far more appropriate that the first woman should cover her shame with leaves about the middle. The resemblance between the two mythological first women could not have been more obvious to these theologians: had not both Pandora and Eve brought affliction and death to mankind? True, Pandora had been expressly manufactured to be evil, while Eve had been fashioned good and merely persuaded to disobey her Creator's commandment by a wily serpent who was perhaps Satan himself; but the net effect for mankind was similarly catastrophic.

The serpent deserves his own story, which in many ways parallels that of female divinity. The hapless reptile's reputation also declined precipitously, and precisely along the same trajectory—from a symbol of life and healing demoted to little more than the Devil's own incarnation. No wonder that woman and snake, beguiling and bewitching creatures both, would be vilified together and in like ways.

The most celebrated poem about *Genesis* in the English language, John Milton's *Paradise Lost,* has Adam liken Eve to the blasted serpent when he angrily denounces her:

Out of my sight, thou serpent, that name best
Befits thee, with him leagued, thy self as false
And hateful, nothing wants, but that thy shape,
Like his, and color serpentine may show
Thy inward fraud, to warn all creatures from thee
Henceforth; lest that too heavenly form, pretended
To hellish falsehood, snare them.[28]

Early in the history of Christianity, Eve and the serpent both became identified with evil and/or sexuality. Eve was seen as morally inferior to Adam, less rational, less disciplined, vain, instinctive, and lascivious. Sexual awareness was likewise connected to the devil and to death, destruction, and evil. The virus of sexuality having infected man through woman, he too became thereby doomed. That virus is—both literally and figuratively—inherited through the sexual act. It goes without saying that the reason why Jesus had to be conceived by a virgin was to avoid corrupting copulation: as man untainted by the sin of intercourse, Jesus would be pure as no human, male or female, ever could.

Logically, the next best thing to being born of a virgin is to abstain from sex altogether. The credit for condemning sexuality almost to the point of deeming it a necessary evil belongs to another famous Christian theologian who hailed from North Africa, known by his beatified name Saint Augustine. He thought woman unequivocally, almost irredeemably evil, for as he wrote in *The Literal Meaning of Genesis,* "It was through her that man sinned." Despite Adam's denial, in *Genesis,* upon divine interrogation, that he had been "seduced" by

Eve, Saint Augustine compares the first man's situation with that of Solomon, who allegedly committed idolatry against his better judgment, having been "unable to resist the love of women drawing him into this evil. . . . So it was in the case of Adam."[29] If even Solomon, one of the wisest men of all time, could be seduced by women, say no more: resisting these insidiously ravishing monsters is nothing short of impossible.

As a result of Adam's sin, writes Saint Augustine, all humanity became lethally contaminated: "By a kind of divine justice the human race was handed over to the devil's power, since the sin of the first man passed at birth to all who were born in the intercourse of the two sexes, and the debt of the first parents bound all their posterity."[30] Inherited concupiscence thus dooms the race; its only hope is salvation through the one man who resisted temptation. That man, though born of woman, is like no other: he is the Son of God Himself, Jesus the Christ.

A number of commentators have remarked on the irony that Saint Augustine, the same man who could so movingly capture the profound turmoil he felt over his early frivolity, in one of the most influential books of all time and the first modern autobiography, *The Confessions*, the grateful son who owed so much to his saintly Christian mother, would become such a militant foe of womankind. One has to wonder too about his long-term relationship with the woman who bore him a son, but whom he never married and whom he mentions in his autobiography but never by name. Did she mean anything to him? And if so, what does that say about the strength of his own ability to imagine a genuinely spiritual marriage of souls? We will never know, but can well wonder.

Saint Augustine describes the human hierarchy of male and female as if he were measuring two sticks of obviously unequal length:

> And just as in man's soul there are two forces, one which is dominant because it deliberates and one which obeys because it is subject to such guidance, in the same way, in the physical sense, woman has been made for man. In her mind and her rational intelligence she has a nature the equal of man's, but in sex she is physically subject to him in the same way as our natural impulses need to be subjected to the reasoning power of the mind, in order that the actions to which they lead may be inspired by the principles of good conduct.[31]

QED Proof complete, conclusion derived with deductive certainty. Unless, of course, the premises are false?

Saint Augustine states with similar—absolute—certainty that man is directed by God to pursue spiritual things and resist his passions "which, in the living soul, are tamed into submission by the practice of chastity, by fasting, and by the soul's regard for its duty to God."[32] This logically leads Augustine to interpret God's commandment urging Adam and Eve to be fruitful and multiply that is nothing short of astonishing.

After an elaborate dialectic exercise, Saint Augustine concludes, "I take the reproduction of human kind to refer to the *thoughts* which our minds conceive, because reason is fertile and productive. . . . I believe that by this blessing you granted us the faculty and the power both to give expression in many different ways to things which we understand in one way and to understand in many different ways what we find written obscurely in one way."[33] Incredibly, instead of a literal meaning, Saint Augustine reads the biblical passage "in a figurative sense,"[34] thus coming perilously close to allowing the possibility that human reproduction is not only unnecessary but indeed the result of weakness.

There is little doubt that subsequent interpretations of woman as the instrument of Satan have left an indelible imprint on Christianity and, indeed, on monotheism in general. Attempts to redeem woman's place by appealing to Mary as the second Eve, though certainly helpful, would hardly suffice to undo, let alone erase, this deeply entrenched negative view of the female sex in general.

I can think of no more heart-wrenching and tragic an expression of female self-loathing than this old Irish lament:

> I am Eve, the wife of noble Adam; it was I who violated Jesus in the past; it was I who robbed my children of heaven; it is I by right who should have been crucified. I had heaven at my command; evil the bad choice that shamed me; evil the punishment for my crime that has aged me; alas, my hand is not pure. It was I who plucked the apple; it went past the narrow of my gullet; as long as they live in daylight women will not cease from folly on account of that. There would be no ice in any place; there would be no bright windy winter; there would be no hell, there would be no greed, there would be no terror but for me.[35]

This passage strikes me as among the most extreme examples of the devastating effects of the Eve-as-sinful-everywoman motif in

Christianity. And the history of the early church could not fail to leave an indelible imprint on Western civilization as a whole.

The Reformation that took place in the sixteenth century in Central Europe did not help much on this account. Although Martin Luther and John Calvin initially read *Genesis* as proclaiming equality among the first helpmates, eventually both theologians came to the conclusion that woman was subservient to man as a consequence of the original sin.

Luther wrote that, among other sorrows such as childbirth, "Eve has been placed under the power of her husband, [which] punishment, too, springs from original sin, and the woman bears it just as unwillingly as she bears those pains and inconveniences that have been placed upon her flesh."[36] Forget stoic subservience: women "indicate their impatience through grumbling. However, they cannot perform the functions of men: teach, rule, etc."[37] Eve's wretched daughters, therefore, far from being "helpers," not only covet jobs for which they are manifestly unfit, but they *kvetch* and make a guy's life more miserable than it already is. John Calvin conceded that woman, like man, had been "created after the image of God" but hastened to add "though in the second degree."[38] In the final analysis, Calvin too agrees with Luther that woman is to be subservient to her husband. Not much comfort there for Eve's daughters.

Notwithstanding the personalities and writings of Luther and Calvin, the Reformation eventually did lead to a fresh interpretation of *Genesis* that was more in line with its original intent. Not only was the Bible translated into vernacular languages so that people unschooled in Latin, Greek, or Hebrew could read the text for themselves, but with the advent of the printing press, the book became far more accessible to millions. It was not long before Eve's well-deserved resurrection would be understood as necessary to a reassessment of human morality and spirituality.

Today, it is not only feminist interpreters of the Bible who agree with Prof. Susan Niditch of Amherst College that using *Genesis* 3 to indict woman "as the gullible, unworthy partner who let loose sin and death," is dead wrong: "*Genesis* 3 has been misunderstood" pure and simple. Niditch goes on to explain:

> Certainly, like Pandora in the comparable Greek cosmogonic tradition, the curious woman is a linchpin in the ongoing process of world ordering. . . . On the other hand, in the lore of all cultures interdictions such as Gen. 2:17 ("But of the tree . . .") exist to be disobeyed

by the tales' protagonists. This is what makes the story. Eve, as she is named in 3:20, is the protagonist, not her husband. This is an important point, as is the realization that to be the curious one, the seeker of knowledge, the tester of limits, is to be quintessentially human—to evidence traits of many of the culture-bringing heroes and heroines of Genesis.[39]

Thanks in part to the eloquence and moral authority of the great Polish Pope John Paul II, as will be seen in chapter 11, Eve may yet be placed alongside her consort on the pedestal of history. Someone may do the same for the Muslim tradition in a manner that will prove not only convincing to scholars but also politically palatable. That is, surely, no small challenge.

Eve after the Quran

"Depart now from Paradise, deceived forever henceforth," said God [to Eve]. "I make thee deficient in mind, religion, ability to bear witness and inheritance. I make the morally malformed, with glazed eyes, and make thee to be imprisoned for the length of days of thy life and deny thee the best things, the Friday congregation, mingling in public and giving greeting. I destine thee to menstruation and the pain of pregnancy and labor, and thou wilt give birth only by tasting the pain of death along with it. Women shall experience more sorrow, more tears shall flow from them, they shall have less patience, and God will never make a prophet or a wise person from among them.
Muhammad Ibn 'Abd Allah Al-Kisa'i, The Tales of the Prophets
(c. 1200 CE)

Islam was last to turn on Eve.[40] It did not take place until after the death of its prophet, following a host of mostly unflattering commentaries about our first ancestress. Here too there was plenty of irony, given the Quran's enlightened view of sexual equality: the Islamic Holy Book had provided the most progressive protection for women to date. Especially seen from the perspective of its time, the Quran was nothing short of revolutionary. During Mohammed's life, in seventh-century Arabia, when, based on wild sexual misconceptions, infanticide, sexual abuse of slave girls, and denial of inheritance to women were rampant, the Quran explicitly and immediately prohibited all these practices and categorically repudiated the entrenched assumption of female inferiority. What is more, Mohammed's own behavior indicates not the slightest lack of respect for his female relatives or any other women. The same, unfortunately, cannot be said of later statements and practices attributed to him by others.

Misconceptions about Islamic views on sexual identity are rampant, both outside and inside the tradition, for diametrically different reasons. Writes Amina Wadud-Muhsin in her widely acclaimed book *Quran and Woman*, "Femininity and masculinity are not created characteristics imprinted into the very primordial nature of female and male persons, neither are they concepts the Quran discusses or alludes to. . . . They have figured very strongly in interpretation of the Quran without explicit Quranic substantiation of their implications."[41]

Indeed, she continues, "with one exception, the Quran always uses the Arabic dual form to tell how Satan tempted both Adam and Eve and how they both disobeyed. In maintaining the dual form, the Quran overcomes the negative Greco-Roman and Biblical-Judaic implications that woman was the cause of evil and damnation."[42] That one exception specifically singles out for reproach . . . Adam:

> And of old We made a covenant with Adam, but he forgot; and We found no firmness of purpose in him. . . . And Satan whispered to him: said he, 'Oh Adam! shall I show you the tree of Eternity and Kingdom that faileth not [does not waste away]?' And they both (Adam and his wife) ate thereof [of the fruit of the forbidden tree]. . . . And Adam disobeyed the Lord, and went astray. (*Sura* 20: 114–119).[43]

The point about forgetfulness is critical: it provides ample reason for the Creator to forgive Adam. As for Eve, she is not even on trial. Yet Islamic tradition turned this on its head as had its older sister-monotheisms, except, alas, eventually more viciously by far.

It started innocently enough, in the seventh century, with the second caliph of the Muslim world, the much beloved and astute Omar. As he was also quite austere and pious, Omar took measures to regulate the roles of men and women, notably by segregating them during prayer—evidently to avoid distraction. But this was still a very far cry from the sexual apartheid that would befall the Muslim world in the not too distant future. Writes Tamim Ansary:

> In Omar's day, education was still compulsory for both boys and girls; women worked alongside men, took part in public life; they attended lectures, delivered sermons, composed poetry for public orations, went to war as relief workers, and sometimes even took part in fighting. Important decisions facing the community were discussed in public meetings, Omar participated in those meetings as just another citizen of the community, and women as well

as men engaged him fearlessly in debate. In fact, Omar appointed a woman as head of the market in Medina, which was a position of great civic responsibility, for it included duties such as regulating construction, issuing business permits, and policing the integrity of weights and measures.[44]

Even so, "Omar did plant seeds that eventually developed into a severe constriction on women's participation in public life."[45]

And there were many other factors contributing to the ominous misogynist turn. Among the most important is that early exegetical works, from the traditional rulings, the so-called *tafasir*, which created "the basic paradigms through which we examine and discuss the Quran and Quranic interpretation[,] were generated without the participation and firsthand representation of women."[46] Another may be found in the various cultural influences to which the Muslim interpreters could not be expected to be immune. In particular, recent scholarship has uncovered a fascinating, complex web of oral and written traditions. In addition to the rabbinical and Christian scholars and storytellers, a sect of particular importance was Gnosticism, which flourished in the Middle East during the second to fourth centuries CE.

Composed of many sects and religious systems, Gnosticism was considered a heretic offshoot of Christianity, Judaism, paganism, or a noxious mixture of all three, which nevertheless proved remarkably influential the mainstream sects, each in different ways. Specifically, many elements of the Gnostic creation myth would later find their way into Islam.

As related by Leigh N. B. Chipman, based on the account from The Apocryphon of John, to be found in the Coptic Gnostic Library in Egypt, the story goes as follows:

> The Demiurge, the creator god of this material world and the son of Sophia (Wisdom—the lowest spiritual divine being), announces that he is the only god. As a result, a heavenly voice proclaims that "There is Man and the son of Man," and the Demiurge and the archons, beings who take part in ruling this world, are vouchsafed a glimpse of the Anthropos, the spiritual First Man who is also the Supreme God. The Demiurge and archons decide to create Adam in the image of the Anthropos, and create "the animate Adam," a non-material being which has a soul (*psyche*) but no spirit (*pneuma*). At this stage, Adam is incapable of movement and lies on the ground, until Sophia persuades the Demiurge to breathe his spirit into him. Thus, the divine spark that Sophia stole in order to give birth to the Demiurge passes from him to Adam. The archons immediately

understand that they have created a being superior to themselves and imprison him in a material body. In other words, Adam is composed of body, soul the "spark," part of the divine power which has fallen into our world and the body was created to ensure that it remains here. In a state of non-salvation, the spirit within the body and soul is not aware of itself and is depicted as paralyzed, asleep or poisoned; it "doesn't know" (i.e., a-gnos-tic, as it were). Awakening and salvation are achieved through gnosis.[47]

In other words, the archons are afraid of Adam, whereupon they reform him and vengefully force him down to the baseness of material existence: to put it bluntly, for the Gnostics, the body is *bad*.[48] The Gnostics assumed that the world is all evil from the outset, and it is necessary to explain how it is possible even for a few elect individuals to be saved at all.[49] This presumption was diametrically opposed not only to the Jewish Bible, the Old Testament, but also to the Quran, which fully embraced the view that a benevolent God created a world that was fundamentally good. Yet the Gnostic contribution to the Abrahamic tradition, and specifically to the development of Islam, has been sufficiently influential to be worth taking seriously.[50]

Disobedience being arguably even more fundamental to Islam— whose the Arabic root "s-l-m" contains the concepts of "submission," and "surrender"—than to its sister Abrahamic sects, the fatal insubordination in the Garden of Eden was bound to be revisited, and Eve fated to bear the brunt of her Arabic sons' anger. Among the most important early documents about the Quran, which is assumed by scholars to summarize the first three centuries of commentaries, written by Abu Ja'far Muhammad ibn Jarir al-Tabari (839–923), illustrates this unsurprising fact. A native of northern Iran, al-Tabari had set out to record the most authoritative and reliable interpretations gathered along his extensive travels. The sources that he specifically traces back to people who lived during the time of Mohammed himself, known as the Companions, fall along two main traditions, neither especially Eve-friendly. One depicts her as merely more subservient to Adam; the other, much more ominous, assigns to her the primary blame for the first rebellion in Eden.

The first tradition uses *Sura* 7:189 (which says that God had had created Adam's "mate that he might take rest in her") as evidence for the claim that Eve had been created expressly for Adam's sake, all but ignoring *Sura* 30:21, which plainly declares the unequivocal reciprocity of the relationship: "He created for you helpmates from yourselves that ye might find rest in them," further underscored by a Divine command—"and He ordained between you love and mercy." This first misogynist tradition then goes one step further, arguing that Eve must have been created secondarily to Adam because the word for life, the etymological root of her name, means that she was "created from something living." This clearly implies the Quran's agreement with the second account of human creation from *Genesis*, which has Eve fashioned from Adam's rib, despite the *absence* of any such account in the Muslim Holy Book itself. Never mind, too, that this reading of her name directly *contradicts* another passage from *Genesis* that explains her name in an entirely different light, Adam having reportedly "named his wife Eve [*hawwah*] because she was the *mother* of all the living" (*Genesis* 3:20; emphasis added), obviously stressing her identity as the *source*, not product, of life.

But the second tradition stemming from the Companions was far worse. Despite the absence of any evidence from the Quran that either first human, male or female, was more culpable than the other, this tradition opts squarely for blaming Eve by portraying Adam as initially having refused to eat the forbidden fruit, Eve repeatedly trying to lure him until she finally succeeded. Later commentaries, incredibly, charge that Eve had used wine and beauty to tempt Adam.[51] For example, al-Tabari alleged that Yazid b. 'Abd Allah b. Qusait had said: "I heard S'id b. al-Musaiyib swear by God: 'Adam did not eat of the tree as long as he was in his senses, but Eve gave him wine to drink, so that when he was drunk, she led him to it and he ate."[52] Never mind that we are talking about a thirdhand (or fourth? or fifth?) hearsay report. What could possibly have been her motivation? Especially if she herself would be punished along with Adam? The logic here is incomprehensible.

The Muslim hostility to Eve only grew with time, reaching a turning point in about the tenth century, when the tone of the scholars' remarks on gender roles became more strident. Tamim Ansary notes that "the radical separation of gender roles into nonoverlapping spheres probably froze into place during the era of social breakdown that marked the latter days of the Abassid khalifate,"[53] around 1000 CE. But the original purpose for relegating women to an unseen private realm, which later would become a form of imprisonment, was, paradoxically, the precise opposite: these happened to be Byzantine and Sassanid practices indicating high status. Wealthy women were spared the indignities of the rough-and-tumble of daily existence. How truly ironic!

Unfortunately, in the Muslim tradition, the isolation of women happened to coincide with the rejection of a more philosophical and humanistic interpretation of religion. Writes Tansary, "The same forces that squeezed protoscience out of Islamic intellectual life, the same forces that devalued reason as an instrument of ethical and social inquiry, acted to constrict the position of women."[54]

It would soon get worse—a lot worse—as may be seen from a later text, dating from around the thirteenth century, entitled *The Tales of the Prophets of al-Kisa'i*. Though primarily a collection of legends from popular culture, *The Tales* both reflected and influenced the attitudes of a large audience. The many wonderful stories about the creation of Adam and Eve that sometimes ascribe qualities of tenderness and care for each other, also mention that she had actually been created from a *crooked* rib out of his sinister *left* side.[55] (In Latin, *sinister* means also, literally, "left.") According to this tradition, God explicitly and unequivocally pronounced her "deficient in reason, religion, ability to bear witness, and in inheritance."[56] Though she is apparently thus cursed only after her fatal transgression, there is some ambiguity regarding whether she may actually have been born that way.[57] Either way, it is clear that simply being born female was no light sentence.

And the worst was yet to come. Jane L. Smith and Yvonne Y. Haddad note that many of the modern commentators on the episode of disobeying the Divine order against eating from the forbidden fruit,

> while agreeing [with the Quran] that Adam was fully responsible, nonetheless come back to Eve as the real cause of the problem. Adam forgot the covenant, says al-Maraghi, and lost all strength of resolution that would help keep him from following his wife. Then citing a *hadith* from Abu Hurayra to the effect that were it not for Hawwa no female would betray her husband, al-Maraghi comments that "She it is who extolled to him the eating of the tree. Woman is created by nature to extol what she desires from man, even though it be by deceitful means" (*Tasfir* 8:120). 'Abbas Mahmud al-'Aqqad agrees when he says that the story of the fall symbolizes eternally the changeless nature of woman who always does what she is

specifically told not to do (*Hadhihi al-shajara*, 7). Every element of a woman's character is represented in the story of the tree, he says, and part of it is her love for that which is forbidden. The only way of preserving the species is through the relationship of one who has control to the other who is controlled.[58]

Mahmud Shalabi, citing several *hadiths*[59] by way of evidence for the all women's "crooked character and the possibility of weakness in their brains," concludes, "It is apparent to us that Hawwa' is created from Adam's rib and that she is crooked in her feelings and emotions similar to the character of the crooked rib from which she was created" (*Hayat 'Adam*, 61).[60]

Evidently, the Islamic exegetic tradition dealt an especially severe blow to the image of Eve. But the other two religions were hardly blameless. The question inevitably arises: why did all three major monotheistic religions depart from the deeply compassionate portrait of the first human marriage as originally depicted? It is nothing short of extraordinary that Eve would end up being targeted as principal scapegoat, the Devil's instrument, her husband's—indeed mankind's—nemesis, instead of his closest friend, his helpmate and lover, God's greatest gift. That vision has been stood on its head.

Nor is it just about Eve—it is equally about Adam. For the vilification of Eve, which abolishes the mutuality, respect, and love among human helpmates, fatally undermines the spiritual basis for the relationship between mankind and God generally. The animosity that fueled the misogyny which infected the Abrahamic religions—admittedly in different ways and varying intensities at different times and places—is surely one of the major calamities to befall civilization. The harm that has already been done is incalculable. Addressing it is imperative, not only in the interest of human survival but because we owe it to one another and ourselves to preserve our dignity and to recover the meaning of being human. By resurrecting Eve, we restore everyone's true identity.

As mentioned earlier, the visceral terror of woman may well be a male propensity, complemented by the equally elemental though manifestly contradictory desire for the proverbial yearning to return to the prenatal condition, the absolute security of the womb. Throughout history, man's relationship to woman has been inescapably ambiguous: simultaneously adored and feared, the prototype of all Nature that is the source of life and death, she has embodied alternately hope and despair. Writes Camille Paglia:

Judaism, Christianity's parent sect, is the most powerful of protests against nature. . . . Judeo-Christianity, like Greek worship of the Olympian gods, is a sky-cult. It is an advanced stage in the history of religion, which everywhere began as earth-cult, veneration of fruitful nature. The evolution from earth-cult to sky-cult shifts woman into the nether realm. . . . Men, bonding together, invented culture as a defense against female nature. Sky-cult was the most sophisticated step in this process, for its switch of the creative locus from earth to sky is a shift from belly magic to head-magic.[61]

In the end, however, head-magic is bound to fail: nature comes back with a vengeance. And Eve reclaims her domain: as sky and earth had been created together on the first day, so male and female are inseparable complements. The point is not to elevate one over the other but to embrace the whole. Conversely, debasing one debases another; and demeaning woman degrades man—in fact more. Unfortunately, religiously condoned misogyny has led to a systematic degradation of women throughout every society, which continues even in the United States and other Western nations, albeit in far attenuated and often insidious, subtle ways. For reasons perhaps entrenched in the structure of the human brain, there may never be a total eradication of gender prejudice. But surely a critical component is cultural, involving archetypal motifs, myths, or narratives, which have persisted over centuries and even millennia and hence must be revisited for a thorough, informed appreciation of our self-conception as human beings.

Notes

1. *Ecclesiasticus* was "received as canonical and divine by the Catholic Church, [which considered it] instructed by apostolical tradition, and directed by the spirit of God" *The Holy Bible*, 713. That said, the history of its compilation, and whether it had been composed by one person or several, continues to be debated.
2. The Jewish bible does include another book, *Ecclesiastes*, unfortunately sometimes confused with *Ecclesiasticus*. Its Hebrew transliteration is sometimes rendered as *Koheleth*, after the name of its presumed author. See *Tanakh*, 1441.
3. Philo, *Questiones et Solutiones in Genesis*, 1:37.
4. Ibid., 1:43.
5. Found also in a rabbinical *midrash* or exegesis, which accuses woman—i.e., Eve—of having "brought death into the world" *Genesis Rabbah* 17:8.
6. A specialty of the otherwise brilliant Camille Paglia; see her superb literary insights in *Sexual Personae: Art and Decadence from Nefertiti to Emily Dickinson*.
7. Raphael Patai, *The Hebrew Goddess*, 221–22.

8. *Eve and Adam*, 162.
9. *Tanakh*, 689.
10. *The Hebrew Goddess*, 225.
11. Ibid.
12. Ibid., 252.
13. Kabbalah refers to the whole range of Jewish mystical activity. Some rabbis regarded the mystical study of God as important but dangerous. See Rabbi Joseph Telushkin, *Jewish Literacy*, 200–3.
14. *The Hebrew Goddess*, 230, citing *Zohar*, I:34b.
15. Ibid., citing Yalqut Reubeni, 68. Admittedly, many consider Kabbalism to be somewhat thinly related to Judaism.
16. Ibid., 204.
17. Daniel Boyarin, *Carnal Israel: Reading Sex in Talmudic Culture*, 23–231.
18. *Eve and Adam*, 75.
19. Leila Leah Bronner, *From Eve to Esther: Rabbinic Reconstructions of Biblical Women*, 22.
20. Louis H. Ginzberg, *Legends of the Jews*, 67.
21. Ibid.
22. Naomi Rosenblatt, *After the Apple: Women in the Bible—Timeless Stories of Love, Lust, and Longing*, xviii.
23. Thus, "since Judaism was not organized around orthodox doctrines or creedal statements, Eve's story could not play the foundational theological role in Jewish thought that it did for later Christian readers," *Eve and Adam*, 3.
24. Northrop Frye, *The Great Code: The Bible and Literature*, 109.
25. Baring and Cashford, *The Myth of the Goddess*, 533.
26. According to Dennis MacDonald, the work of Paul "has come down to us from the hands of pious, dedicated, and skilled men" whose perspective on the nature, role, and function of women had hardened when Christianity became the religion of the Roman state. (See Cullen Murphy, *The Word According to Eve: Women and the Bible in Ancient Times and Our Own*, 227.)
27. Ibid., 517.
28. John Milton, *Paradise Lost*, Book X: 867–73.
29. Saint Augustine, *Confessions*, Book XI: 42.
30. Ibid., 534.
31. Ibid., ch. 32, 344.
32. Ibid., Book XIII, Ch. 23, 334.
33. Ibid., Book XIII, Ch. 24, 336–37 (emphasis added).
34. Ibid., 336.
35. David Greene and Frank Connor, *A Golden Treasure of Irish Poetry, 600–1200*, 158.
36. Martin Luther, *Lectures on Genesis*, 69.
37. Ibid., 115.
38. John Calvin, *Commentary on Genesis*, Book II, 9.
39. Carol A. Newsom and Sharon H. Ringe, eds., *The Women's Bible Commentary*, 12.
40. Technically, the Quran does not use a specific name for Eve—or indeed for any other woman, with the notable exception of Mary (Mariam). The

words are either *imra'ah* (woman), *nis'* (women), or *zawj* (spouse or mate) pl. *azwaj*, along with the name of a particular male. *Quran and Woman*, 32–33.

41. Ibid., 22.
42. Ibid., 24–25.
43. *The Koran*, 209.
44. Tamim Ansary, *Destiny Disrupted*, 51. Also, 113–14.
45. Ibid.
46. Ibid., 2.
47. Leigh Chipman, "Mythic Aspects of the Process of Adam's Creation in Judaism and Islam," 7.
48. For the Gnostic attitude to the body, and to matter in general, see Brown, *The Body and Society: Men, Women and Sexual Renunciation in Early Christianity*, 106–12, cited in ibid., 15.
49. Ibid., 18–19.
50. A brilliant analysis may be found in *The Mind of Jihad* by Laurent Murawiec, especially the section on "Etiology," 81–89.
51. *Eve and Adam*, 158.
52. Cited in ibid.
53. Tamim Ansari, *op. cit.*, 114.
54. Ibid.
55. *The Tales of the Prophets of al-Kisa'i*, 31 and 54.
56. Ibid., 40.
57. *Eve and Adam*, 159.
58. Jane L. Smith and Yvonne Y. Haddad, "Eve: Islamic Image of Woman," 142.
59. The *hadith* consists of edicts, letters, and treatises dictated by the prophet himself, followed by his sayings recorded in the 'pages' (sahifah) of his Companions and the next generation, usually known as the Followers, or tabi'un." Seyyed Hossein Nasr, *Islam: Religion, History, and Civilization*, 54; see also 55–58.
60. Ibid., 143.
61. Paglia, *Sexual Personae*, 8–9.

6

Eve's Muslim Daughters

In these [Muslim] states, however, the ability of women is not known, because they are merely used for procreation. They are therefore placed at the service of their husbands ... But this denies them their [other] activities. Because women in these states are considered unfit for any of the human virtues, they often tend to resemble plants.
                          Averroes (Ibn Rushd) (1126–1198)

By the twelfth century when Averroes was thus deploring the plight of Muslim women, the pedestal of equality the prophet of Islam had outlined for them in the Quran had long since vanished. It seems very hard to believe that Eve/Hawwa had been portrayed in the Quran as Adam's devoted helper and lovely companion. Yet so it was. Nowhere does Islam's Holy Book accuse her of disproportionate guilt for eating the forbidden fruit, nor is she portrayed as inferior to her mate. More frequently mentioned in the Quran than she had been in the Bible, her reputation as Adam's equal was not only presupposed but underscored. According to one major tradition of commentaries on Muhammad's teaching, stemming from his Companions, contemporaries who had interpreted his creed according to everything they knew of him and his beliefs, God had created woman as a source of rest for the man. And when God discovers their transgression, after they both repent and ask for mercy, saying that they realized they had wronged both God and themselves (*Sura* 7:23),[1] God forgives them both and bestows upon them as well as all of mankind the garment of righteousness. Says God:

> O children of Adam! Now have we sent down to you raiment to hide your nakedness, and splendid garments; but the raiment of piety—this is best. O children of Adam! Let not Satan bring you into trouble, as he drove forth your parents from the Garden, by despoiling them of their raiment, that he might cause them to see their nakedness. (*Sura* 7:5–26)[2]

Though sent away from paradise into the world of strife, the two humans had not been banished from the heart of God.

But it did not take long for Eve to become unrecognizably distorted in the Islamic tradition, through exegetical commentaries of learned patriarchs, bits of folklore steeped in pre-Islamic mores, and mystical contemplations that departed radically from the Quranic text itself. Doomed to inherit a woefully skewed portrait of their symbolic mother, for the ensuing millennium and a half, the vast majority of Eve/Hawwa's Muslim daughters would suffer enormously, far more than most of her Jewish and Christian offspring.

Barbara Freyer Stowasser writes that classical Muslim interpretations of the Quranic telling of the story distort the original script in numerous ways: "Extraneous detail transmitted in Hadith form and frequently originating in the Bible and Bible-related sources not only fleshes out the story but dramatically changes it, especially with regard to the woman's role." Specifically, "medieval interpretation of woman's origin and nature denies female rationality and female moral responsibility."[3] As a result, woman's subservient place in society was institutionalized and justified with the presumed weight of divine accession. She continues, "The Hadith materials on women's inferior nature were accepted and propagated by the consensus (*'ijma'*) of the learned doctors of law and theology until eighteenth century premodern reformists began to question their authoritative status"[4]—followed, a century later, and again in the twentieth, by new studies that boldly return to . . . the original text. In other words, the self-proclaimed fundamentalists, the extremist Islamist clerics, stand accused of engaging in a distorted reading of the Holy Book, and charged with . . . blatant blasphemy!

The origin of this erroneous yet prevalent reading that is responsible for the plight of women in Saudi Arabia, post-1979 Iran, Somalia, Yemen, and many other societies where conservative, misogynist clerics have been waging an undeclared asymmetric war against their disenfranchised, muted, occasionally even mutilated female population may be found in an exegetic tradition that focused on Eve's role as the first rebel against God who was held fully responsible for Adam's sin. The Egyptian scholar Nawal El-Saadawi points out that the infamous veil, whose complex symbolism continues to mystify foreign commentators, is the most tangible example of that tradition's legacy. Writes El-Saadawi:

> A historical study of how the veil arose shows that it began with the rise of Judaism as a religion and the myth of Adam and Eve. It originates with the fact that Eve is looked upon as the source of evil and sin, and must feel shame for her corrupt nature. She must therefore cover her body including the head and face, and refrain from exhibiting any part of it. It is also inspired by the idea that Eve (woman) is a body without head and that Adam (her spouse and man) is her head.[5]

According to this reading, it was Eve who allegedly successively tempted Adam to eat from the forbidden tree, treacherously eroding his reluctance by drugging him with alcohol. Abu Ja'far Muhammad Ibn Harir Al-Tabari, for example, noted in his *Commentary on the Quran*, probably written in the late ninth century, that one Muslim follower had heard "Sa'id b. Al-Musaiyib swear by God: 'Adam did not eat of the tree as long as he was in his senses, but Eve gave him wine to drink, so that when he was drunk, she led him to it and he ate.'"[6] This sinister view of Eve would soon gain preeminence throughout the Muslim world.

For Eve's character was a hot subject of discussion not only among theologians and wise men otherwise disconnected from the daily life of ordinary people; it also preoccupied the common folk. Stories about the first woman abounded in the popular culture, and for good reason. The seminal event that was mankind's creation, with such enormous implications for inter-gender relations, could not but fire the imagination. A remarkable collection dating from around the end of the twelfth century, titled *The Tales of the Prophets*, intended principally to entertain yet also guide people's conduct, became immensely popular in many different regions of Islam. And they did not bode well for Eve.

The *Tales* are certainly imaginative. Some seem faithful—in spirit at least, if not in letter—to the Quranic account of the first couple as loving and supportive mutual helpers. Thus Adam and Eve reportedly articulated their mutual affection, after being separated by God following their disobedience, in a most tender fashion. For the most part, however, the general thrust of the *Tales* is categorically, even viciously, antifeminine. In a section entitled "The Address of Eve," God is said to have expelled Eve from paradise with anger and vindictiveness, making her "deficient in reason, religion, ability to bear witness, and in inheritance."[7] For good measure, she is also destined to be "morally malformed, with glazed eyes," and even condemned "to be imprisoned for the length of days in life." And lest there be any question as to whether the sentence is cast only upon Eve, the "Address" specifically has God declare that all ensuing "women shall experience more sorrow, more tears shall flow from them, they shall have less patience, and God will never make a prophet or a wise person from among them."[8] Guilt carried by every X (and never the Y) chromosome was presumably morally recessive, intended to spare her sons. But though its primary victims were women, men were by no means spared the consequences—in ways they did not realize.

This was hardly the kind of treatment one might have expected from an all-merciful Creator. The legacy of such a curse would weigh heavily, albeit in varying degrees at different times and in different places, upon the entire Muslim world. Despite occasional moments of emancipation, the plight of Muslim women has been a painful and pathetic saga of cruelty. While early in the twentieth century a number of Muslim countries allowed women to vote, hold jobs, and even make important decisions about their lives, the tide would turn against such policies, in reaction against Arab nationalism and globalization that seemed to threaten the culture and traditions of Islam. Only slowly have women started to emerge once again in the twenty-first century, however tentatively, in a few Muslim states, asserting their ancient rights with felicitous consequences for their families and the nations themselves. But there is a very long road still to travel.

Recent studies by the UN Development Program, notably the widely acclaimed 2005 *Development Report on Gender in the Arab World*, the 2009 Freedom House report on women's situation in Arab countries in the Gulf region, and various global surveys gauging popular perceptions of women's status all indicate that while Eve's Muslim daughters may be up for parole or at least a milder sentence, they continue to face very serious problems.

The 2009 Freedom House report notes encouraging signs of progress, yet it concludes with the following negative findings:

> [W]omen throughout the Gulf continue to face systematic discrimination in both laws and social customs. Deeply entrenched societal norms, combined with conservative interpretations of Islamic law, continue to relegate women to a subordinate status. Women in the region are significantly underrepresented in senior positions in politics and the private sector, and in some countries they are completely absent from the judiciary. Perhaps most visibly, women

face gender-based discrimination in personal-status laws, which regulate marriage, divorce, child custody, inheritance, and other aspects of family life. Family laws in most of the region declare that the husband is the head of the family, give the husband power over his wife's right to work and travel, and in some instances specifically require the wife to obey her husband. Domestic violence also remains a significant problem.[9]

Not much has changed since. In September 2010, the American Islamic Congress released *A Modern Narrative for Muslim Women in the Middle East: Forging a New Future,* including case studies from Egypt, Jordan, Morocco, Saudi Arabia, and Iraq. They document a pervasive trend, confirming that women throughout the Arab world "though a slight statistical majority—remain disenfranchised and hold an inferior status as a result of their gender."[10] In the end, scorecards and statistics cannot capture the full magnitude of the problem that is very deeply rooted, as Muslim men's perception of women is the result of centuries-old archetypal preconceptions.

There are certainly important similarities between Western misogyny and Muslim, specifically Arab, prejudices against Eve and her daughters. But, paradoxically, in Western culture, woman's biological second place has long been taken for granted: even Aristotle, the first empiricist who observed and classified with superhuman thoroughness rarely equaled in human history, didn't bother to count a woman's teeth, merely assuming them to be fewer than a man's since she was assumed worse in every respect. Aristotle is merely one of the pioneers of the Western misogynist tradition, whose later exponents are very much with us today. In the Muslim world, by contrast, woman's currently benighted plight is based on a very different premise. Fatima Mernissi observes that "[i]n Islam, there is no such belief in female inferiority. On the contrary, the whole system is based on the assumption that women are powerful and dangerous beings. All sexual institutions (polygamy, repudiation, sexual segregation, etc.) can be perceived as a strategy for containing their power."[11] In other words, the West had turned against woman because of her alleged inferiority and weakness; the Arab, and more generally Muslim world, did so because of her strength!

The Quranic conception of the two sexes as one another's helpmates was thus gradually set on its head: male and female are in fact nothing less than each others' sworn tormentors. Mernissi continues: "At stake in Muslim society is not the emancipation of women (if that means only equality with men), but the fate of the *heterosexual unit*. Men and women were and still are socialized to perceive each other as *enemies*."[12]

Come again? Women are perceived as dangerous adversaries? This is difficult to accept, considering the incredible disparity between the status of men and women, particularly in conservative societies throughout the Middle East and other Muslim cultures, especially in Africa. Sometimes the plight of Muslim women seems little better than that of slaves; but slavery has traditionally been justified on the basis of the subhuman nature of the victims rather than their superiority! Given the manifestly inferior status of women throughout the Muslim realm, how can they possibly be seen as more powerful than men?

The answer lies in the attitudes of Islamic culture toward sexuality. Unlike Christianity, and particularly Catholicism, which has always held asceticism in high esteem, Islamic culture has traditionally considered abstinence not only ill-advised but outright dangerous. Sexual frustration is feared. Pious men, therefore, are advised to marry pious women; they certainly must not stay celibate. Man's dependence on a woman's willingness to engage in intercourse thus gives her a strange, ominous advantage, which proves ultimately detrimental to her status as his intellectual and spiritual equal. For since the only type of intercourse that is condoned is within the institution of marriage, in order to avoid sexual frustration, a man is under considerable stress to seek a wife, and marriage ends up being more about physical satisfaction than about mutuality and friendship.

In addition, it is easy to see how sexual arousal can become a real problem for men who are conditioned to avoid and even fear it. If her mere presence can cause havoc, a woman obviously possesses great power—but it is no blessing. Rather, it motivates men to seek to control her, so she may be available to satisfy him, and incapable of refusing him. What is more, she is, or certainly can be, easily the recipient of his rage: she is to blame for the effect she has on him. What sorry state for them both.

Polygamy is one logical next step: if his first wife becomes too old or proves otherwise undesirable and incapable of satisfying him, a man can take another wife—up to four, presumably according to the Quran. Whatever its original intent—and some scholars have suggested that its principal rationale was political rather than psychological, reflecting the prophet's conviction that the family unit was superior to the tribe as a unit of socialization[13]—polygamy soon became an instrument of control over women. What can only be deemed a hysterical attitude against the rise of female self-determination among elite Muslims (especially in the Arab world, which is predominantly Sunni, but also among fundamentalist Iranians and other Shiia) and deserves no sympathy must nevertheless be explained in historical context. Writes Mernissi, "Female self-determination, female initiative, whether in the home of the outside world, is the very embodiment of the absence of order, the absence of Muslim laws."[14] In other words, woman power is thought to lead to chaos, to the pre-creationist disorder that God had ended with His establishment of law and harmony.

The inordinate fear of women, which had been assiduously resisted and even opposed by the prophet, led to the pathological oppression that defines their destiny in most—though by no means all—Islamic societies today. But it would be a gross distortion of Islam to consider this attitude a necessary, let alone irreversible, component of the religious culture. Rather what has emerged from the complicated tradition of post-Mohammedan Islam is a multifaceted feminine legacy. Barbara Freyer Stowasser observes that the richly poetic Quranic style, which invites and indeed engages the full panoply of psychic faculties—above all, the heart and the imagination—has also encouraged the tendency of Islamic scripturalist scholars to mold the images of the female figures in the Quran to reflect and enforce their societies' prevailing values "in ways that often changed the images' Qur'anic nature and role," since these were consistently androcentric (male-centered). Unfortunately, as a result, most medieval Islamic exegesis, "viewing women's innate nature as weak but also dangerous to the established moral order, largely excluded the Qur'anic theme of female spiritual freedom and moral responsibility."[15]

Yet that theme was difficult to suppress entirely, as evidenced by some of the key symbols of womanhood that have emerged over the course of nearly two millennia in the Islamic world. Eve's Muslim daughters have included the bride-soul prototypical wives Zulaikha and the Queen of Sheba (traditionally called Bilqis), which both appear in the Quran, followed in the popular lore by Layla and Shirin; the patient and intelligent Scheherazade; the ascetic, saintly Rabi-a al-'Adawiyya; as well as the quintessential generative-mother figure. And finally, there are the tortured Lolitas, the silent child virgins who live in putatively pious patriarchal societies, mostly though by no means exclusively illiterate women whose stories may be read in lifeless, tear-drained eyes, mutilated bodies, and premature deaths.

Each of these metaphorical daughters illustrates an aspect of Eve's stifled, distorted sexuality. The ideal woman's love is thus commonly imagined as either motherly, unrequited—ideally, even ascetic, or at least postponed—tamed by patience and intelligence, and of course, most problematically of all, as innocently prepubescent. But love they would and love they did, in many ways strengthened by suppression. We will return to the more egalitarian Quranic conception of Hawwa in chapter 9, when we examine Mohammad's idyllic marriage to his beloved Kadija.

The Saintly Mother

Just as Eve was created from Adam without a woman, so was Jesus created from Mary without a man.
Isma'il ibn Umar Abu l-Fida Ibn Kathir, Quisas Al-Anbiya'

The Quran adopts the Old Testament commandment to honor one's father and mother, but preeminence is given to the latter: for "paradise lies at the feet of their mothers." According to one tale, when a youth came to Mohammed and asked who was most deserving of his love and care, the prophet allegedly replied, "Your mother!" "And the next most deserving?" "Your mother!" "And the third?" The prophet replied, "Your mother!"[16] (My mother should have heard this; she may well have converted.)

Clearly indicative of her exalted status, Mary (Maryam) is the only female dignified in the Quran with a proper *name* rather than described by her relationship to someone else—merely as a wife, sister, or daughter. Also, improbably enough, she figures even more prominently than in the New Testament! She is said to have been surrounded by miracles even in childhood, having been chosen by God above all the other women as "an example for the believers" for her chastity, faith, and obedience. Both classical and modern Islamic interpretations of the Quran assume that Mary had been a virgin when she conceived her child from God's spirit, which would have enhanced her reputation among males. Islamic scholars have used her story to emphasize the duty of women to be virgins on the eve of their marriage, stay faithful to their husbands, and demonstrate their obedience to God through obedience to their mates.

> But males were not her only or even main admirers. As Barbara Freyer Stowasser points out, Mary's importance to Muslims, especially Muslim women, is far different and far greater than what

126

these scholarly formulations might suggest. Recitation of "her Sura" (*Sura* 19) is a favorite especially with women circles throughout the Muslim world, believed to confer special blessings on reciter and listeners alike. Many women in Syria are said to pray through Mary (and Fatima) in moments of anguish, as women elsewhere pray through (other) female saints.[17]

Fatima, the prophet Mohammed's youngest daughter, had died only a few months after her father. Having married his cousin, Ali ibn Abi Talib, she bore him two sons, whom Mohammed reportedly adored. In the Shiite tradition, reports the celebrated Islamic scholar Annemarie Schimmel, Fatima was granted a special position that can well be described as that of *mater dolorosa*, a status arguably comparable with that of the grieving Mary. Although dead for almost fifty years before the demise of her second son, to the Shiites Fatima stands higher than all other people except for Mohammed and Ali.[18] Yet her reputation is by no means restricted to the Shiites. Writes Schimmel:

> Indeed, Fatima has come to be a role model for Muslim girls . . . Her veneration is also great in the Sunnite world . . . Most [Muslim] people would probably agree with Sana'i (d. 1131 in Ghazna, today's Afghanistan), who sings:

The world is full of women
yet where is there a woman like Fatima,
the best of women?[19]

Perhaps the most eloquent demonstration of the mother's place in Islam is found in the countless examples of pious men carrying their old mothers to Mecca so they too may perform their sacred duty in pilgrimage. Famous poets, saintly men, and other notable figures throughout the history of Islam have offered heartfelt tribute to their mothers. According to the thirteenth-century Persian poet Jalal ad-Din Mohammad Balkhi, the most celebrated poet of Sufism, better known as Rumi (so named after the city where he lived), a human being is like a pregnant mother who carries within herself the mystery that grows ever larger. That mystery is likened to the proverbial hero's journey, the development of self-knowledge and spiritual maturity. Schimmel points out that "even a glance at the literature of mystical Islam shows that this whole genre, however unconsciously at times, actually did identify the human soul with the feminine element. . . . Pain is an essential aspect of all development and growth, and if Mary, having suffered the pangs of childbirth, was rewarded with a shower of sweet dates, then it follows that the sight of the beautiful Beloved will expunge all memory of pain from the soul."[20]

The mother's pain and that of all mankind finds resonance in the figure of Mary/Maryam and Fatima. But there is pain also in unrequited love, whether from unpropitious circumstances or death. Small wonder, considering their plight over the course of many centuries, that women's fate is invariably treated in the Islamic literary tradition as somehow interconnected with suffering.

The Lovesick Lover

Like your happiness, I am separated from you, but I am your companion, even when I am far away from you. . . .
Nizami, Kahmseh

The story of Layla and Majnun is best known through the version written by the twelfth-century poet Nizami (who spent most of his life in what is today Azerbaijan) as one of five stories included in the epic *Khamseh* (Quintet). Later imitated by Persian and Turkish poets, the story of Layla and Manjun is typical of the unrequited love between two young people whose marriage is prohibited by the woman's stern father. Layla, who according to some versions of this story met Majnun while they were both children, in Koran school (an example of egalitarianism not uncommon among the Islamic upper classes of early Islam[21]), later falls hopelessly in love with him. When forced by her father to marry a man she does not want, she obeys, but after her marriage, she refuses to give herself to her husband. She soon becomes terminally ill and confesses her secret to her mother, who dresses the young woman as a bride. Majnun of course dies as well, on her grave, driven almost to madness by his passion—thus pre-dating the celebrated Shakespearian plot of the star-crossed child-lovers of Verona by many centuries.

Indeed, historian Wiebke Walther believes the doomed Muslim couple to be "better known throughout the Islamic New East than are Romeo and Juliet in Europe."[22] Notwithstanding the striking similarity between the two couples separated both culturally and chronologically, however, the differences are crucial. For example, Juliet, true to Eve's negative image, had engaged in a plot to deceive her family by planning to elope with Romeo, then proceeds to commit suicide, after finding her lover dead, having killed himself at the sight of what he took to be her corpse. Juliet is not only oblivious to the fact that suicide, unlike lovesickness, is prohibited in Christianity—as indeed in all monotheistic religions; her suicide also expressly seeks to *avoid* the experience of longing. Majnun and Layla, quite the opposite, succumb to lovesickness, which they are powerless to avoid—but they never actively seek to do so. In fact, Layla lacks precisely the fatal flaw of insubordination that had allegedly doomed Eve and hence mankind. Indeed, Layla simultaneously obeys both her father and what she considers to be her destiny, which is to love Majnun. She submits, and succumbs.

The feeling of longing to be united with the other half, which Layla and Majnun symbolize, has left a deep imprint on Islam. Writes Annemarie Schimmel, "The idea that Eve, created from Adam's rib, and thus a part of him, constantly yearns for the undivided whole . . . is reminiscent of Gnostic ideas about the splitting of the primal principle into the two aspects of the heavenly masculine and the earthly feminine. . . . [C]enturies later Rumi took up the same theme . . ."[23] In turn, the unconsummated woman represents mankind's yearning for love. She continues, "In the Ismaili poetry of Indo-Pakistan, the *virahini*, the woman yearning in unfulfilled love, can be understood as a symbol of creation separated from God."[24]

Note, however, that Rumi advises a woman beholding her beloved to be frozen and passive; she must "sit before him like a mirror"—which connotes truthfulness, clarity, and purity. In one of his quatrains, he has a lover say, "I created a mirror, clear to you; its face is the heart, its back the world" . . . and in another, Rumi writes, "My heart is like water, clear and limpid, /like the water that reflects the moon."[25] A woman must avoid being aggressive; she should await her fate.

It is interesting that in his best known and last work, the epic *Masnavi*, Rumi specifically mentions the story of Adam's fall as having been caused by Adam's having "tried to interpret [God's admonition] on his own [and] He couldn't leave forbidden fruit alone" (verses 1259–60). In line with the Quranic account, nowhere does Adam blame Eve. On the contrary, Adam's attempt to interpret God's Words seems altogether understandable; continues Rumi, "If I don't see a snare by God's decree /I'm not the first who can't see destiny" (verses 1265–66).[26] If God seems cruel, it is only an illusion: "By frightening you, know that He's being kind /In His safe kingdom space for you He'll find" (verse 1270).

Throughout his famous writings (as recently as 2007, the BBC referred to him as the most popular poet in America), Rumi's principal theme was love in all its aspects. Fascinated by mysticism and the feminine aspect of the soul, he painted the many hues of longing—at its darkest when unrequited. Woman's plight transcends her sex: Layla represents not only one face of Eve but mankind itself, yearning for God without any hope of meeting Him before death. Yet death is not to be feared; Layla's bridal attire symbolically anticipates her union with her lover yet also—perhaps through him?—with their Creator, whose children they are.

So can Islamic tradition sublimate the ideal feminine lover's passion into a union with the divine—through death. By transforming lovesickness into spiritual longing, thus seamlessly morphing from carnal lust to chaste desire for infinite salvation, the uniting of Eve with Adam is rescued from both banality and the ire of misguided clerics.

Layla had been preceded in the Quran by two legendary stories— that of Zulaikha, who in the Old Testament was said to have been Potiphar's wife who fell desperately in love with Josef (named Yusuf in the Quran), and second, that of the Queen of Sheba (Bilqis in Arabic), another biblical figure that Schimmel considers "rather reminiscent of Zulaikha"[27] for she is similarly smitten with a holy man. As Stowasser points out, in Zulaikha's complex story as related by Mohammed, "the themes of female desire and cunning are woven together with those of love, repentance, honesty, and fidelity." Of course, traditional scholarly commentaries drastically reduced its sophistication through the predictable "exegetic emphasis on this woman's nature as symbol of the sexually aggressive, destabilizing, and dangerous nature of women as a whole. The love motif, on the other hand, was fully developed in the pious popular storytelling traditions past and present, and also underlay the enduring power of female selfless love and faithfulness, which (according to most of this literature) is rewarded with the bliss of reunion with the beloved."[28]

That distant reward notwithstanding, what emerges from the various stories of lovesick women lovers is the yearning, the passion, the deprivation—in brief, the un-consummation and the ensuing fidelity, an all-encompassing devotion and spirituality. Some Islamic mystics, in a curious reversal of fortune for Eve, even consider woman superior to man in her ability to love purely, to wait for him for as long as necessary, and to love him even when he does not return her love for whatever reason. The obvious palliative effect of such a narrative for ordinary women, who throughout the history of Islam have had to cope with deprivations ranging from solitude and isolation to outright rejection, is clear. But leaving aside the hope for postmortem retribution, many found solace in the legendary quality of women's cleverness.

And no other female figure from the entire corpus of the Arabian folk tradition captured this quality better than the captivating, ever alive, Scheherazade.

The Clever Companion

Shahrazad turned to King Shahrayar and said, "May I have your permission to tell a story?" He replied, "Yes," and Shahrazad was very happy and said, "Listen."
The Arabian Nights (*a.k.a.*, The Thousand and One Nights)

Her name is a composite: Scheherazade, which is the Arabic pronunciation of the Persian *tchir* ("born") and *zad* ("to a good race"). The aristocratic Persian women's stories, told over the course of a thousand nights, represent what Fatima Mernissi calls "a symbol of Islam's genius as a pluralist religion and culture, unfold[ing] in a territory that stretches from Mali and Morocco on the Atlantic Coast of North Africa to India, Mongolia, and China."[29] Yet she adds the startling, and disconcerting, observation that "the tales' cosmopolitan grace, their capacity to transcend cultural boundaries, does not extend to the relationship between the sexes. That is portrayed as an abysmal, unbridgeable frontier, a bloody war between men and women."[30]

The fabulous fable, well-known in the West, begins in the wake of the king's determination to wed and then immediately kill his bride, by way of retaliation against the female sex for the betrayal he suffered at the hands of his adulterous wife. His name, Shahrayar, a composite of *shar* and *dar*, meaning "owner or ruler of the kingdom," implies that he is in essence the god of his people and hence can do with them as he wishes. After killing practically every other virgin in the land, the eldest daughters of the king's beloved *vizir* (his right-hand man), Scheherazade insists despite her father's protests that she be presented to the king as his next bride. Convinced that she would not only survive by her wits, intelligently able to read the king's mind and mesmerizing him with stories, she eventually saves not only herself and other potential victims but the king himself, who would have been doomed to a life of loneliness and slaughter. In a sense, she is the post-Lilith Eve, or even a kind of female Noah who saves humanity with her mind and soul from eventual destruction. The enmity between (faithful) man and his (presumed unfaithful) woman could have resulted in the extinction of the entire species but for a brilliant woman of truly "noble birth"—one might almost call it divine.

The Iranian-born British writer Shusha Guppy credits Scheherazade, "the archetypal example of a woman who through the magic of story-telling saves her life and changes her own destiny and the course of events,"[31] with inspiring Persian women to overcome their patriarchal society. Throughout history these "women had to rely on their strength of character and inner resources, and they drew on a variety of stratagems to survive and exercise power. One of the most effective of these was the telling and spinning of stories, and since most of the population was unlettered, they passed them down the generations by word of mouth; they were the guardians of memory." As such, anonymous women played the roles of Homer, Thucydides, Herodotus, Shakespeare, and the unnamed biblical chroniclers, constituting "not only the biological mothers of the nation, but the creators and transmitters of its cultural inheritance."[32] Their handicap—illiteracy, political and economic ostracism, and domestic isolation—became their principal tool in fulfilling Eve's original destiny: the creation and preservation of human experience.

Azar Nafisi is right to call Scheherazade "our own lady of fiction";[33] she is indeed far more. Her persona is mythological in the sense defined earlier: she symbolizes woman—at her best. Though hardly "Everywoman" in the sense that Eve, as the first woman, would necessarily be envisaged, Scheherazade is clever without being deceptive, she is beautiful though defined principally by her mind, and every bit the equal of her husband—indeed, superior, for he succumbs to boundless rage while she stays calm in the face of mortal danger. She argues for mercy and nonviolence, which is at the heart of the Quran. In the story, King Shahrayar ultimately admits that a man should use words to settle his disputes, not the sword—evidently emulating Scheherazade, who represents the triumph of reason over violence. Here is how Mernissi defines her importance in Muslim culture: "To understand the emergence of the storyteller as a symbol of human rights in the modern Orient, one has to remember that for centuries, the conservative elite, with a few exceptions, scorned *The Thousand and One Nights* as popular trash of no cultural value whatsoever, because the tales were transmitted orally [and hence] a symbol of the uneducated masses."[34]

This is far worse than misguided: ignoring the central place of this treasure trove of tales in the culture of Islam is a very serious error.

Daniel Beaumont is one of many scholars who praise the collection for its enormous intellectual value, specifically for "reenacting the manner in which Islamic culture borrows from all of these cultures [Persian, Indian, Arabic, and Hebrew[35]] to create cultural synthesis." Like Mernissi, he is saddened by its reception within Islam itself: "The irony is that *The Thousand and One Nights* —rather like Ishmael, after all—became and has remained an outcast from the Arab-Muslim tradition that gave birth to it."[36]

The reason for its secondary place is to be found in the specific style, which was primarily oral. Suspicion of fictional narratives as frivolous was widespread. In fact, one explanation for the combination of genres, adventure or quest alongside moralizing, was to "entertain audience while fending off criticism from religious scholars and legal authorities."[37] Consisting of pre-Islamic Arab materials, which from the start competed with Persian material, the first version of *Arabian Nights* has been estimated to date as far back as the late eighth century.[38] Mohammed himself is said to have loved many of these tales, as did his first and dearest wife Aishah as well as, after her death, the other members of his harem.[39]

Scheherazade herself has become an idol for all Muslims, not only women, who feel that a commitment to human rights is not only compatible with Islam but is in many ways coextensive with it. Besides her own example as an exceptionally courageous, intelligent, enterprising, and successful woman who is able to lure her husband away from his rage against his treacherous Eve-like first wife, there are other important themes in Scheherazade's stories that center on topics closely identified with man's banishment from paradise. Notable among them is the symbolism of the Forbidden Doors, coupled with that of the idyllic but dangerous Garden. Insubordination as evidenced by opening a door against advice, which was invariably related to doomed love and eventual death, appears in several of these magical stories.

An unusually perceptive analysis by W. F. Kirby, published in 1887, centers on five tales of *The Thousand and One Nights,* all based on just two simple ideas: the existence of a door which the hero is forbidden to open, and his falling in love with a beautiful woman whom he sees from the housetop.[40] In every case, what is discovered behind open doors is a woman: being kept indoors, away from men's eyes, would be a woman's fate in Muslim culture. The only way she might be able to escape would be through intelligence and ingenuity.

Fatima Mernissi, whose mesmerizing autobiography is poignantly titled *Dreams of Trespass*, explains how Scheherazade had inspired her as a child:

> When Mother finished Scheherazade's story, I cried, "But how does one learn how to tell stories which please kings?" Mother mumbled, as if talking to herself, that that was a woman's lifetime work. This reply did not help me much, of course, but then she added that all I needed to know for the moment was that my chances of happiness would depend upon how skillful I became with words.[41]

At the conclusion of her book, little Fatima Mernissi asks her aunt Mina, "Why can't men and women keep on playing together even when they are older? Why the separation?" No explanation is given, because there is none. Mina says, sadly, that as soon as little girls and boys are separated, "a cosmic frontier splits the planet in two halves. The frontier indicates the line of power because wherever there is a frontier, there are two kinds of creatures walking on Allah's earth, the powerful on one side, and the powerless on the other." Little Fatima's question how she could find out on which side she stood, however, is answered very easily: "If you can't get out, you are on the powerless side."[42] She would eventually get out by trespassing with her mind, which then sets her body free as well.

Exactly like Scheherazade—as her mother had told her. And also like Scheherazade, Mernissi and her husband would become, to the extent that is humanly possible, soulmates. At least, they would try.

The Silent Virgin

The desperate truth of Lolita's story is not the rape of a twelve-year old by a dirty old man but the confiscation of one individual's life by another. . . . Lolita belongs to a category of victims who have no defense and are never given a chance to articulate their own story. As such, she becomes a double victim: not only her life but also her life story is taken from her. . . . Humbert was a villain because he lacked curiosity about other people and their lives, even about the person he loved most, Lolita.
Azar Nafisi, Reading Lolita in Tehran

Throughout literature and art, Adam and Eve are always depicted as young adults: How else would their nakedness have been a cause for shame? And how else could God have held them responsible for disobeying Him? A child, prepubescent and barely rational, is only a future Eve, a not-yet sinner, a malleable soul. An innocent, nubile creature is best suited for a man conditioned to abhor the mature woman as treacherous by nature and threatening. In modern Western culture, the fictional character that most aptly approximates this scenario has come to be associated with the protagonist of Vladimir Nabokov's exquisitely crafted novel *Lolita*. Little did that aristocratic Russian émigré know how ideally his heroine would capture the tragic situation of women in the Middle East and specifically, very soon after his death, in Iran. Yet this is exactly what inspired Azar Nafisi to write her autobiographical *Reading Lolita in Tehran*, which became an instant bestseller after its publication in 2003.

In this extraordinary memoir, Nafisi describes how she decided to continue teaching clandestinely, after leaving academia in a regime that not only prescribed what she should wear but also dictated her curriculum. Her students, who risked their lives by gathering at her home for an illegal class on English and American fiction, found their own lives immeasurably enriched by the discussions, enhancing their appreciation of their condition and deeper self-knowledge. In that setting, the Tehran of the 1980s, Nafisi's choice of Lolita to help her students grapple with the Khomeini regime's treatment of innocent female victims could not have been more appropriate: a child kidnapped and raped by a pedophile whose intellectual abilities thinly camouflage his pathological obsession provided a subtle yet honest, brutally graphic picture of their own, seemingly unrelated plight. The Ayatollah's ruthless, fanatic supporters eerily resemble Humbert, Vladimir Nabokov's sophisticated, sinister narrator: they too murder in cold blood while at the same time coveting child-women whose innocent beauty they find irresistible. Although the differences between the two types of pederasts far exceed the similarities, what they share is an inability to see their victim as anything but an extension of their own repulsive obsessions.

Nafisi records, for example, the story of Nassrin, a young woman who recounted the following incident she had witnessed while briefly jailed:

> There was one girl there—her only sin had been her amazing beauty. They brought her in on some trumped-up immorality charge. They kept her for over a month and repeatedly raped her. They passed her from one guard to another. They married the virgins off to the guards, who would later execute them. . . . If I were not privileged, she said with rancor, if I were not *blessed* with a father who shared

their faith, God knows where I would be now—in hell with all the other molested virgins or with those who put a gun to someone's head to prove their loyalty to Islam.[43]

As it happens, Nassrin had also been translating the Leader's magnum opus entitled *The Political, Philosophical, Social and Religious Principles of Ayatollah Khomeini*. Or, more precisely, she was translating them . . . again. Earlier versions of the translation having become the butt of jokes in embassies abroad, they had been confiscated in droves by the Iranian regime. And no wonder, since the tome stated, among other things, that men could find relief for their sexual urges by having intercourse with animals—including chickens. (And in case you were wondering whether or not a man who has had sex with a chicken can then eat the chicken afterward, the answer is *no*, neither he, nor his immediate family, nor his next-door neighbors can eat of it; but it's OK for a neighbor who lives two doors away[44]—"so good meat isn't completely wasted."[45] Aren't you sorry you asked?) Is it any wonder that one of Khomeini's first acts of "reform" was to lower the marriage age for women from twelve to . . . nine? Nor are such marriages mere formalities.

Yet Nafisi's genius discerns a far more profound rationale for the perversion shared by Nabokov's male antihero Humbert and the Ayatollah. She insists that Lolita represented not merely a critique of the Islamic republic; it was a statement that "went against the grain of all totalitarian perspectives." Few writers could be better suited to write on this topic than the Russian émigré Nabokov, whose compatriots had been subjected to the longest, most vast and brutal dictatorship of the twentieth century. Nafisi understood perfectly that these two seemingly opposing male figures, the consummate intellectual anti-Christ Humbert and the fire-breathing Islamist cleric, share the essential trait of tyrants: a complete lack of empathy, a lack of the slightest curiosity about other people. "Humbert," observes Nafisi, "like most dictators, was interested only in his own vision of other people."[46] Lolita existed only as his creation; she had no independent will that deserved even to be heard, let alone respected. What is more, she had been taken as a child, her voice denied before having had a chance to find itself.

Nafisi's students described their own sense of entrapment, caused in part by the ruthless censorship imposed in the Islamic Republic of Iran that had robbed them of a past, of language and symbols through which they could engage in self-reflection. Like Lolita, they had been not only violated but muted. They were condemned to absolute submission, both physically and intellectually. Nabokov's self-absorbed Humbert too became enraged at Lolita's slightest attempt at independence, even mere curiosity, followed by the briefest remorse which "was all of no avail. . . . [for] soon [Lolita] was to enter a new cycle of persecution."[47] In the context of her father's release from jail with all charges dropped but one—insubordination—Nafisi remembered a sentence she had read in Nabokov: "curiosity is insubordination in its purest form." Hungry to know about the world and themselves, Nafisi's curious young students were guilty of the most subversive sin: they were unwilling to remain voiceless and ignorant, even upon the threat of death.

Yet, however, inhuman the situation of women in such fundamentalist states as the Shiia Islamic Republic of Iran and Sunni Saudi Arabia certainly is, the routine mutilation of female children in many regions of Muslim Africa, notably Somalia, all but defies imagination. The harrowing description of genital circumcision in Ayaan Hirsi Ali's bestselling *Infidel* is difficult even to read; I expect that a visual account would be just about unbearable. Yet such an account exists—and Hirsi Ali is paying for it. After agreeing to collaborate on a movie about that barbaric practice with Theo Van Gogh, who was brutally murdered shortly after its production, she is now required to live in utter seclusion. The movie, which is called *Submission* from the literal translation of "Islam" as "submission to the Will of the One God"—a composite of *taslim* (submission to Him) and *salam* (peace)—confronts Islam's very meaning as it has come to be interpreted in her native land.

In her riveting autobiography, Hirsi Ali describes how in Somalia little girls are made "pure" by having their genitals cut out, typically around the age of five. After the brutal excision that is performed with no benefit of anesthesia, "the whole area is often sewn up so that a thick back of tissue forms a chastity belt made of the girl's own scarred flesh."[48] Although the practice predates Islam, in Somalia (where virtually every girl is so mutilated) the practice is always justified in the name of Islam. "Imams never discourage the practice: it keeps girls pure."[49]

She refers to her own pain as having been "indescribable." But her younger sister—she was only four—had it even worse: the cut tore, and she had to be re-sewn. "I will never forget the panic in her face and voice as she screamed with everything in her and struggled to keep her legs closed." She was never the same. She became ill for several weeks, had horrible nightmares, and preferred being alone. "My once cheerful, playful little sister changed. Sometimes she just stared vacantly for hours."[50] Her little sister's name—how ironic!—is . . . Hawwa.

This grotesque practice is the extreme, logical extension of the Lolita syndrome in the name of Islam: little girls prevented from ever becoming women by guaranteeing that every penetration by a male takes place within a child's minuscule orifice. But the barbaric custom is obviously designed to condemn women to abhor sexual intercourse while seemingly satisfying an utterly bizarre form of male sadism. It also seeks to further ensure the abject subordination of the female. According to Raphael Patai, writing in *The Arab Mind*, since "female circumcision, in contrast to male, is typically carried out in privacy and surreptitiously, the operation is calculated to impress the girl with her own inferiority in relation to boys."[51] According to one observer, commenting on the procedure as performed in Sudan, "causes a shock so severe that those responsible for female education say that girls are often permanently dulled."[52] Lolita is not allowed to grow up, either physically, intellectually, or sexually. Eve's egregious sins had to be guaranteed never to be replicated in any way. A little girl subjected to a clitorectomy becomes a sacrificial lamb, her life snatched away before it could ever begin.

Here is how Nafisi explains the relevance of Nabokov's heroine to the Muslim world: "Lolita belongs to a category of victims who have no defense and are never given a chance to articulate their own story. As such, she becomes a double victim: not only her life but also her life story is taken from her."[53] The only possible form of rebellion that seemed available to Nafisi and her wisdom-seeking students was to turn to fiction, to learn from fairy tales and world literature. For every work of art "is a celebration, an act of insubordination against the betrayals, horrors and infidelities of life."[54] Insubordination again: Eve's alleged sin, turned into a wonderful celebration of freedom. That is what Eve's Muslim daughters want for themselves: like Scheherazade, they want to tell stories, including, indeed especially, their own. And they want a soulmate who can understand and love them for who they are—preferably without first having to escape death by resorting to their wits.

Lost in Translation

I am gonna go where the desert sun is, where the fun is;
go where the harem girls dance;
go where there's love and romance. . . .
To say the least, go East, young men.
You'll feel like the Sheik, so rich and grand, with
dancing girls at your command.
When paradise starts calling, into some tent I'm crawling.
I'll make love the way I plan. Go East
and drink and feast.
Elvis Presley in "Harum Scarum" (1965)

If Edward Said's stubborn hostility to veracity has given Orientalism a bad name, at least among those who are uncomfortable with overly facile West-bashing, the fact that Occidental (not only American but also European) views of Islam are simplistic at best, and do it little justice, is uncontestable. No wonder Westerners oscillate erratically and incoherently between Islamophilia and Islamophobia: mistranslation of the Muslim's culture's exceptionally intricate symbols earns second place only to rank ignorance of the tradition's roots and contexts. That ignorance, while understandable, is not only shortsighted but incalculably dangerous. We cannot formulate effective dialogue among cultures without recognizing the inherently flawed nature of all interpersonal, but especially cross-cultural, perceptions. If Muslim publics are notoriously misinformed about the West and about America in particular, that is to a considerable degree the result of censorship, illiteracy, and deliberate distortions by elites bent either on maintaining or on gaining power, and America is a convenient scapegoat for homegrown ills. We in the West, on the other hand, blessed with a free press and the privilege of leisure to engage in self-education, have little excuse. We can and must do better.

The image of the Muslim woman in the West has suffered from an inexplicable paradox: on the one hand, she has been portrayed as the sensual dancing girl willingly ready to do a man's bidding, while on the other she is portrayed as the great victim of demonic exploitation that many consider intrinsic to Islam. No lesser exponent of this Manichean oversimplification was the late Samuel Huntington, the Harvard professor who popularized the term "The Clash of Civilizations" (which he admitted to have borrowed from Bernard Lewis, though failed to credit Adda Bozeman[55]). First introduced in 1993 in a controversial *Foreign Affairs* article, expanded into a bestselling book published in 1996, Huntington simplistic and indeed dangerous version of this concept proclaimed the following: "The underlying problem for the West is not Islamic fundamentalism. It is Islam, a different civilization whose people are convinced of the superiority of their culture and are obsessed with the inferiority of their power."[56] So much for blaming the vast right-wing conspiracy for this simple-minded us-versus-them mentality.

Part of the blame for the largely skewed American perception of Islam itself goes to Hollywood, of course, that perennial scapegoat, all the more convenient for propagating quite shamelessly the most crass inaccuracies, which are also exceptionally influential.[57] But domestic politics of race and gender have also contributed to the problem, as indicated in Melani McAlister's *Epic Encounters: Culture, Media and U.S. Interests in the Middle East, 1945–2000*. Tracing the simple—and simplistic—parallelism of the male-gendered "West" as against the female-gendered "Orient" back to the nineteenth century, she observes that it has since evolved into a "racialized binary that made maleness equal to 'Europeanness' [and, more generally, 'Westernness'] and femaleness the equivalent of 'otherness.' That rhetorical logic . . . underlay a range of imperialist discourses that posited the 'subject' of history as white, male, and bourgeois."[58] As the gender divide was thus awkwardly superimposed upon civilizational, racial, and ideological antinomies, the Muslim woman remained as misunderstood as ever—perhaps even more misunderstood by their fellow Muslim men.

Fatima Mernissi captures the various dimensions of those misunderstandings with delightful wit:

> In both miniatures and literature, Muslim men represent women as active participants, while Westerners such as Matisse, Ingres, and Picasso show them as nude and passive. . . . While Muslim men describe themselves as insecure in their harems, real or imagined, Westerners describe themselves as self-assured heroes with no fears of women. The tragic dimension so present in Muslim harems—fear of women and male self-doubt—is missing in the Western harems.[59]

Mernissi insists—and this is exceptionally significant—that the dimension is tragic not only for women but, perhaps in some way even more, for the men themselves. At the same time, however, she chuckles at Western men's subtly insidious self-assurance. "The Western illusion of gender equality," argues Mernissi, "belies the existence of an invisible yet none the less powerfully real Western harem." "In the Orient, men use space to dominate women; Imam Khomeini, for example, ordered women to veil when stepping into public space. But in the Occident, men dominate women by unveiling what beauty ought to be"[60]—what they should wear, and how they should look. Reflecting on a recent experience in a Western boutique, Mernissi says to herself: "I am so happy that the conservative elite does not know about it. Imagine the fundamentalists switching from the veil to forcing women to fit size 6."[61] She calls this "the tyranny of the 'size 6 harem.'" The cult of the young, the thin, the innocent: Is that not the very cult of . . . Lolita?

But, of course, that was a quintessentially Western novel—capturing a most typically Western, and specifically American, pathology. Our own little Lolitas, used to adorn magazine covers and help sell everything from lipstick to mufflers, are no less silent and drained of soul for being ubiquitous. About which more will be said in the next chapter.

Notes

1. "They said, 'O our Lord! With ourselves have we dealt unjustly; if thou forgive us not and have pity on us, we shall surely be of those who perish'" *Koran*, 96.
2. Ibid., 97.
3. Barbara Freyer Stowasser, *Women in the Qur'an, Traditions, and Interpretation*, 28.
4. Ibid.
5. Nawal El Saadawi, "Woman and Islam," *Women's Studies International Forum* 5, no. 2, 193–206.
6. Kristen E. Kyam, Linda S. Schearing, and Valarie H. Ziegler, eds., *Eve and Adam: Jewish, Christian, and Muslim Readings on Genesis and Gender*, 189.
7. Ibid., 159.
8. Ibid., 194.
9. *Women's Rights in the Middle East and North Africa, Gulf Edition*, "Overview Essay: Recent Gains and New Opportunities for Women's Rights in the Gulf Arab States" by Sanja Kelly.
10. *A Modern Narrative for Muslim Women in the Middle East: Forging a New Future*, 4.
11. Fatima Mernissi, *Beyond the Veil*, 19.
12. Ibid., 20 (emphasis added).
13. See Montgomery Watt's *Muhammad at Mecca and Muhammad at Medina*, discussed by Mernissi, *Beyond the Veil*, 79–85.
14. Ibid., 84.
15. Stowasser, *Women in the Qur'an, Traditions, and Interpretation*, 21.
16. Annemarie Schimmel, *My Soul Is a Woman*, 89.

17. Stowasser, *Women in the Qur'an, Traditions, and Interpretation*, 81.
18. Schimmel, *My Soul Is a Woman*, 30.
19. Ibid., 31.
20. Ibid., 96.
21. Wiebke Walther, *Women in Islam*, 158.
22. Ibid.
23. Schimmel, *My Soul Is a Woman*, 108.
24. Ibid., 111.
25. Ibid., 113.
26. Rumi, *The Masnavi*, 79.
27. Schimmel, *My Soul Is a Woman*, 60.
28. Stowasser, *Women in the Qur'an, Traditions, and Interpretation*, 50.
29. Fatima Mernissi, *Scheherazade Goes West*, 43.
30. Ibid., 44.
31. Shasha Guppy, *The Secret of Laughter: Magical Tales from Classical Persia*, xiv.
32. Ibid.
33. Azar Nafisi, *Reading Lolita in Tehran*, 6.
34. *Scheherazade Goes West*, 55.
35. He could definitely have added Greek. See Gustave E. von Grunebaum, "Greek Form Elements in the Arabian Nights."
36. Daniel Beaumont, "'Peut-on . . .': *Intertextual Relations in the Arabian Nights and Genesis*," 134.
37. This is argued by David Pinault; see his review of *The Thousand and One Nights in Arabic Literature and Society*, in the *Journal of the American Oriental Society*, 119, no. 3 (1999): 537.
38. Nabia Abbott, "A Ninth Century Fragment of the 'Thousand Nights': New Light on the Early History of the Arabian Nights," 156.
39. Ibid., 157.
40. W. F. Kirby, "The Forbidden Doors of the *Thousand and One Nights*," *The Folk-Lore Journal*, 112.
41. Fatima Mernissi, *Dreams of Trespass: Tales of a Harem Girlhood*, 16.
42. Ibid., 242.
43. *Reading Lolita in Tehran*, 212.
44. Ibid., 35.
45. Ibid., 71.
46. Ibid., 48–49.
47. Ibid., 43.
48. Ayaan Hirsi Ali, *Infidel*, 31. Given her family trauma, it does not seem difficult to sympathize with Hirsi Ali's eventual abandonment of Islam.
49. Ibid.
50. Ibid.
51. Patai, *The Arab Mind*, Ch. VIII, "The Realm of Sex," 124.
52. Ibid.
53. Nafisi, *Reading Lolita in Tehran* 47.
54. Ibid.
55. Elaborated in such superb, if somewhat plodding, books as *Politics and Culture in International Relations*.

56. Samuel Huntington, *The Clash of Civilizations: Remaking of the World Order*, 217.

57. For a thorough history of American perceptions concerning the Middle East, as reflected by Samuel Huntington, see Michael B. Oren's Power, *Faith and Fantasy: America in the Middle East 1776 to the Present*, esp. 572–73. See also his discussions of Hollywood's contribution to the fantasies, *passim*.

58. Melani McAlister's well-documented book *Epic Encounters: Culture, Media and U.S. Interests in the Middle East, 1945–2000*, 271.

59. Mernissi, *Scheherazade Goes West*, 16.

60. Ibid., 112.

61. Ibid., 219.

7

Born Again in the New World

In the beginning, all the world was America.
John Locke, Second Treatise on Government *(1690)*

In thus describing the beginning of human society, Locke had in mind not America, of course, but its ideal image: a virgin territory scarcely populated by pre-civilized yet civil individuals, who generally respected each others' property and settled disputes in the absence of organized government. He also called such a pristine condition *the state of nature*, but meant it as a theoretical construct rather than a historical reality, a model that could facilitate understanding important questions of political philosophy by going back to basics, obviously *not* to be taken for an anthropologically accurate fact. The Reformation of the sixteenth century, which led to a proliferation of Christian sects, and the concurrent Scientific Revolution catapulted by the Polish astronomer Copernicus (1473–1543) who had suggested that planetary trajectories revolved around the sun rather than the earth (an idea soon to be reinforced by Johannes Kepler and later by Galileo Galilei), precipitated a reconsideration of many timeless questions.

At the dawn of modernity, especially after the rediscovery of Aristotle,[1] some fundamental questions were being reassessed not only by a few overzealous theologians but also by a wide spectrum of ordinary mortals—questions such as, What is man? May any man rule over another? What is the basis of legitimate authority? If God created everyone in His Image, who decides what belongs to whom, and why? Doesn't every person have the right to decide his or her own fate? After all, isn't everyone endowed with reason capable of understanding God's Law, the Natural Law, also known as the Law of Reason? If people landed on virgin territory, how would they decide to rule themselves? The answers differed from sect to sect,

145

indeed from individual to individual. A brave new world was being born—quite literally—rapidly becoming populated by brave new immigrants.

The enormous territory that came to be known as America, upon which Christopher Columbus had landed accidentally, shortly before the dawn of the sixteenth century, had seemed to provide the perfect opportunity for just such a fresh start. Those eager to escape the Old World's endemic corruption and religious persecution, the restless and bold looking for land and riches, the haunted and persecuted, and the criminal and the foolhardy were eager to start again in what would soon indeed be called the New World. Its defining feature was the repudiation of the old, even of history as such.

Whether explicitly articulated or subliminally assumed, the premise of the hopeful emigrant to America was that a new birth was possible in the Garden that this yet unmapped continent was imagined to be. In that Garden, man (and perhaps even woman) would become a new *Adam*, as it were, ready to take on life with its endless possibilities, unencumbered by the sins of history. That nation, which had emerged improbably at first, blessed by both circumstance and seemingly providential good fortune, is now the sole world superpower—*hyperpower* or *uberpower* to its detractors. Consistently defying perennial predictions of its imminent decline, the United States' culture and technology continue to shape the new century, as much if not more than it did the old. America's symbols, its mythology, its image of *Homo modernus*, define the global conversation.

The Adamic Eve

Our national birth was the beginning of a new history . . . which sepa-rates us from the past and connects us with the future only.
Editorial from The Democratic Review *(1939)*
I, chanter of Adamic songs,
Through the new garden the West,
The great cities calling.
Walt Whitman, Children of Adam *(1860)*

We celebrate the national birth of the United States of America on a specifically assigned date, the Fourth of July, but in truth, we ripened slowly. It took us about two or three centuries of social, economic, and political evolution, the product of genius, bravery, and very good luck, to mature into the liberal democratic system that subscribed first to the Lockean—most commonly known to us as the

Jeffersonian—premise that God created all human beings equal because equally endowed with Reason.

What is more, around the middle of the eighteenth century, a strong consensus had emerged, especially among the educated classes of New England, that the principles of individual freedom and responsibility, free markets and free minds, and self-government by elected representatives who served their constituents had to be expressly captured in a founding constitution, whose principles were to be faithfully implemented. At the same time, however, the ethos of the civil society had to both reflect and be nurtured by such a document. A free people could survive without a government that would defend them, but neither would it last long if the government itself extinguished that sentiment. Luckily, a providentially fine-tuned group of Founding Brothers (historian Joseph Ellis's apt term) crafted what was needed: a blueprint for a nation fit to govern self-reliant American Adams—rugged individuals determined to start anew, for whom anything was possible with hard work and sufficient commitment.

That legendary rugged individual was only part myth; its basis in reality was solid, further reinforced by the culture that soon blossomed, seeking to reinforce and nourish the human soul in the difficult surroundings it had found on the more pristine side of the Atlantic. That culture adapted old themes to the New World, endowing time-honored myths with new meanings. As R. W. B. Lewis explains in his superb study *The American Adam,* a remarkable modern version of what may well be called "the American myth" was being created from the biblical story of creation that seemed perfectly suited to the new circumstances:

> The new habits to be engendered on the new American scene were suggested by the image of a radically new personality, the hero of the new adventure: an individual emancipated from history, happily bereft of ancestry, untouched and undefiled by the usual inheritances of family and race; an individual standing alone, self-reliant and self-propelling, ready to confront whatever awaited him with the aid of his own unique and inherent resources. It was not surprising, in a Bible-reading generation, that the new hero (in praise or disapproval) was most easily identified with Adam before the Fall. . . . His moral position was prior to experience, and in his very newness he was fundamentally innocent.[2]

"Self-reliance," the title of a celebrated essay by Ralph Waldo Emerson (1803–1882), had inspired his close friend Henry David

Thoreau (1817–1862) to seek to live in the wild, close to nature, far from the materialism and superficiality of the crowd. Self-reliance had apparently rescued, at least for a little while, the admittedly rather cash-stripped Thoreau (who, like many others in the bohemian Transcendentalist circle, depended on Emerson's largesse), from the rampant immorality and materialism that he felt eroded the national fiber. The decadent society surrounding him had officially sanctioned the continued practice of slavery, which Thoreau rebelled against by refusing to pay any taxes. "Civil disobedience"—a term coined by Thoreau that would later inspire Mohandas Gandhi and then Martin Luther King—was pitting the individual against society, personal morality against the all-too-often flawed standards of the community. And as expected, the lone individual who came to symbolize the new Adam was usually male.

It fell to a Frenchman, the astonishingly astute Alexis Charles Henri Maurice Clerel de Tocqueville (1805–1859), to detect what would become the principal subject of the American literary imagination. In a fascinating essay titled "Some Sources of Poetry among Democratic Nations," Tocqueville reveals the nature of this new subject: it would be "man himself, taken aloof from his country and his age and standing in the presence of Nature and God."[3] The American hero would thus represent man in his universal adventure on earth: "Man springs from nowhere, crosses time and disappears forever in the bosom of God; he is seen but for a moment, wandering on the verge of the two abysses, and there he is lost."[4]

R. W. B. Lewis wholeheartedly agrees: this did indeed become the main theme of American literature, as many novelists, poets, and critics focused on the "Adamic person, springing from nowhere, outside time, at home only in the presence of nature and God, who is thrust by circumstances into an actual world and an actual age"[5]—a myth no less noble for being unrealistic, no less powerful an inspiration for being idyllic, and no less tragic for promoting the pursuit of happiness to the point of desperation. Interestingly enough, in principle, the "Adamic person" could actually be . . . a woman. Self-reliant, strong, defying the group with personal conviction and courage, her eventual triumph, however, would come at the price of her very femininity.

Unquestionably the single most poignant example is the epic figure of Hester Prynne, the heroine of Nathaniel Hawthorne's *The Scarlet Letter*. Portrayed as a feisty emigrant from a poor Old England family, having sailed to Puritan New England as the wife of a sinister, crippled old man, Hester is first introduced as she stands serene, if inwardly mortified, before an outraged crowd ready to punish her for adultery. The issue of her crime is a baby, asleep in her lap, whose father could not have been her long-absent husband. Yet she refuses to name the culprit, to spare him opprobrium or worse. Condemned to wear forever a scarlet A on her lovely bosom, she displays it instead with ostentatious, regal elegance and an almost contemptuous dignity. Comforted by the conviction that her alleged sin was genuine, heartfelt love, whose triumph was an innocent child, she goes on living alone, undaunted, exuding an inner peace as an exquisitely eloquent refutation of the popular verdict. The child's name, Pearl, could not have suited the precious little beauty better. The shell's traditionally feminine sexual symbolism also underscores the girl's unique origin: a wild yet perfect creation of nature, further hinting at Hester's quasi-virginal majesty. Little Pearl herself is a budding Eve, a precious jewel of nature.

Hester's story is the transformation of a strong human being from a shunned outcast into a respected, indeed revered, member of the community. However mysterious her choice to not return (as she was free to do) either to her birthplace in England or to any other European city, apparently her sin and her ignominy "were the roots which she had struck into the soil. It was *as if a new birth*, with stronger assimilations than the first, had converted the forestland, still so uncongenial to every other pilgrim and wanderer, into Hester Prynne's wild and dreary but lifelong home. All other scenes of earth—even that village of rural England, where happy infancy and stainless maidenhood seemed yet to be in her mother's keeping, like garments put off long ago—were foreign to her, in comparison."[6] Hester had been reborn a self-determined free Adamic American.

She supported herself easily with needlework, an art that she mastered to perfection. And with time, as she helped everyone who was in need, "quick to acknowledge her sisterhood with the race of man, whenever benefits were to be conferred,"[7] the letter she had magnificently embroidered on her blouse glimmered with comfort, transformed from a token of sin to the taper of the sick-chamber. Many people refused to interpret it by its original meaning any longer, for it had become "the symbol of her calling . . . . They said that it meant 'Able'; so strong was Hester Prynne, with a woman's strength."[8] And as such, it proved immeasurably greater than that of her Adam, the guilt-ridden Rev. Dimmsdale, whose cowardly silence would eventually kill him. The letter's audacious, disdainfully elaborate, embroidery gradually acquired a strange new effect, like that "of a cross on a nun's bosom. It imparted to the wearer a kind of sacredness which enabled her to walk securely amid all peril."[9] So had Hester resurrected herself, at once Adamic and Christlike, gaining a saintly beauty along with a sublime serenity.

But the price was steep. In the end, the vulnerability and fragility that had infused her feminine allure would be sacrificed at the altar of sheer endurance. "Some attribute had departed from her, the permanence of which had been essential to keep her a woman," as nothing was left in her face "for Love to dwell upon," nor in her form and bosom anything "to make it ever again the pillow of Affection."[10] In other words, she was becoming asexual—all but masculine. She even began to think for herself on matters rarely of concern to others of her sex. "Standing alone in the world . . . the world's law was no law for her mind" as she transcended not only moral but intellectual conventions: "thoughts visited her, such as dared to enter no other dwelling in New England."[11] Having thus become a freethinker, an individual in body and soul, society had failed to prevail in the war it had meant to wage against her as a person. But had Hester emerged unscathed? By no means. After all, she was still a woman, and "a tendency to speculation, though it may keep woman quiet, as it does man, yet makes her sad."[12]

For sad she truly was, and lonely to the end—yet hopeful that some day, "in Heaven's own time, a new truth would be revealed, in order to establish the whole relation between man and woman on a surer ground of mutual happiness."[13] Not surprisingly, she was convinced that "the angel and apostle of the coming revelation must be a woman . . . the ethereal medium of joy; and showing how sacred love should make us happy, by the truest test of a life successful to such an end!" That Eve, thus luminously resurrected, would then experience how sacred love can be in an ideal relationship between two people on the basis of mutual happiness. Till then, however, the best that Hester was able to achieve was to join her prematurely deceased lover's grave, her own resting place next to his, separated only by a space, a kind of concrete admonition, a concrete reminder that the dust of the two sleepers had no right to mingle. No right, at least, according to mere convention, and on this earth; for in Heaven, the two would surely meet, to celebrate at last the love that had reflected God's own love for this difficult, beautiful world.

No similar comfort would soothe the loneliness of the poet who, more than any other American writer, captured the essence of the American Adam: Walt Whitman (1819–1892), author of the epic *Song of Myself* and *The Children of Adam*. R. W. B. Lewis describes the eccentric Adamic romantic as an early example, "perhaps the most striking one we have, of the self-made man, with an undeniable grandeur which is the product of the manifest sense of having been responsible for his own being—something far more compelling than the vulgar version of the rugged individual who claims responsibility only for his own bank account."[14] Yet he was doomed to indescribable loneliness.

Consider, for example, Whitman's poem about a live oak he had seen growing in Louisiana:

All alone stood it and the mosses hung down from the branches,
Without any companion it grew there uttering joyous leaves of dark green,
And its look, rude, unbending, lusty, made me think of myself.[15]

Except . . . the oak tree cannot express its despair as can a poet, with excruciating vividness:

I wondered how it could utter joyous leaves standing alone
There without a friend near, for I knew I could not . . .
And though the live-oak glistens there in Louisiana solitary in a wide flat space,
Uttering joyous leaves all its life without a friend a lover near,
I knew very well I could not.

Nor indeed can anyone. So does Whitman introduce, according to Lewis, "what more and more appears to be the central theme of American literature, in so far as a unique theme may be claimed for it: the theme of loneliness"[16]—the loneliness of the first man. But Whitman's is a loud and busy loneliness: speaking to himself and to everyone, manically traversing the self-described "chanter of Adamic songs" he sweeps "through the new garden the West" across America the modern Eden, its "great cities calling." The poet revels in his figurative and literal nakedness:

As Adam early in the morning,
Walking forth from the bower refresh'd with sleep,
Behold me where I pass, hear my voice, approach,
Touch me, touch the palm of your hand to my body as I pass,
Be not afraid of my body.[17]

As Adam, yes, but also as Eve, for Whitman proclaims to speak for all the world.

Thus he begins *Song of Myself*:

I celebrate myself, and sing myself,
And what I assume you shall assume,
For every atom belongs to me as good belongs to you . . . .
I am the poet of the woman the same as the man,
And I say it is as great to be a woman as to be a man,
And I say there is nothing greater than the mother of men.[18]

Whitman is not merely everyman/everywoman, he is everywhere and everything:

I know that the hand of God is the promise of my own,
And I know that the spirit of God is the brother of my own,
And that all the men ever born as also my brothers, and the
    women my sisters and lovers,
And that a keelson of the creation is love . . .[19]

The poet is literally a part of everything, eternally; his bold if not outright blasphemous pantheism refers ultimately to himself.

And as to you, Death, and you bitter hug of mortality, it is idle to
    try to alarm me . . . .
And as to you Corpse I think you are good manure, but that does
    not offend me,
I smell the white roses sweet-scented and growing . . .
And as to you Life I reckon you are the leavings of many deaths,
(No doubt I have died myself ten thousand times before.)[20]

The robust, raw, honest, almost offensively direct quality of Whitman's writing startled his readers. Self-published, the poems would undoubtedly not have gained such acclaim and immediate recognition had it not been for Emerson's enthusiastic support at the outset. (Emerson later came to regret his precipitous reaction). But Whitman would emerge over time as the spokesman for America's new ethos: he had struck a powerful chord. The poet who had declared "I contain multitudes" managed to speak for them with thunderous resonance.

The critic John Burroughs reflected a widespread opinion when he stated, in 1896, that "Whitman appears as the Adamic man reborn here in the nineteenth century." So he was, truly, a chronicler of the future being created right before their eyes. Adds Lewis, "It was this that gave *Leaves of Grass* its special quality of a Yankee Genesis; a new account of the creation of the world—the creation, that is, of a new world; an account this time with a happy ending for Adam its hero; or better yet, with no ending at all; and with this important emendation, that now the creature has taken on the role of creator."[21] The comment is not meant to be profane: though he admits to not understanding God, Whitman did not mean to imply that God does not exist, let alone that the poet himself, or mankind as such, plays that role. But the metaphor of the self-made individual, the self-reliant human being, does reflect the conviction that every citizen of the New World is in a fundamental sense reborn, ready and able to make a life worthy of the name, unencumbered by useless prejudices: in brief, each American is, at bottom, *innocent.*

At Whitman's hands, "innocence," writes Lewis, "replaced sinfulness as the first attribute of the American character"—directly contradicting the original Puritan and Calvinist conviction that every individual had inherited the first couple's original sin. Hester Prynne was but one epic character who sought to refute that cruel assumption. But this seemed easier for the male Adam than for his consort, Eve. Hester herself is an excellent example: for while the dignity and generosity of her penitence had all but erased any trance of shame, the author seems to find it impossible to declare her fully innocent and absolve her completely. Her ultimate punishment was to become less feminine over time, devoted only to her work and daughter, morphing into an Adam-like female, not quite a prototypal human being, for a sexless individual is incomplete. Even the self-described bisexual Whitman (who may have been homosexual) celebrates his hirsute strength and raw virility. So overwhelming is that power that he is able to assume, like Zeus, both male and female functions to gestate then give birth to the world within himself. Yet paradoxically, an uber-sexual (which is not quite synonymous with "oversexed") human, though seemingly at the other end of the spectrum from the asexual, is less role-model than freak.

Whitman, the American Adam, is ultimately transsexual, beyond sin and beyond death, whose one flaw is a too vigorously (and hence unconvincingly) denied sense of alienation from the human condition. He declares himself beyond resurrection, a quasi-mythical new Adam, more than human yet also less: the price of his *ersatz* immortality is to have never quite lived.

Yet unbeknownst to either of them at the time, he did have a formidable female counterpart: Emily Dickinson (1830–1886). The diminutive introvert mistress of deceptively delicate but in reality brutally muscular verse proved to be one of America's most iconoclastic, truly great artists. Her cryptic language, as if she were writing for herself alone, underscores the intense solipsism of her vision, obscuring the shocking violence of her sexual allusions. Camille Paglia captures brilliantly the twin vision of these two giants of the American narrative: "Emily Dickinson and Walt Whitman, apparently so dissimilar, are Late Romantic confederates of the American Union. Both are self-ruling hermaphrodites who will not and cannot mate."[22] They are both excruciatingly alone even as they embrace life passionately and completely.

But Emily Dickinson's voice reflects a decidedly feminine anguish, as illustrated by this poem written around 1861:

Forever at His side to walk—
The smaller of the two!
Brain of His Brain—
Blood of His Blood—
Two lives—One Being—now—
Forever of His fate to taste—
If grief—the largest part—
Is joy—to put my piece away
For that beloved Heart—
All life—to know each other—
Whom we can never learn—
And bye and bye—a Change—
Called Heaven—
Rapt Neighborhoods of Men—
Just finding out—what puzzled us—
Without the lexicon.[23]

So she imagines herself walking with her lover—smaller than him, blood of his blood and even brain of his brain, Eve-like to his Adam as their two lives intertwine and become one, eventually, almost seamlessly, continuing the walk in heaven. That celestial setting, which Dickinson explores often in her little gems of poetry, with bemused skepticism and a touch of trepidation, is here seen as merely a setting for "neighborhoods of men," rapt perhaps in awe, at last able to find out what had "puzzled" us all before: the nature of eternity. It seems that alongside her lover, she does not mind the change in status from life to afterlife. And yet, even as she rejoices in having a whole lifetime "to know each other," she quickly adds a caveat: "whom we can never learn."

Communion seems forever elusive to us all; it certainly did to Emily Dickinson. And yet she persists to dream of it, as in the poem she wrote immediately thereafter:

Wild Nights—Wild Nights!
Were I with thee
Wild Nights should be
Our luxury!
Futile—the Winds—
To a Heart in port—

Done with the Compass—
Done with the Chart!
Rowing in Eden—
Ah, the Sea!
Might I but moor—Tonight—
In Thee![24]

Her yearning is palpable, and heartbreaking, but never self-indulgent. A poem written in the following year perfectly captures the majesty of her distancing. Her suffering is lightly borne, her dignity is magnified by the surgical accuracy of the description:

After great pain, a formal feeling comes—
The Nerves sit ceremonious, like Tombs—
The stiff Heart questions was it He, that bore,
And Yesterday, or Centuries before? . . .
This is the Hour of Lead—
Remembered, if outlived,
As Freezing persons, recollect the Snow—
First—Chill—then Stupor—then the letting go.[25]

The nerves sit "ceremoniously," not unlike Hester Prynne, with seeming respect for formality but in fact stunned by the greatest pain, anesthetized. The heart can hardly believe or remember whether it was "he" that suffered it, and if so, when. Perhaps it was centuries ago, someone else's pain altogether that the poet, Christlike, has appropriated in Whitman-like fashion. The moment is described as infinitely heavy, remembered *only if* it is outlived: the way a frozen person recollects the snow that caused him to let go eventually, after the chill. A small word like "chill" stuns with a blunt Anglo–Saxon thud, bespeaking torment that will not—cannot—be spoken. As the poet records the moment after having let go, the reader is left wondering if that leaden moment is in reality devoid of breath, if her recollection is not actually postmortem.

For, like Whitman, she is in the habit of describing herself beyond the grave, accustomed to imagining herself apart from her own body and soul. Consider the first line of her possibly most famous poem: "I heard a Fly buzz—when I died—"[26]. She too, like Whitman, is everywhere, having transcended both life and death, gender and social companionship, tradition and history, and—of course—sin. Self-made and self-sufficient, the "Belle of Amherst," as she was called, also contained multitudes, speaking for them all with a tiny but deafening voice. In a mirror reversal of Whitman's ubiquity, Emily Dickinson is everywhere in her singleness: she will not give birth to anything, because as nothing is capable of ending, neither can it ever begin. And unlike Christ who sought to lessen pain through his own suffering, Dickinson defines pain as the status quo: To live is to die, not the other way around. In a sublimely ironic reversal, her Adamic Eve is not the mother of life but the mother of death: her stoicism is the most devastating retort to God Himself. For God cannot curse the human race with awareness of death if mankind embraces that awareness with equanimity. ("You can't fire me; I resign.")

What these Adamic American poets share, however, is the profound sense of alienation that is the ultimate price of their peculiar innocence: the not-knowing, specifically the not-knowing another human being. After all, Whitman's all-encompassing self who proclaims to *be* another—in fact, *every* other—is the very essence of solipsism the absolute denial of any separateness, the logical impossibility of merging with something outside oneself for the simple reason that out there, there is . . . *nothing*.

The pens of some remarkable American writers—some, though by no means all, women—would soon expose, with subtlety and insight, the ironic consequence of this narrative. Evidently the New World could not stay pristine for long. Eventually the American Adam, in both male and female guises, would have to—and indeed want to— travel beyond paradise, to the East of Eden. And the Age of Innocence would have to come to an end, even if America neither would nor could ever quite abandon its idyllic illusion of an exceptional, new identity.

The Age of Innocence

If you would live innocently, seek solitude.
Publilius Syrus, Moral Sayings *(First century BC)*
A man is not to aim at innocence, any more than he is to aim at hair;
but he is to keep it.
Emerson, Journals *(1855)*

Innocence, unfortunately, is often even harder to keep than hair: mere time and experience erase it, no matter how hard we try to hold on to it. Not only is solitude excruciating, it eludes most of us whose souls are unlike Emily Dickinson's:

The Soul selects her own Society—
Then—shuts the Door—
To her Divine Majority—
Present no more—[27]

In her case, that company was confined to the figments of her imagination, a majority perhaps less divine than supernatural, a human—even antihuman—demon. Someone who could spend a lifetime within the confines of a small house in Massachusetts may be capable of writing exquisite poetry, but her loneliness would render most ordinary people quite mad. Even if they tried to shut the door of their souls metaphorically, social conventions would inevitably intrude.

Hester Prynne had suggested to her lover that they run away from the village that had condemned her to shame and him to torture from guilt and fear of ostracism. She certainly could have done that, but not he. In the New World, it seemed as if the option to run away to still another virgin territory, to build one's own Eden in a forest yet undiscovered by civilization, was always open. Eventually, however, folks settled down, and the new became old. The Land of Innocence was harder to reach and even to imagine as America's original Age of Innocence receded in time.

The novel by the incomparable Edith Wharton (1862–1937) with that title was met with enthusiasm when published, in 1921, earning her the first Pulitzer Prize ever won by a woman. But *The Age of Innocence* was not its original title: she had first called it *Old New York*.[28] The deliberate irony of the oxymoron "old–new" captures the novel's underlying theme: the nation's most modern city had lost whatever innocence it might have ever had. It was also symbolic of America's predicament.

Whitman could praise the magnificence of the grand city's architectural wonders facilitated by the antediluvian rock of Long Island, geologically most appropriate for the commercial and artistic center of a New World: they stood as proof of implicit divine approval in encouraging contrast to its ominous absence in the aftermath of Babel, the first skyscraper that had famously incurred God's thunderous wrath for presuming to reach the heavens. Wharton's perspective, though following Whitman's by a mere half-century, complements his mania with the depressing reality of pseudo-innocence, which desperately tries to pretend its age is not yet past, while watching itself wilt away. The tragedy of the high society sometimes described as "old New York" is its insistence on being simultaneously old and new, holding on to traditional mores imported from Europe in a setting devoted to the ever-changing. Like every self-contradiction, that old culture had been stillborn.

And yet, what Edith Wharton's whole oeuvre, but especially *The Age of Innocence*, amply demonstrates is the aftereffect of the American quest for a new rebirth on its Adamic creatures in the self-described Eden bounded by seemingly ever-expandable frontiers. The true paradise of communion is bound to elude them; still they continue to imagine that somewhere, someday, it may be found. And that illusion seems to hit especially hard the woman who dares to play the singular Adam by striking out alone, defying society and following her will, intellect, and sentiment; she is judged more harshly not only by others but also, albeit unconsciously, by herself.

The main protagonists of this classic narrative are Newland Archer, the scion of an aristocratic family, and the beautiful Countess Olenska (played in the movie version of this novel by the luminous Michelle Pfeiffer), who represent two halves of the author's own conflicted psyche. Archer eventually marries the pretty young socialite that everyone had expected he would. He is too cowardly, or too psychologically, castrated by a sclerotic society whose vitality is sapped by degenerating, increasingly irrelevant conventions, to dare submit to his unquenchable passion for the stunning woman who so deeply, disturbingly, fascinates him.

The whole affair was doomed from the start. Having left her worthless husband back in Europe, the countess had just returned to her family in New York when she met Archer. She fell in love with the weak-willed patrician perhaps by default, since he is surely a curious choice for the bold young woman. When it becomes fully clear that he will not marry her after all, even while protesting that he cannot bear to part with her, she asks him directly whether he merely wants her to be his mistress. Archer answers, "I want—I want somehow to get away with you into a world where words like that—categories like that—won't exist. Where we shall be simply two human beings who love each other, who are the whole of life to each other; and nothing else on earth will matter."[29] Obviously: *Eden*.

The countess retorts with a sigh, "Oh my dear—where is that country? Have you ever been there?" She answers her own exasperated, contemptuously rhetorical question, "I know so many who've tried to find it, and, believe me, they all got out by mistake at wayside stations" with predictable disappointment. Archer defers to her better judgment and asks, pathetically, "Then what, exactly, is your plan for us?" Since she had been the first to break away from her fate, by leaving her marriage, she seems again to be the one suited to decide matters. She immediately rejects his presumptive plural: "For *us*? But there is no *us* in that sense! We're near each other only if we stay far from each other." She sees clearly that their only choice together would be on the sly, "trying to be happy behind the backs of the people who trust them." Dejected, he groans that he is "beyond that." But she lashes back, startling him, with her own confession: "'No, you're not! You've never been beyond. And I have,' she said in a strange voice, 'and I know what it looks like there.'"[30] Wharton describes the pitiful Archer's silence at this revelation as "dazed with inarticulate pain." She is not innocent—and neither is he. But she has tasted of the fruit and knows its aftertaste; he is too timid to do so.

Countess Olenska is typical of Wharton's most sympathetically rendered women characters who, as the late feminist writer Marilyn French observed, are all "women who risk . . . [and] have moral courage, something even Wharton's most sympathetic men lack. They are not passive victims of their lives, although there is no question of their triumphing over circumstances. What they do is live their lives out fully, by feeling and thinking through whatever occurs, by refusing to blind themselves They risk discovering their own dark sides, their sexuality, their guilt, their jealousy."[31] In other words, they risk tasting the fruit of knowledge. As a result, "their lives are rich not because of what they are able to take from life but because of what they are. Thus, in a sense, all Wharton's work aims toward a definition of what constitutes full humanity: it is not victory over circumstance, but knowledge of the deepest sort, the full living of life."[32] Such "knowledge of the deepest sort" is won dearly; it takes much courage to venture the risk. But oh, the joy of it while it lasts . . . .

In the epilogue, Archer and the countess have a chance to meet again three decades later in Paris, Archer a widower and the countess now a widow as well, never in fact having returned to her husband after leaving New York for Europe in the aftermath of Archer's marriage. When Archer's son, who accompanies him in Paris, indiscreetly but with callous precision asks his father if she had been his great love—"the woman you'd have chucked everything for, only you didn't"—Archer hesitates at first. His son protests, "Dash it, Dad, don't be prehistoric!"[33]

The son belongs to an even newer world, soon to be known as "the Roaring Twenties." America obviously could not stay "old" for long; its mission was to travel ever further, break new boundaries. But the destination was still Eden, no matter how far the journey, East or West.

And the search was still for innocence, long after anyone dared call it that, for fear of seeming "prehistoric."

Black Eves: Jezebel and Mammy

My mistress had taught me the precepts of God's Word: "Thou shalt love thy neighbor as thyself." "Whatsoever ye would that men should do unto you, do ye even so do unto them." But I was her slave, and I suppose she did not recognize me as her neighbor.
Harriet Jacobs, Incidents in the Life of a Slave Girl: Written by Herself *(1861)*

No discussion of the Age of Innocence that was to be the New World could be complete without an examination of the fate endured by the one group of inhabitants who arrived very much against their will: the Africans who were declared property rather than human beings. But so, in a different but not unrelated sense, were all white women, even in the Southern states, which rather disingenuously prided themselves for their gentility. Writes Deborah Gray White in her book *Ar'n't I a Woman? Female Slaves in the Plantation South*, "The slave woman's condition was just an extreme case of what white women as a group experienced in America. . . . So inhibitive were society's norms that many women's rights advocates likened the husband-wife relationship to that of master and slave."[34] Adam may have found his Eden, but Eve decidedly had not.

Black women were stereotyped, the ensuing composite paradoxical, if not outright contradictory:

> From the intricate web of mythology which surrounds the black woman, a fundamental image emerges. It is of a woman of inordinate strength, with an ability for tolerating an unusual amount of misery and heavy, distasteful work. This woman does not have the same fears, weaknesses, and insecurities as other women, but believes herself to be and is, in fact, stronger emotionally than most men. Less of a woman in that she is less "feminine" and helpless, she is really *more* of a woman in that she is the embodiment of Mother Earth, the quintessential mother with infinite sexual, life-giving, and nurturing reserves. In other words, she is a superwoman.[35]

Either way, a superwoman, whether "more" feminine as a nurturing life-giver, a sexually insatiable Jezebel, or as strong as a male both emotionally and physically, was in the final analysis treated as less than a human being.

No one could have spoken more eloquently on behalf of the black woman slave than did the celebrated Sojourner Truth, whose heart-wrenching cry slices the soul to the quick: "I could work as much and eat as much as a man (when I could get it), and bear de lash as well—and ar'n't I a woman? I have borne thirteen children and seen em mo' all sold off into slavery, and when I cried out with a mother's grief, none but Jesus heard—and are'n't I a woman?"[36] What additional proof need there be that she too was a daughter of Eve, no less than were her white owners. She too was a mother who grieved when separated from her children, knowing they would be doomed to a life of bondage and suffering. Her piety was hardly inferior to her white-skinned sisters whose scriptural exegesis seemed to rule out compassion for their darker fellow humans. Little did they realize how they were all doomed in the process.

As Truth's contemporary, Harriet Jacobs (1813–1897), observed in her own extraordinary journal, those "sisters" did not even acknowledge the black women as neighbors, let alone equal descendants of Adam's spouse. But Jacobs is not resentful so much as compassionate, especially of those ignorant Northern women who marry Southern slaveholders without understanding the full reality of slavery. Writes Jacobs:

> The young wife soon learns that the husband in whose hands she has placed her happiness pays no regard to his marriage vows. Children of every shade of complexion play with her own fair babies, and too well she knows that they are born unto him of his own household. Jealousy and hatred enter the flowery home, and it is ravaged of its loveliness.[37]

Southern women know better. Sometimes they marry a man who has already fathered little slaves, but consider the brood little more than property, "as marketable as the pigs on the plantation"—and often make a point of exchanging them for currency at the earliest opportunity (though Jacobs adds, generously, "I am glad to say there are some honorable exceptions").[38]

In some ways, the black woman played the role of Lilith to the white woman's Eve. As White observes, "Jezebel was the counterimage of the mid-nineteenth-century ideal of the Victorian lady. She did not lead men and children to God; piety was foreign to her."[39] Southern men often claimed that slavery uplifted white women, exempting them from the menial work of the lower strata of society. Far from recognizing that slave women were treated as inferiors, George Fizhugh claimed that, while in the North a woman had to suffer being "thrown into the arena of industrial war," by contrast, "be she white, or be she black, she is treated with kindness and humanity in the slaveholding South."[40] What he did not—because he could not—claim was that she was treated as an equal, as her husband's helpmate.

White men sometimes justified intercourse with their slave women by appealing to the "Jezebel" image of the promiscuous, oversexed persona representing the paradoxical complement of the Mother Earth or "Mammy" image, which together represented the black female. Explains Deborah Gray White:

> In sum, the forces that made the Mammy image were many. It cannot be fully understood independent of the Jezebel conceptualization because they are inverse images that existed simultaneously in the Southern mind. They are black images but, being almost as old as the images of Eve and the Virgin Mary, they are also universal female archetypes.[41]

While the image of Jezebel served to justify miscegenation, the Mammy ideal rationalized the intimate relationships developed between white children and their nurses who were often very nurturing, as well as the close quarters in which whites and blacks necessarily had to live.

White women were portrayed as delicate, beautiful, and if educated at all, only to the extent of entertaining and pleasing their husbands. The Founding Father who could declare that all men were created equal, the immensely erudite Thomas Jefferson, confessed to a friend that "a plan of female education has never been a subject of systematic contemplation with me. It has occupied my attention so far only as the education of my own daughters required." This is the same man who directed that his tombstone define him as the founder of the University of Virginia. The casual manner in which he mentions female education, almost as an afterthought—"a subject on which I have not thought much"—speaks volumes.

Jefferson does concede that a study of French "is an indispensable part of education of both sexes." So, of course, are the "ornaments" of life which, "for a female, are dancing, drawing, and music. The first is a healthy exercise, elegant and very attractive for young people," though he hastens to add that "the French rule is wise that no lady dances after marriage. This is founded in solid physical reasons, gestation and nursing leaving little time to a married lady when this exercise can be either safe or innocent."[42] On the other hand, he rails against that "great obstacle to good education," to which the fair sex seems uncommonly susceptible, namely "the inordinate passion prevalent for novels and the time lost in that reading which should be instructively employed." He warns his unwitting fellow females against the immorality masquerading "in all the figments of fancy" that will corrupt an innocent maiden's pretty little brain presumably no less effectively than was Eve's by Satan's reptilian mouthpiece.

The American Adam was conflicted about the role of his female cohabitants in the New World, whether black or white, evidently insufficiently secure in his newfound independence to understand the full value of a genuine soulmate. Whether he claimed to place his white woman on a virginal pedestal and his black Mammy on an altar of nurturing sexuality, or on the flip side, treated his white counterpart as naturally inferior and black women as hardly human, the ultimate result was still loneliness—his own and every one else's.

That loneliness was further exacerbated by an exaggerated optimism fueled by advertisements and self-absorption, and an obsession with youth and beauty. If man could not eat from the Tree of Life, at least he would try to drink at the soda fountain of eternal youth, imbibing its aroma. With the advent of photography, cosmetics, botox, and the democratic proclamation—bolstered by advances in plastic surgery—that anyone could be anything, every woman could at least in principle aspire to the status of an Aphrodite. The subtle tyranny of that creed, and its subversion of spiritual communion among human beings who yearned not only for sexual compatibility but for life (and lifelong) companionship, was harder to detect.

Pinup Eve: The Pictured Girl East of Eden

Come slowly—Eden!
Lips unused to Thee—
Bashful—sip thy Jessamines [jasmines]—
As the fainting Bee—
Reaching late his flower,
Round her chamber hums—
Counts his nectars—
Enters—and is lost in balms!
Emily Dickinson (c. 1860)
God has marked the American people as His chosen nation to finally
lead in the regeneration of the world. This is the divine mission of
America and all it holds for all the profit, all the glory, all the happi-
ness possible to man.
John D. Rockefeller (1900)

Have you ever noticed the thought in the eyes of a pictured girl?
Evelyn Nesbit, My Story *(1914)*

America's self-image as the leader of a regenerated—that is, both reborn and consciously recreated—brave new world, a man-made Eden to rival the original, was bound to condemn its misguided architects to grandiose visions. Happiness, that mesmerizing, elusive grail, the sanctity of whose pursuit had been declared absolute by the nation's most revered founding document, would bless the energetic and optimistic men and women of the New World with unprecedented vitality and imagination, allowing millions to reach unbelievable heights of prosperity and creativity, the envy of the world. Yet at the same time, it cursed them with the allure of impossible dreams, whose pursuit could doom to loneliness, spawning a spiritual poverty far more abject than the material variety. The custodians of the New Eden, who encouraged the planting of every splendid fruit with no thought of aftertaste, would unwittingly condemn its inhabitants to a self-inflicted emotional desert.

Undeterred, America chose to see it as the perfect soil for the fountain of youth. And since youth implies life, and youth is beautiful, the translation of beauty into the promise of immortality came naturally. Beauty, after all, is the elixir of love, which has traditionally served as a euphemism for sex, which looks to many like the straightest road to happiness. As such, so it must be: Eden is what Eden seems. But while Americans of both sexes pursued self-reliance, the female of the species would soon learn that, if she was to get what she wanted (or what she thought she wanted), she had to make herself into the idol her partner convinced himself he needed: a young, beautiful, pure, yet savvy and resilient, Eve. The American woman figured she had to be able to—or look like she was able to, which amounts to the same thing—inspire a man to the greatness he was, or rather believed himself to be, capable of reaching. The longer she could sustain that illusion the better. America was reaching for perfection: the national anthem itself proclaimed "America, the Beautiful" forever, praying that "God mend thine ev'ry flaw," fully expecting that The Divine Surgeon would do just that.

And in the new Eden, with everyone created equal by a benevolent Deity, everyone may well aspire to be (or at any rate become), if not beautiful at least reasonably attractive—as demonstrated daily on the makeover shows that have proliferated on cable television. Plain Jane and Nerdy Ned morph into worthier facsimiles of the Ideal, actualizing a potential they had always secretly presumed they possessed—the Ideal that confronted them all their lives on the screen, the pages of magazines, and advertisements both explicit and subliminal, driving our hormones to distraction. As the novelist Kathryn Perutz writes in her insightful book *Beyond the Looking Glass: A Glimpse into America's Beauty Culture*, images found in fantasy handbooks enticingly titled *Allure, Cosmopolitan, Vogue,* and *Glamour,* "are archetypal creatures whom no one really recognizes, though all readers sense that something in themselves corresponds to one of these figures."[43] That something is the universal desire to be desired, even if the subject is not exactly oneself but what we each think others want us to be or, at least, seem.

Perutz says of the wannabe American Eve that "she's hooked on beauty." She speaks with authority, for as a self-confessed representative member she knows the species up close and personal:

> Beauty is the hope for salvation, for Pandora's box, which offers treasures most desired by men . . . The search for beauty is one of the great quests, and if in America we seek it in ourselves, this is because we seek everything in ourselves, even God. . . . America is studded with ornamental humans who challenge the authority of their deaths through their advocate, beauty.[44]

These ornamental, archetypal humans, though hardly sacred, are a quintessential part of what makes up the modern American ethos, which "above all," according to Perutz, "adulates the individual as an end in himself, and this unbearable responsibility leaves man with a sense of reality more ephemeral than the dust on rose leaves."[45] To say nothing of woman—though she may neither realize it nor admit it.

One of the most notorious such women was the legendary, though in the end tragic, Evelyn Nesbit. Deemed "the American Eve" by her biographer Paula Uruburu, hers was "an image that spoke of both the vitality and freshness of an antediluvian world and the brave new world of the Century of Progress."[46] That happened to be the twentieth, but could well have been any other, since, after all, Progress *defines* America. Continues Uruburu:

> As with Eve before the Fall, Evelyn's natural charms and air of innocence created an overwhelming and immediate impression of

incorruptibility in certain poses. Yet the deceptive maturity of her heavy-lidded gaze and ever so slightly open-mouthed expression of apparent self-satisfaction in photo after photo suggested an Eve who had already tasted the forbidden fruit.[47]

How perfect: the reborn American Eve as pinup model, camouflaged in prepubescent simplicity. At once sultry and childish, Evelyn Nesbit was utterly seductive: "All the feminine myth and mystique of the ancient world seemed to coalesce and form a 'beguiling new creature'"—the new Edenic feminine that would fit the requirements of the New World about to inaugurate not merely a century but a new era for mankind. This, at least, is the impression she usually conveyed, although she did not fool everyone: the sculptor Augustus Saint-Gaudens declared, just before he died, in 1907, that "she had the face of an angel and the heart of a snake."[48] The serpent as Eve impersonator!

Evelyn Nesbitt could have played the young demonic Eve in the movie version of John Steinbeck's monumental, partly autobiographical epic entitled *East of Eden*, published in 1952—his most ambitious and by far his most important novel. (Though superbly acted, its screen adaptation is so lame by comparison as not to deserve even a mention.) Explicitly created as an American *Genesis*, Steinbeck's masterpiece portrays the New World versions of Cain, Abel, Adam, and inevitably, a sinister Eve who in the novel bears the deceptively unthreatening name "Cathy."

Steinbeck captures Cathy-Eve's essence in a brief sentence: "There was a time when a girl like Cathy would have been called possessed by the devil."[49] This beautiful Pandora-like monster first kills her parents, then a man for whom she worked as a prostitute, abandons her children after shooting her husband (though not killing his body—only his spirit), and finally kills a madam to whom she had endeared herself so as to take over the management of her whorehouse which the gullible woman had willed to Cathy. East of Eden is where Cain had been sent by God after the murder of his brother Abel. We live there.

Steinbeck's Salinas, California, was already forsaken territory at the turn of the twentieth century. Comments the author who is also the narrator, "It is my belief that Cathy Ames was born with the tendencies, or lack of them, which drove and forced her all of her life."[50] Though fiercely independent, unwilling to be subject to anyone's control, quite capable of supporting herself, Cathy is the very caricature of self-reliance—compelled to hurt others as well as herself. Her life is defined by absolute loneliness: incapable of love, she defies the illusion that beauty has anything whatever to do with happiness. Her eventual suicide is almost beside the point: Cathy had never quite lived. Steinbeck's portrayal of Adam's unhappy consort Cathy-Eve embodies the very refutation of the beauty myth in all its grotesque superficiality.

But he does not end on a hopeless note. The young couple that redeems the ideal of human love demonstrates the possibility of hope predicated on the ability to forgive both oneself and others. As they come to understand the power of generosity and humble acceptance of mortality, they manage to glimpse as much of Eden as is possible beyond its borders, East or West.

Still the image, the appearance (literally the "surface," or that which is accessible, usually visually) to the human sense rather than discerned upon reflection, continues to dominate the contemporary scene, with less than salutary consequences. An interesting, highly symbolic example is the enormous success of a movie released in 1999, which James Greenberg of *The Los Angeles Magazine* at the time dubbed "one of the best of the year, maybe the decade."[51] The Oscars would soon reinforce his enthusiasm with several awards. Its title: *American Beauty*.

American Beauty

I stand to the beauty culture much as I do to America and have with it an uneasy, respectful, guilty, religious involvement from which I can't exile myself because there is nowhere to go that wouldn't remind me what I had left.
Kathrin Perutz, Beyond the Looking Glass: America's Beauty Culture

It was meant ironically, as a spoof on the triumph of superficiality, of epidermis over epithet.[52] The glib-is-cool crowd resonated to its message: poetry be damned, metaphysics be damned—why, damnation be damned. Yet David Denby of *The New Yorker* found it "a funny movie that hurts."[53] He was aware, however dimly, that the irony masked something very disturbing. Its audience, after all, was not only in on the joke but an intrinsic part of it. A public that accepts the damning message, embracing it both unwittingly and witlessly, cannot go to the extra step and reflect upon that irony, transcending it. As a result it too is—you guessed it—damned.

Yes, the movie really is sad, and not simply because the main character is shot at the end senselessly. His death is irrelevant anyhow: the eerie commentary from beyond the grave is a brilliant device, for it proves that he is posthumously no less aware of his fate than the characters who are still on earth but are equally powerless to change it. That fate is captured in the dissonance between the antiseptic title and the brutal reality depicted in the movie—at once funny and sad because pointless. In brief, beauty in America emerges as little more than an oxymoron.

The deliberately ambiguous noun is at once concrete and abstract, descriptive but also sarcastic. "Beauty" denotes the little nymphet who epitomizes everything that American beauty both is and is not. She is real and yet an illusion, she is and is not what she seems. Blonde and slender, she becomes the object of her best friend's middle-aged father's sexual fantasies. But she is a temptress in dream only: she boasts to her friends of sexual conquests that turn out to have been invented. Epitomizing the ultimate perversion that results from a glorification of the purely visual, she appears fully satisfied to inhabit the imaginations of masturbating males. This is sex by pure proxy. Her life ambition is to become—what else?—a model, a pinup Eve. She is what she appears—which is to say, less. Indeed when faced with the prospect of a real, live prospective lover, she confesses, terrified, that she is not merely a virgin, not simply incapable of knowing what to do, but has no clue what she might want from an actual sexual encounter with a man. The beast thus decides to forgo the frigid beauty; for what would be the point of possessing her? It would merely detract from the fantasy.

But fantasies are notoriously thin, metaphysically speaking: they barely exist. Some are especially shallow. For example, the wife of the protagonist wants to succeed in her real estate business because, well, that is what one does in America, right?—succeed. Doomed to "joylessness," in the words of her husband, she ends up having an affair with a one-dimensional man like herself, whose single-minded pursuit of the maximum number of sales broke up his own marriage. The affair is inescapably self-centered for both. He is merely attracted to his reflection in her eyes, while she succumbs to his success which she actually craves for herself. As she gazes at his picture on the ubiquitous billboards, she wishes for the same. Oh, to be seen . . . . Does one even *exist* otherwise?

How pathetic: the hysterical wife of the Adamic protagonist—an Eve turned Lilith, the original closeness of the couple having long evaporated—ends up having an affair with . . . a face on a billboard. A fellow real estate broker, whose advertisements litter buses and fences, she looks longingly and admiringly at his fake smile and is smitten. Such unpropitious prelude leads to the predictably campy moment of climax, when the self-absorbed salesman, whose appropriate name is King, demands that she scream out "The King!" (More ludicrous than funny, though the audience laughs, obligingly.) But she is hardly better: in the aftermath of the egotistical copulation, she reports that her "tenseness" is gone and it was "exactly what she needed." For her it was all just erotic aspirin, therapeutic coitus. *Beauty*? *Love*? What outworn words . . . like, totally not cool. What can they possibly mean?

Alas, even the young couple—for whom one might have had some hope—doesn't know. The neighboring voyeur, a young man addicted to videotaping, claims to find Jane, the daughter of the Lolita-obsessed protagonist and his ambitious wife, "interesting." We learn that this word has odd connotations for him—he uses it, for example, to describe an old woman about to be evicted, whom he decides to capture on film. Since he finds Jane interesting and/or beautiful, he presumably loves or at least cares for her—but then why does he videotape her without her consent, obviously violating her privacy? In fact, her first reaction upon discovering the strange intrusion is a natural revulsion. His "love" becomes a form of stalking. While his perversion is partly explicable by his abnormal home life, it is still altogether off-putting bordering on creepy. These are not soulmates—their lives are merely parallel, untouchable. Jane is fully aware that to him, she is merely an object to be captured on film.

Not surprisingly, Jane is obsessed with her own appearance—and specifically, the size of her breasts. Her goal is to save all her babysitting money in order to afford breast augmentation surgery. And naturally, she is desperately lonely: she hates her parents even though they try, however lamely, to reach her. For good measure, she also dislikes her best friend. When Jane does decide to give in to her obtrusive neighbor, allowing him to videotape her as she undresses in front of him, she does so without really knowing who he is. Evidently she does not care; all that matters is his interest in her appearance. And like everyone else, she eventually copulates with someone because he boosts her own self-image and alleviates the pain of ineffable, inescapable insecurity. At least Narcissus loved himself; these characters love only their reflection—if that.

The relatively most sympathetic of the characters, the male protagonist, seems victimized by both a compulsive wife and a terrible boring job (which he quits in a flurry of self-assertion—to then take a job flipping hamburgers, hardly the epitome of creativity). But when he once attempts to make love to her (because she "looks good"), as soon as she points out that he is about to spill his beer, he goes into a wild rage and comments, as she leaves the scene: "I was only trying to help you!" They simply do not know how to reach one another.

Can such hapless creatures living for nothing that seems worthwhile ever hope to appreciate genuine beauty? The young voyeur claims to do so. He invites his girlfriend, for example, to watch "the most beautiful thing in the world." Whereupon comes the picture of . . . a paper bag flying in the wind. Charming enough, one may agree, but . . . THE most beautiful thing in the world? Admittedly, the assessment must be seen in light of the young man's broader, near-indiscriminate aesthetics: he claims that he finds so much beauty all around him that "it hurts." It apparently does not hurt quite enough for him to stay away from drugs. Or does he turn to drugs *because* it hurts? One wonders whether the paper bag gains special qualities to him mainly when he is under the influence. Or does the ubiquitous beauty hurt just because he is always hurting? Is beauty itself a kind of pain? If so, has it not morphed into its very opposite?

It is this anti-esthetics that is adopted by the narrator as well, admittedly in a comment made postmortem—perhaps to further underscore its absurdity. The dead man tells the audience that beauty is "everywhere." But that only serves to trivialize it. Certainly among soulmates, beauty requires sublime ingredients such as generosity, innocence, nobility of sentiment, harmony, reverence for life, connection, and respect. Otherwise, are we not just glorified paper bags, flailing in the wind of fate and senselessness?

The issue, however, is not merely the trivialization of beauty, but the inability to appreciate what constitutes genuine human value. In order for the New World to represent a new beginning, it must be capable of regeneration. Its roots must be able to nourish the souls of its human creatures and sustain them to reflect the image of God. But that image will not be found in a mirror.

Notes

1. Described in great detail by Richard E. Rubenstein in his superb study *Aristotle's Children: How Christians, Muslims, and Jews Rediscovered Ancient Wisdom and Illuminated the Middle Ages*.
2. R. W. B. Lewis, *The American Adam: Innocence, Tragedy, and Tradition in the Nineteenth Century*, 5.
3. Cited in Ibid., 88.
4. Ibid.
5. Ibid., 89.
6. Nathaniel Hawthorne, *The Scarlet Letter*, 70–71 (emphasis added).
7. Ibid., 144.
8. Ibid., 145.
9. Ibid., 146.
10. Ibid., 147.
11. Ibid., 147–48.
12. Ibid., 149.
13. Ibid., 240.
14. Lewis, *American Adam*, 49.
15. From Walt Whitman, *Leaves of Grass*, "I Saw in Louisiana a Live Oak Growing," 105–6.
16. Lewis, *American Adam*, 49.
17. Whitman, *Leaves of Grass*, "As Adam, Early in the Morning," 95.
18. Ibid., section 21, 45.
19. Ibid., section 5, 32.
20. Ibid., section 49, 77.
21. Lewis, *American Adam*, 45–46.
22. Camille Paglia, *Sexual Personae: Art and Decadence from Nefertiti to Emily Dickinson*, 673.
23. *Final Harvest: Emily Dickinson's Poems*, section 57, 31. This text preserves the original punctuation of the author.
24. Ibid., section 58, 32.
25. Ibid., section 122, 73.
26. Ibid., section 184, 111.
27. Ibid., section 95, 55.
28. Cynthia Griffin Wolff, *A Feast of Words: The Triumph of Edith Wharton*, 334.
29. Edith Wharton, *The Age of Innocence*, 290.
30. Ibid., 291.
31. Marilyn French, "Introduction," in Edith Wharton, *Summer*, xxvii–xxviii.
32. Ibid.
33. Ibid., 356.
34. Deborah Gray White in *Ar'n't I a Woman? Female Slaves in the Plantation South*, 15.
35. Cited in ibid., 27.
36. Cited in ibid., 14.
37. Harriet Jacobs, *Incidents in the Life of a Slave Girl—Written by Herself*, 39.
38. Ibid., 40.

39. Ibid., 29.
40. Ibid., 45.
41. Deborah Gray White, *Ar'n't I a Woman? Female Slaves in the Plantation South*, 60–61.
42. Ibid., 491.
43. Kathrin Perutz, *Beyond the Looking Glass: A Glimpse into America's Beauty Culture*, 28.
44. Ibid., 323.
45. Ibid., 318–19.
46. Paula Uruburu, *American Eve: Evelyn Nesbit, Stanford White, the Birth of the 'It' Girl, and the Crime of the Century*, 14.
47. Ibid.
48. Ibid., 15.
49. John Steinbeck, *East of Eden*, 72.
50. Ibid.
51. James Greenberg, "America the Beautiful," *The Los Angeles Magazine*, October 1999.
52. See my "Shadows: Comments on the Modern Cave," *Humanitas* XII, no. 2 (1999).
53. David Denby, "Transcending the Suburbs," *The New Yorker* 27, September 20 (1999).

Part III

Resurrecting the Soulmate

8

Transcending the Goddess

The Old Testament was the first alphabetic written work to influence future ages. . . . The words on its pages anchor three powerful religions: Judaism, Christianity, and Islam. Each is an exemplar of patriarchy. Each monotheistic religion features an imageless Father deity whose authority shines through his revealed Word, sanctified in written form.
Leonard Shlain, The Alphabet Versus the Goddess

The idea that monotheism and patriarchy are interconnected is so widespread it has become practically a commonplace. But likening the rise of an abstract ("imageless") deity to the decline of the visual, presumably the predominantly "feminine" domain, is far more problematic, even paradoxical. Which is it: was woman's downfall the inevitable result of the ascendancy of word over image or, rather, does the cult of the visual a.k.a. the "superficial" lead to reducing woman to a mere sex object? Is there a grain of truth—while also, correlatively, a grain of falsehood—in both approaches? No doubt writing facilitated a more abstract approach to religion in the form of monotheism, which soon took on a patriarchal quality—suggesting that the triumph of the male Yahweh over "the goddess" amounts to the triumph of the alphabet over pictorial communication. Yet, on the other hand, as we have just seen in the previous chapter, the idolatry of the image (with apologies for etymological redundancy) is no less inimical to the female gender, if perhaps not to her divine counterpart, the goddess. How to reconcile this seeming inconsistency?

First, let us concede that both word and image are necessary to a full appreciation of life and of the human condition: ideally there should be no opposition of word *versus* image, god *versus* goddess. The abstract as well as the concrete, the word and the picture, masculine and feminine, are equally necessary to achieve the fullest understanding of human destiny. Might one say, metaphorically, that each of us embodies both god and goddess?

Virginia Wolf had explored this notion nearly a century ago, in her revolutionary autobiography, *A Room of One's Own*, first published in 1929. She reports having wondered

> whether there are two sexes in the mind corresponding to the two sexes in the body, and whether they also require to be united in order to get complete satisfaction and happiness. And I went on amateurishly to sketch a plan of the soul so that in each of us two powers preside, one male, one female; and in the man's brain, the man predominates over the woman, and in the woman's brain, the woman predominates over the man. If one is a man, still the woman part of the brain must have effect; and a woman also must have intercourse with the man in her. Coleridge perhaps meant this when he said that a great mind is androgynous. It is when this fusion takes place that the mind is fully fertilized and uses all its faculties.[1]

Neurophysiology, whose job is to sketch a plan if not of the soul then certainly of the brain, reinforces Woolf's poetic insight. Humans do indeed have a bilobed brain—two hemispheric lobes performing more or less the same type of tasks, though specialized in important respects. It was a French physician, Paul Broca (1824–1880), who first noted that patients whose left frontal lobes had been injured experienced various speech problems. And since the left side turned out to be involved primarily in reasoning, while the right is the more emotional (read: feminine), the latter was considered subordinate to the more "masculine" left.

It was not until the 1960s when Roger Sperry experimented on epileptic patients that "hemispheric lateralization" was properly understood: while each hemisphere take on certain types of functions, neither can be considered secondary or inferior in any way. For example, the left brain processes information logically and sequentially, but the right synthesizes it simultaneously. A bridge of neuronal fibers, the amygdala, connects and integrates the two cortical lobes. And while the earlier, simplistic parallelism between the left-masculine *versus* the right-feminine brain was tempered by a more nuanced understanding of the relationships between the two hemispheres, the dualism pitting male and female gained widespread acceptance in popular culture.

Venus and Mars were soon declared planetary and mythological opposites, separated from one another by light-years both literally and figuratively. Determined to defy a fate that seemed to condemn us to staring at one another across a gaping sexual ravine, we all turned to the experts. Self-help books instructing the members of each gender on how to traverse the Great Gender Gap offer tips (of uneven effectiveness) on how to at least tiptoe around the yawning abyss, even if most (maybe all?) of us are doomed never to cross it.

The pro-Venus crowd is quick to emphasize various ways in which the right hemisphere is better. First of all, it precedes the left in embryonic development, an urgency that would seem to imply added value. And if that doesn't convince, consider that it is the seat of environmentally motivated as opposed to left-brain, self-motivated behavior.[2] (This might suggest that women are more attuned to facts, while men are more self-centered? Maybe. Then again, maybe not.) And though the left brain admittedly handles language, women possess a greater density of neurons than do males in parts of the temporal lobe cortex associated with linguistic processing and comprehension.[3] Density is destiny, linguistically speaking.

Meanwhile, the macho Martians flaunt their larger parietal cortex that is involved in space perception. And so on and so forth. It would be easy to dismiss the entire gender game as too little knowledge being a dangerous thing, for indeed there is no such thing as "his brain" and "her brain." That said, there is no question that neurological differences among the sexes are real, with important wide-ranging implications, from gender-specific medical treatment to more enlightened social attitudes. But the attitudes that shape our culture, thinking, and behavior continue to follow along decidedly Mars-centric lines.

The history of the unfortunate prominence of masculinity as manifested through reason, *logos*, cold, mechanistic calculation, dispassionate thinking, as against the feminine instinct, compassion, warmth, sensuality, and the visual, is the subject of *The Alphabet versus the Goddess: The Conflict between Word and Image* by Leonard Shlain. That prominence, he believes, must be reversed if we are to survive as a species. A surgeon by profession, Shlain argues that "the demise of the Goddess, the plunge in women's status, and the advent of harsh patriarchy and misogyny occurred around the time that people were learning how to read and write."[4] It is reading itself, not merely "the word" as such, and thus the written word—the oral tradition having previously reigned supreme—against which he inveighs.

And since it was the Hebrews who turned reading into a ritual, guess who is principally to blame for this calamity. Shlain, a Jew himself, accuses them of having dealt a decisive mortal blow to the Goddess. Just look for yourself. Even though the Bible invariably describes "wisdom" as female, those Jewish scholars, those little *yeshiva bochers*, those *schlemiels*,[5] "all long for book learning! With the rising importance of alphabet literacy in Jewish culture, young men are instructed to turn their eyes away from desirable young women and instead, pore over written words. In one of the strangest aberrations to occur in the 3,000,000-year-old human condition, men substituted dry scrolls in place of a woman's beauty."[6] Although this sounds like the sort of thing my mother might have said, he is quite serious. Shlain goes on to charge that "the aleph-bet broke the spirit of women and banished the Goddess."[7]

Once again, the dialectical antagonism pits one extreme over the other, male *versus* female, and the recommended solution to this conflict where the female loses is for her to be rehabilitated and duly enthroned again as co-goddess. Why this concern to deify woman? One reason seems to be that mythology is considered to be inescapable: human beings necessarily think in such terms. We need archetypes to articulate our feelings. And since we are basically theophiles (god-lovers)—even when we deny it, and substitute quasi-secular deities such as "the nation" or "the proletariat," as do nationalists and communists—the answer is to populate the mythological realm with the proper cast.

Which would seem to argue in favor of reinstating the primeval goddess on her rightful throne, would it not? At first blush, perhaps. But the trouble is that her glittering crown was hardly all gold, let alone twenty-four carats. More importantly, neither did her fame correlate directly, if at all, with a higher regard and appreciation for her mortal subjects. As far back as archeologically grounded inference permits us to venture, we find signs of goddess worship—temples, statues, and later explicit writings. But alongside the adulation, there is also evidence of widespread hostility to women in prebiblical times. Negative female images of divine or symbolic stature reflected uncontrollable, even murderous anger, jealousy, and capriciousness. The goddess would eventually fade away, but her allure would persist, along with a yearning for its glow.

The Original Holy Princess

I say, "Hail!" to the Holy One who appears in the heavens!
I say, "Hail!" to the Holy Princess of Heaven!
Sumerian hymn *(cc. 3500 BC)*

The oldest extant figure of a goddess, a small (4.5 inches) sculpture of a pear-shaped woman with arms crossed over her breasts, dates back to the Paleolithic era, about 20,000 BCE. Evidently, ancient man worshiped a wide variety of gods ranging from the asexual, bisexual, homosexual, and animal to the chameleonic who change their appearance at will. Scholars Anne Baring and Jules Cashford, however, decided to embark specifically on an exploration of the feminine, wondering whether they might find a pattern. Far from being disappointed, they soon discovered "such surprising similarities and parallels in all the goddess myths of apparently unrelated cultures that we concluded that there had been a continuous transmission of imagines throughout history." So startling was the evidence that they felt "entitled to talk of 'the myth of the goddess,' since the underlying vision expressed in all the variety of goddess images is constant: the vision of life as a living unity."[8]

They explored how and why the goddess myth would gradually be lost. "It soon became clear that, from Babylonian mythology onwards (c. 200 BCE), the Goddess became almost exclusively associated with 'Nature' as the chaotic force to be mastered, and the God took the role of conquering or ordering nature from his counterpole of 'Spirit.' Yet this opposition had not previously existed."[9] The dialectic became entrenched: Humanity and Nature were polarized, and the opposition between Creative Spirit and Chaotic Nature would persist until well into the eighteenth century when the Scientific Revolution would declare that the Laws of Nature were in fact the Laws of Reason and hence the Laws of God. By the time Reason became Queen, however, the goddess was long gone.

Writing in 1991, Baring and Cashford summarize their findings as follows:

> We concluded that, for the last 4,000 years, the feminine principle, which manifests in mythological history as "the goddess" and in cultural history as the values placed upon spontaneity, feeling, instinct and intuition, had been lost as a valid expression of the sanctity and unity of life. In Judeo-Christian mythology there is now, formally, no feminine dimension of the divine, since our particular culture is structured in the image of a masculine god who is beyond creation, ordering it from without; he is not within creation, as were the mother goddesses before him.[10]

The solution, they argue, is to bring the myth of the goddess back into consciousness, by recovering the stories people have told for millennia. So, since back in the Bronze Age, for example, a sacred marriage of the goddess and the god ritualistically assisted the regeneration of nature, perhaps the human imagination could reenact that lovely story once again. The ancient stories should thus help us appreciate how ancient man regarded the position of women. According to Tikva Frymer-Kensky, "goddesses are the 'women' of the divine world and behave much as women are expected to behave," which is to say, they are "women writ large, with the same positions in the god-world that women have in the human world."[11] This certainly sounds encouraging.

The most important goddess to throw light on the complex attitudes toward women in the ancient world hails from the great civilization of Mesopotamia. According to one myth originating some twenty-two centuries BCE, the goddess Ninlil, daughter of the grain-goddess Nisaba, is wooed and then wed by the god Enlil, one of the main triumvirate of gods, including the first creator An and the supreme mother goddess Ninhursag. After their marriage, Enlil decrees that Ninlil will be known as the mother goddess Nintu, "the lady-who-gives-birth" (or its appallingly inelegant equivalent, "lady-of-the-open-legs"), placed in charge of all the secrets pertaining to women, thus taking over a function previously attributed by the Sumerians to Ninhursag. The importance of identifying Ninlil with the supreme goddess is seen as an ominous portent of the patriarchal cosmology that would soon dethrone her altogether: on the one hand, it elevates Ninlil to the company of the greatest of gods, but, on the other hand, her power, rather than self-generated, is endowed by another male.

A very interesting detail of this story, however, relates to the courtship of Enlil and Ninlil: according to one version, although they are betrothed, Enlil propositions her prior to their marriage. She allegedly rebukes him, but he eventually prevails, sleeps with her, and she becomes pregnant. The good news is that she does fall in love with him and wants to bear his children. The bad news is that, in the first place, Enlil is subsequently sent by the angry gods to the underworld for his improper behavior: how did he dare have sexual relations prior to marriage? The even worse news is not that Ninlil follows him there—that in itself is actually good news, indicative of her love—but that on her way down she meets him in his three successive disguises and sleeps with him all three times, thus engaging in precisely the kind of behavior that had him sent there in the first place. Nor is that the worst of it. It turns out that there is no reason to assume she knows it is actually

Enlil she had thus thrice bedded! The myth does not elaborate, but it does not have to: this is not exemplary behavior in any culture. The lady may be a goddess, but she is still a tramp.

In the end, the story concludes happily for Enlil and Ninlil: they are both hailed—Ninlil as the great mother, Enlil as the protector of fertility. But the triumph of Ninlil as the great goddess is double-edged: for it appears that her premarital behavior may have been just what young women roaming alone were expected to do: act promiscuously. That was bound to bode ill in the end for womankind.

Another Sumerian tradition has the goddess by the name of Inanna, who is betrothed to Dumuzi, similarly faced with prenuptial propositions, which she duly rejects—and unlike Ninlil, does not succumb. Instead, she protests, "What lies could I tell my mother?" Irresistibly demure, the goddess of sexual attractiveness and desire, Innana, eventually does become Dumuzi's lawful wife. That, however, is where the good news ends. It turns out that she does not take on the job of wives, nor does she bear children. As a result, she is marginalized and, frankly, has little to occupy her time. Underemployed and restless, she ends up frequently on the move, during daytime and often at night, thus becoming known as the goddess of morning and evening stars. One of her descriptions, *sahiratu*, means "the one who roams about." Unfortunately, the same expression is also used to refer to the baby-stealing she-demon Lamashtu, who can also enter houses at will as she, well, . . . roams about. In sum, Innana's freedom from domestic duties makes her at once unfeminine and frightening yet also appealing. She is both attractive and repulsive, encompassing in one supernatural symbol the conflicted attitudes of a culture toward its own women. In a Semitic incarnation called Ishtar, Innana would continue to haunt the ancient imagination with the same ambivalent, contradictory emotions—as, of course, would the mythical first Eve, Lilith, already discussed in chapter 4.

According to Tikva Frymer-Kensky, the goddess Innana/Ishtar, "who combines the passions of sex and violence, has had a long hold on the human imagination," and with good reason. It must be that "this fusion of sex and ferocity had to make psychological sense."[12] Innana/Ishtar is supposed to bring marital harmony, but she can also doom the relationship to calamity. Frymer-Kensky cites the following passage from a Hittite Hymn to Ishtar: "A man and his wife who love each other and carry their love to fulfillment, that has been decreed by you, Ishtar. But [if] a woman is ha[ted] by her husband [then you,

Ishtar] have caused [her] to be hated."[13] She is also the patroness of adulterous liaisons, which can lead not only to personal anguish but to larger, social strife. The inherent double-edged nature of the woman goddess is thus inescapable.

Other fascinating tales of Babylonian goddesses reveal still more layers of complexity. One version, for example, from the Old Babylonian period that has come down to us through a copy estimated to have been written in Akkadian around 1500 BCE, relates the creation of mankind after Enlil summons a divine council to consider the suggestion of Enki's son to create a worker whose job would be to relieve the gods. The council appeals to the mother goddess, but she refuses to take on this job as "not properly [hers] to do these things."[14] In the end, she agrees to help, albeit reluctantly, by mixing clay shaped by Enki with the blood of an unknown god, thus endowing it with rationality, then goes on to divide it into fourteen pieces, upon each of which she recites an incantation, as Enki prompts her to do. As a next step, fourteen goddesses proceed to incubate the humanoid embryos for a period of nine months, whereupon the resulting humans emerge at last. There is great praise for the initially unwilling mother. But the myth evolved: by the latter half of the second millennium, as recorded in the Babylonian epic *Enuma Elish*, man's creation is entirely the work of Enki, who is given the special name Nudimud, meaning "the man-creator." The goddess has receded much further into the background.

But she is not gone. "The tale of Dumuzi and Innana," writes Frymer-Kensky, "had a very long life. Special songs for Inanna/Ishtar and Dumuzi were still recited in the first millennium, and even the women of Jerusalem were still weeping for Tammuz (Dumuzi) in the times of Ezekiel."[15] Ishtar not only persisted but in fact "continued to grow in importance."[16] Her role as representative of sexual attraction simply could not be relegated to a male god. Her ambivalent image as both sensual temptress and fierce goddess of warfare, as both nurturing mother goddess and wanton demon, persisted. Over the centuries, "alongside hymns to Ishtar's glory and preeminence, we also find negative portrayals and ultimately a demonization of her image."[17]

By the end of the second millennium BCE, Mesopotamian religion imagined the universe to be controlled by male gods; the older goddesses were all gone except for Ishtar. Yet despite her survival, the evidence suggests that the status of Sumerian women had already declined significantly over the course of a millennium. The great goddess could no longer protect her female worshippers, not even ambiguously. "The existence and power of a goddess, particularly of Ishtar," warns Frymer-Kensky, "is no indication or guarantee of a high status for human women. In Assyria, where Ishtar was so prominent, women were not.[18] The intrinsic tension within her very image would guarantee that the "vision of unity" her cult had presumably fostered, as Baring and Cashford had claimed and hoped, was little more than an illusion. Civilization had a long way to go before marriage would be seen as the crowning fulfillment of equal loving partners.

Woman in Search of Her Goddess

We may find ourselves wondering to what degree the suppression of women's rites has actually been the suppression of women's rights.
Merlin Stone, When God Was a Woman

In the past half century, there has been a veritable revival of the goddess myth, after Merlin Stone published her book *When God Was a Woman* in 1978, followed a year later by *Ancient Mirrors of Womanhood*. Stone inspired such enthusiastic followers as Riane Eisler, who presented a picture of pre-monotheist societies in her book *The Chalice and the Blade*, published in 1987, that is nothing short of rosy. "In the goddess religions," writes Eisler, "just as the head of the holy family was a woman, called the Great Mother, so too in the secular family descent was matrilineal (it took place through the mother) and the domicile matrilocal (at her home)." Both men and women were children of the Goddess; "neither half of humanity ranked over the other, and diversity [was] not equated with inferiority or superiority."[19]

No wonder Baring and Cashford had decided to embark on the project to revisit the myth of the goddess. It turned out, however, that upon closer examination the picture was somewhat more complicated: while the Goddess had vanished from the official stories, she continued to linger on behind the scenes. Indeed, even when the goddess myth was "debased and devalued," it managed to stealthily stick around. "In Hebrew mythology the goddess went, so to speak, underground": it took on a feminine persona as Yahweh's consort "Wisdom," sometimes also known under her Greek name, "Sophia"; embodied in the Sabbath as "God's Bride"; and the most tantalizing Shekhinah which, throughout history, Jews took to be God's spiritual consort.[20] Christianity too belatedly came to recognize the great goddess when at last the Virgin Mary, also known as "the 'Second Eve,' was declared 'Assumed into Heaven, Body and Soul' as Queen [, though] only in the 1950s."[21]

Not that Mary was easily comparable to Eve. Mary the Virgin had borne the Son of God immaculately. Eve, by contrast, created to help her consort, counterpart and mate, was hence his equal. Mary was unique in having born God's son who is himself a God. Eve was in no way a goddess, but was meant to be—and to stay—human: the moment she and Adam ate the forbidden fruit that rendered them both "like the gods," they were forced to leave Eden, their mortality reinforced by exile: to dust they would irrevocably return.

And yet, being portrayed as the quintessential Mother—the Mother of God, no less—Mary seems at once divine and human. The dissonance is aptly captured by Baring and Cashford:

> Paradoxically, it is Mary's very humanity as a mother—our readiness to identify with a woman about to give birth with nowhere to go—that predisposes us to take the symbolism of virginity literally because she does not 'feel symbolic.' . . . But rendering Mary as human and virgin together is [certainly] perplexing, for it also confuses the archetypal and the human dimensions: symbolically virgin is only for goddesses and literally virgin is not for human mothers. Christianity has taught that the "miraculous" birth without the "sin" of sexuality is believed to redeem the Eve of its own invention, but it perpetuates the Judaic tradition of belittling the human order to honor the divine. It exalts a woman to the level of a goddess, creating as a goddess creates—at once mother and virgin—yet denies her either the title of goddess or the complete humanity of a woman.[22]

Or, in the words of Marina Warner, author of the seminal book about the Virgin Mary entitled *Alone of All Her Sex*: "In the very celebration of the perfect human woman, both humanity and women were subtly denigrated."[23] The real resurrection of Eve's image would have to take on a different form and serve a very different purpose. Any suggestion of her divinity, no matter how metaphorical, would completely defeat her biblical purpose. By contrast, Mary's function is in a very important sense neo-divine.

I must add a word of clarification about the expressed intent of Baring and Cashford's seminal book. While carefully researched, their tome is not restricted to enriching academic discourse for its own sake. Rather, it is an effort to change what the authors perceive as "the predominant mythic image of the age—which could be characterized as 'the god without the goddess'—[which] continues to support the very oppositional and mechanistic paradigm that the latest scientific discoveries are refuting."[24] In the process, however, they seem to have exchanged one flawed ideology for another. While true that a monotheistic orientation that is not only overly anthropomorphic but neo-pagan, having simply eliminated all the deities but one, can serve to distort human relationships, it is unclear that the solution is to opt instead for a Divine Couple.

I would argue that, perhaps unwittingly, the righteous foes of patriarchy have subliminally appropriated the very premise they profess to oppose. What they offer to combat the preeminence of the male is to elevate the female to the same job, as co-sovereign of the universe. But the challenge is to re-appreciate not only woman as eminently, rightfully worthy of respect and power, but to revisit intimacy itself, which has been lost in the theological shuffle. That relationship should not pit the right hemisphere of the brain against the left. Intimacy, perhaps the most difficult of all feelings, encompasses all we are and all we can be.

Merlin Stone, one of the pioneers of the goddess-resurrection movement, notes in *When God Was a Woman* that Yahweh's transcendence ended up preventing the human tribe from identifying divinity with nature. What had once been sacred in itself was now merely a place from which the sacred spoke.[25] The alienation of the sacred from nature thus resulted in the simultaneous alienation of mankind—as part of nature—from the sacred. At the same time, the receding of the goddess into the background resulted in the alienation of man from woman—disunity undermining not only the vision of harmony between man and his universe but also a supportive, mutually reinforcing relationship between the sexes.

Inspired by both Stone and Erich Neumann, the Jungian analyst Jean Shinoda Bolen, in her book *Goddesses in Everywoman: A New Psychology of Women,* defends restoring the goddess in order to bolster the self-image, self-respect, and coping mechanisms of women—an approach she found in the course of her medical practice to have succeeded remarkably well. Her technique involves identifying several categories, based on several types of Greek goddesses, which a woman may recognize as most aptly capturing her own personality (although complex interactions among categories are frequent). Mere fairy tales will not do: it is important that these be goddesses, to provide that heightened sense of importance. Her explanation is Jungian: "Myths evoke feeling and imagination and touch on themes that are part of the human collective inheritance," and Greek myths especially tend to "remain current and personally relevant because there is a ring of truth in them about shared human experience."[26]

Dr. Bolen's social consciousness had been raised by the pioneer feminist Betty Friedan in 1963, with the publication of her manifesto *The Feminine Mystique*, Friedan had been appalled by the results of the Commission on the Status of Women commissioned by President John F. Kennedy indicating that "women were not being paid the same as men for doing the same job . . . [a] glaring unfairness [which] was further evidence of how women's roles were devalued and limited."[27] Bolen's book, which did not appear until 1985 when American feminism was already in full swing, seemed an appropriate response to the cultural and political tides that swept the nation. She wanted "for women to discover the goddesses within themselves,"[28] which could not fail to heighten their higher self-esteem, social power, and prestige.

She recounts having started with the Psyche myth, because it helped her understand "women who put relationships first." But then she went on to other Olympians—including "the virgin goddesses" Artemis (goddess of the hunt), Athena (goddess of wisdom and crafts, born directly from Zeus's head), and Hestia (goddess of the hearth and temples). Not surprisingly, renowned feminist Gloria Steinem writes in the Foreword to the book how pleased she was to find herself cited—correctly, in her personal opinion—as an example of the Artemis archetype, "who bonded with other women and who rescued her mother while wishing not to be like her."[29] She then goes on to confess, without a trace of false modesty, having recognized within herself traits of other goddesses as well, fully endorsing the methodology to open new paths "as we lead ourselves out of unequal societies [when] gods and goddesses may become one and the same."[30]

Ah, the insidious allure of monism: yearning for the time when gods and goddesses, Adam and Eve, will become "one and the same" . . . This is rather different from the message implicit in the Adam–Eve story. Labeling "Psyche-like" personalities as referring to women who prefer a particular type of lifestyle, women who "put relationships first," is to really miss the whole point of the story. First before *what*? Career, one assumes? But Psyche put intimacy before *lack* of intimacy. In that sense she put both herself and Eros first. Otherwise, they were both losers.

In any event, why do relationships have to be placed in queue, instead of asserting their simultaneous validity alongside whatever priorities we choose to follow in our varied lives? To live alongside another is not a choice at the expense of someone or something else; it not only can but *should* accompany whatever we choose to do with our lives.

The more liberated women, then, as Bolen describes them, presumably resemble one of the so-called virgin goddesses: they prefer the company of other women and hope not to be "like their mothers." They hope some day for women and men to "become one and the same." Except, one wonders, for a few negligible gender differences? The subliminal message implied by this attitude is unjustly denigrating those who cherish a woman's nurturing role and who consider it a priority. At its most extreme, this leads to a paradoxically misogynist pseudo-feminism that worships a quasi-male goddess whose gender is purely anatomical but whose soul is bare. For Eve that would truly constitute the ultimate defeat, at the hands of her own daughters.

Renascence

The heroine must become a spiritual warrior. This demands that she learn the delicate art of balance and have the patience for the slow, subtle integration of the feminine and masculine aspects of herself.
Maureen Murdock, The Heroine's Journey

Eventually Psyche is indeed immortalized and becomes a goddess, but that had never been her goal—and should not be ours. The denouement of the Greek myth that vindicates her; promotion to Olympus may be seen as tantamount to obliterating any lingering stigma from her original transgression. But she was not intended as a role model merely for women: instead, as her name explicitly indicates, she is the symbol of the *soul* as such, of its symbiosis with love, and the primacy of that fusion. For that to resonate again in our century, and resonate it should for there is aching need, the goddess is not what must be resurrected. At issue is not simply the re-empowerment of women: it is the proper role of Eve-for-Adam. Eve, after all, is not simply the first mortal woman; she is the first mortal *soulmate*. No goddess can come close to that status, since every goddess is handicapped by immortality, and most are doomed either to self-sufficiency or promiscuity or both.

The yearning for life—mortal, *human* life—can be most properly conveyed through poetry. Such a poem was composed by Edna St. Vincent Millay at the age of nineteen, in 1911. Its perfect title *Renascence* captures with exquisite precision the yearning for rebirth that is the only resurrection worthy of Eve. I offer it here in summary, though it is obviously best appreciated in its entirety.

In a manner vaguely reminiscent of Emily Dickinson, Millay starts by beholding "three mountains and a wood," followed by "three islands in a bay," and finally the sky above, which she could at first "almost touch," then reaching up her hand to try, she "screamed to feel it touch the sky."[31]

I screamed, and—lo!—Infinity
Came down and settled over me;
Forced back my scream into my chest,
Bent back my arm upon my breast,
And, pressing of the Undefined
The definition on my mind,
Held up before my eyes a glass
Through which my shrinking sight did pass
Until it seemed I must behold
Immensity made manifold . . .

Followed by the gossiping of friendly spheres and the creaking of the tented sky, she could hear at last the ticking of eternity.

I saw and heard, and knew at last
The How and Why of all things, past,
And present, and forevermore.
The Universe, cleft to the core,
Lay open to my probing sense . . .

But there is a price:

For my omniscience paid I toll
In infinite remorse of soul.
All sin was of my sinning, all
Atoning mine, and mine the gall
Of all regret. Mine was the weight
Of every brooded wrong, the hate
That stood behind each envious thrust,
Mine every greed, mine every lust.
And all the while for every grief,
Each suffering, I craved relief
With individual desire,—
Craved all in vain! And felt fierce fire

About a thousand people crawl;
Perished with each,—then mourned for all!

No, Jesus, she finds the weight of "every grief" unbearable; she yearns for relief like Job: "Ah, awful weight! Infinity/Pressed down upon the finite Me!" At last relief does come, as quietly the earth beneath gives way, and she sinks six feet under ground, then sinks no more. Cool is the hand of earth and soft its breast beneath the head "of one who is so gladly dead."

And then, suddenly . . . there is rain. She welcomes its friendly sound, which seems to her lovelier than ever, as if she was hearing it for the first time. She suddenly exclaims:

I would I were alive again
To kiss the fingers of the rain,
To drink into my eyes the shine
Of every slanting silver line,
To catch the freshened, fragrant breeze
From drenched and dripping apple trees . . . .

And soon the rain will be over and the world will rejoice with "answering mirth," each round drop of rain shaking off the blades of grass . . . . She cries:

How can I bear it; buried here,
While overhead the sky grows clear
And blue again after the storm?
O, multi-colored, multiform,
Beloved beauty over me,
That I shall never, never see
Again!

She begs God to give her "new birth" and put her "back upon the earth!"

Miraculously, she slowly regains her self. "I know not how such things can be!—/I breathed my soul back to me." As she, at last, beholds "the face of God," she vows never to fail to see Him, to hear and feel Him: "God, I can push the grass apart/And lay my finger on Thy heart!"

This resurrection is merely temporary, of course. The almost-death experience induces her metamorphosis from casual bystander in a seemingly ordinary world—three mountains, three islands, whatever—to humble worshipper at last capable of appreciating the splendor, that is rain and dew and sunshine. Only a soul capable of grasping the ineffable, devastating realization that all of this beloved beauty will "never, never" be seen again is blessed with the knowledge of its unfathomable goodness.

But this poem is best read in conjunction with another by Millay called "Interim"[32] to fully appreciate the meaning of "becoming one flesh." The poem begins with a lament over the passing of her lover, "the fairest thing God ever made,/I think." The brief refrain threaded through the poem captures her pain with powerful simplicity: "I had you and I have you no more." How can mere language convey all she feels? "O little words, how can you run so straight/Across the page, beneath the weight you bear?" She wishes God would "set back the world a little turn or two!/Correct its griefs, and bring its joys again!" If only for a little while, a brief renascence of a love unexpectedly, untimely interrupted.

We were so wholly one I had not thought
That we could die apart. I had not thought
That I could move,—and you be stiff and still!
That I could speak,—and you perforce be dumb!
I think our heart-strings were, like warp and woof
In some firm fabric, woven in and out;
Your golden filaments in fair design
Across my duller fiber. And to-day
The shining strip is rent; the exquisite
Fine pattern is destroyed; part of your heart
Aches in my breast; part of my heart lies chilled
In the damp earth with you. I have been torn
In two, and suffer for the rest of me.

Incapable of easy solace, she knows not where he is—because she knows he is not. Nor will he ever be again; so she pretends to speculate, trying to numb the agony. If Heaven hold him "or if the earth transmute, body and soul," into the earth again—dust unto dust—she honestly cannot say. She lets the world "drip its easy tears"; her sorrow, un-consoled, "shall be dumb!"

How much she wishes for divine solace . . . . "Would to God I too might feel that frenzied faith whose touch makes temporal the most enduring grief." In the end, she is mercifully graced by a flash of knowledge:

O God, I see it now, and my sick brain
Staggers and swoons! How often over me
Flashes this breathlessness of sudden sight
In which I see the universe unrolled
Before me like a scroll and read thereon
Chaos and Doom, where helpless planets whirl
Dizzily round and round and round and round,

Like tops across a table, gathering speed
With every spin to waver on the edge
One instant—looking over—and the next
To shudder and lurch forward out of sight—

Beholding the unfathomable universe, she reflects on the "helpless" motion of its planets of which Earth is but one, hardly unique. She reads it "like a scroll," to find only Chaos and Doom, each creation teetering on the edge of the abyss—one instant "looking over" and the next "out of sight." The human condition is to be, then not to be. It is no longer a question but an icy statement of fact.

She had him and now has him no more. The poem ends:

I am wearied out—
It is too much—I am but flesh and blood,
And I must slee Though you were dead again,
I am but flesh and blood and I must sleep.

She dispenses with melodrama, opting for the simple majesty of acquiescence: *Thy will be done.*

To know the grief of death—one's own and another's—is the price man pays for beholding the overwhelming beauty of life. Only art may capture the solace and mystery of intimacy. If graced, that spiritual solace may open us to faith, which offers the ultimate grace. Not ready to ascend beyond her present misery quite yet, the poet begs only for a little sleep: "O, let me sleep a while! Would I could sleep, and wake to find me back/In that sweet summer afternoon with you." A brief respite, an interim renascence, is all she asks. Yet isn't life itself little more than just such an interim from dust to dust?

Eve was willing to risk knowing that; and with her by his side, Adam could do the same. This is no ordinary blessing; suffering is the prerequisite for understanding how God's creation is *good*. Yet a blessing it is, truly. So writes Millay in another little poem entitled "God's World":[33]

O world, I cannot hold thee close enough!
Thy winds, thy wide grey skies!
Thy mists, that roll and rise!
. . . .—Lord, I do fear
Thou'st made the world too beautiful this year;
My soul is all but out of me,—let fall
No burning leaf; prethee, let no bird call.

Perhaps death, far from being a punishment, is simply what it takes to attain the deepest, most genuine knowledge. God had meant us to feel absolute joy; the price was its brevity.

The life of the beautiful, rebellious, promiscuous, and enormously talented Edna St. Vincent Millay, unfortunately, ended in tragedy. Lonely and ill, she fell to her death, perhaps a suicide, at the age of fifty-eight, feeling unfulfilled and deeply disappointed in her life despite having won a Pulitzer Prize for poetry in 1923. Her personal renascence was not to be. She was never to surrender to grace, to the larger meaning that could sustain her spirit.

One reason may be that she, like many women who seek to find harmony by reconciling themselves to their quintessentially feminine, rather than Adamic, hero-emulating paths, ended up doing it alone. The psychologist Maureen Murdock, in her book *The Heroine's Journey*, published in 1990, is right to observe that "when a woman reduces the emphasis on the outer heroic quest for self-definition, she is free to explore her images and her voice."[34] She is also correct that "the intense focus on feminine spirituality at this time is a direct result of so many women's having taken the hero's journey, only to find it personally empty and dangerous for humanity." They did so presumably because "there were no other images to emulate."[35] But the answer is not to find the duality within oneself, but to be able to reach out beyond oneself.

This brings us finally to the principal reason why a search for the goddess is not merely unhelpful, not simply inappropriate, but fundamentally antithetical to the Abrahamic tradition. Leonard Shlain's claim that "each monotheistic religion [Judaism, Christianity, and Islam] features an imageless Father deity"[36] is just plain wrong. The God of Abraham was certainly beyond imagining, but He was not imageless. It had been in His image that mankind had been created: man and woman were His image *together*, not singly. The way to understand the profound meaning of this admittedly abstract creed is not to deny the feminine, nor to re-anthropomorphize God along with a consort for the purpose of providing humans a useful psychological model. We do not have any need of the goddess when we have a perfectly good example of the mutual love among the female and the male in ourselves, a love that our merciful God fully embraces, having created it Himself.

Notes

1. Virginia Wolf, *A Room of One's Own*, 101–2.
2. Peter F. MacNeilage, et al., "Evolutionary Origins of Your Right and Left Brain," *Scientific American Magazine*, June 24, 2009.

3. Larry Cahill, "His Brain, Her Brain," *Scientific American Magazine*, April 25, 2005.

4. Leonard Shlain, *The Alphabet versus the Goddess: The Conflict between Word and Image*, viii.

5. "A foolish person, a simpleton." See Leo Rosten, *The Joys of Yiddish*, 264–66 and 348–50.

6. *The Alphabet versus the Goddess*, 118–19.

7. Ibid., 119.

8. Anne Baring and Jules Cashford, *The Myth of the Goddess: Evolution of an Image*, xi.

9. Ibid., xii.

10. Ibid.

11. Tikva Frymer-Kensky, *In the Wake of the Goddesses: Women, Culture, and the Biblical Transformation of Pagan Myth*, 14.

12. Ibid., 67.

13. Hans Gutterbock, "A Hurro-Hittite Hymn to Ishtar," *JAOS* 103, no. 1 (1983): 155–64.

14. Stephanie Dalley, *Myths from Mesopotamia: Creation, the Flood, Gilgamesh and Others* (Oxford and New York: Oxford University Press, 1989), 1–38.

15. *In the Wake of the Goddesses*, 76.

16. Ibid., 77.

17. Ibid., 78.

18. Ibid., 80.

19. Riane Eisler, *The Chalice and the Blade*, 28.

20. Raphael Patai, *The Hebrew Goddess*, ch. IV, "Shekhinah," 96–111.

21. Ibid., xviii.

22. Baring and Cashford, *The Myth of the Goddess*, 564.

23. Cited in Ibid.

24. Ibid., xiv.

25. 228 (in Bolen, 21).

26. Jean Shinoda Bolen, *Goddesses in Everywoman: A New Psychology of Women*, 6.

27. Baring and Cashford, *The Myth of the Goddess*, 438.

28. Ibid., 11.

29. Ibid., xi.

30. Ibid., xii.

31. Edna St. Vincent Millay, *Renascence and Other Poems* (New York: Dover Publications, 1991), 1–8.

32. Ibid., 9–16.

33. Ibid., 23.

34. Maureen Murdock, *The Heroine's Journey*, 10.

35. Ibid.

36. *The Alphabet versus the Goddess*, 7.

9

The First Wives

The first and highest service which Eve renders Adam is to throw him out of paradise.
William James Sr., Society the Redeemed Form of Man *(1879)*

Such is the verdict of the good doctor who is known, insofar as he is known at all, as "the elder James"—his reputation all but eclipsed by his illustrious progeny, which included the great novelist Henry James and pioneer Harvard psychologist William James. Far from damning Eve, the elder James applauds her, not altogether whimsically, for helping Adam . . . grow up. (Many a wife will consider this insight hardly startling.) James argues, sensibly enough, that in order to become a man, the individual first has to "fall," in the sense that he has to know the meaning of evil—indeed, must encounter it, experience it directly—so as to combat and counteract his innate egotism. Instead of deploring man's demise from paradise, he deems it necessary. As James controversially (certainly too condescendingly) observes in his book *Christianity, the Logic of Creation*, published in 1857, that "[a]ny one with half an eye can see . . . that 'Adam's fall,' as it is called, was not that stupid lapse from the divine favor which it has vulgarly been reputed to have been, but an actual rise to the normal human level. . . . And accordingly, every son of Adam . . . welcomes this puny, silly death, which inwardly is his proper consciousness, as his inevitable and unconscious resurrection to life."[1]

In other words, what Adam needed was to be jolted into reality and appreciate that his freedom comes at a price. His helpmate's function is not only to provide that jolt but accompany him in the aftermath, thus rescuing him from self-absorption and an innocence that superficially seems idyllic but does not equip man for the hard job of living, let alone the much harder job of dying. The two soulmates are one another's solace till death do them part, as death must.

After Eden, the first male and female become parents, whereupon they are necessarily faced with the challenges of family life. The all-merciful God, however, sees to it that they meet obstacles together, side by side, sharing the good and the bad, for richer or (mostly) for poorer. And as they age, they are able to learn to appreciate one another more, while they travel alongside one another on their lives' journey—not surprisingly becoming spiritual templates for the subsequent legendary couples of the three principal monotheistic religions. In each case, the woman plays a critical role, proving herself indispensable to the survival of the respective branch of the biblical creed. In many ways, the stories of the "first wives" of each monotheistic sect reinforce the original narrative of creation with uncanny, and by no means accidental, clarity.

Abraham and Sarah

Abraham is so to speak "given" a wife who is also his sister in order to educate him—and the reader—in the crucial difference between wife and sister and to lead him—and us—to embrace with understanding the singular meaning of woman as wife.
Leon Kass, The Beginning of Wisdom

"Go forth from your native land and from your father's house to the land I will show you!" Thus does God address the first member of the Judaic tribe, and hence the man who inaugurated the tradition that would bear his name. The first male who would eventually receive God's formal Covenant through circumcision, he had to prove himself worthy of that honor. Most important, Abram (Abraham's original name) had to learn the meaning of marriage prior to receiving the Divine promise of protection and prosperity for himself and his progeny. If Adam and Eve were the first soulmates, Abram and Sarai (later renamed by God Sarah) were the first to elucidate the concept in a social setting—hence the notion of "marriage." For despite the fact that both would have other sexual partners during the course of their very long lives, for reasons illustrated in book 12 of *Genesis,* they were the first to learn the real meaning of spiritual communion and commitment between husband and wife.

Their story begins rather inauspiciously. Abram, though no youngster at age seventy-five, is told by God to leave his home to settle in Egypt. Commendably obedient to the Creator, he nevertheless proves ignorant of what it means to honor his wife fully: Abram chooses to sacrifice her honor, thinking it necessary for his own survival and also God's purpose. What happens is that Abram, anticipating that Sarai's striking beauty will attract the Egyptians who might well kill him in order to take her, decides to ask her to *please* pose as his sister. Admittedly, Naomi Rosenblatt notes that Abram's use of the word "please" is "rare in the language of biblical husbands, which indicates his respect and consideration for his wife's opinions."[2] But it must have been a very small comfort to the poor woman, whose feelings on the matter are not recorded in the Bible. She is merely reported to have complied without protest, even if this meant that she would have to be both unfaithful and raped. Demonstrating exemplary piety, she acquiesces to being taken into Pharaoh's harem, thus choosing the survival of the Covenant and of her husband over her personal interests and desires.

Since Abram at this point shows no indication of understanding that he had done something very wrong, he will first have to appreciate the selfishness and immorality of his act before he can be entrusted with the Covenant. This would happen only after one more suitor—Abimelech, the king of Gerar—takes hold of Sarai, whom he believes to be unmarried and hence available. Fortunately, God intervenes: He appears to Abimelech in a dream and reveals to him the truth about the hapless couple. Whereupon Abimelech confronts Abram, who lies by telling a half-truth, namely that Sarai is actually his half-sister (which she is), but conveniently leaves out the small matter of their wedding. Abimelech, who already knows the full truth, pretends to accept this explanation, mindful not to hurt Sarai. He proceeds to teach her culpable husband the requisite lesson: he offers them a gift of a thousand pieces of silver as "a covering of [her] eyes" and declares that "before all men [she is thereby] righted"—in other words, her shame has been wiped clean.

Leon Kass interprets this episode as follows:

> This time around, thanks to the virtuous Abimelech, who bears moral witness against Abraham and who displays a clear appreciation of the honor due to Sarah as a wife, Abraham is forced to confront the sinfulness of his own conduct. Very likely he sees what the reader is told, in so many words: that God insists on the dignity and honor of the woman as wife; and that the blessings of fertility and progeny—the promised great nation of innumerable descendants—depend upon man's proper regard for the status of wife and the meaning of marriage, informed by the call to transmit a righteous and holy way. . . .[3]

Chastened, Abram finally understands. He is thus ready to become a true husband and a father.

But decades pass and Sarai is still barren. No less desirous than Abram that he sire a new breed of men, she would once again set aside her own feelings and desires in the interest of her husband and God's wish. This time, however, she does it of her own initiative. Concluding, on reasonably good grounds (presumably having entered menopause about half a century earlier), that childbearing is no longer an option for her, Sarai decides to tell Abram to bed her maid[4] Hagar who, Sarai hopes, might give him a son. He agrees, and Hagar gives birth to a boy who is named *Ishmael*, meaning "God Heeds." Through Ishmael, God's promise has technically been fulfilled: Abram, though already eighty-six, finally has a son.

It would not take long before Hagar would become insubordinate, further stoking Sarai's already inevitable jealousy. Eventually, Sarai demands that Abram evict both Hagar and Ishmael. Abram agrees reluctantly, having grown very fond of his firstborn son, but complies with his wife's request. Their marriage had to take precedence over his paternal feelings.

It would take still another thirteen years before God would re-name him Abraham—allegedly "father of multitudes" in Hebrew (though this etymology is controversial)—and Sarai would be known as "Sarah" (an arguably negligible modification, since the word still meant "princess"—which as his *wife*, she had always been). God then announces that, as originally promised, the two of them at last would be blessed with offspring as Sarah herself would now bear a child. Abraham is dismayed by his new name, for he cannot imagine how Sarah, herself no spring chicken at (by then) eighty-nine, could make him father of anyone, let alone "multitudes." It is important to note that Sarah is the only woman in the Bible whose name is explicitly bestowed by God, which He does immediately after explaining the ritual of circumcision—symbol of God's Covenant with his people. The Jewish tradition has taken this divine gesture to imply that woman too, despite being anatomically incapable of undergoing circumcision, is tacitly included in that Covenant.[5]

Upon hearing this prediction, Abraham is first to laugh, followed by Sarah, stunned by the suggestion that she could still be fertile. Was it an expression of incredulity or of joy? Undoubtedly a mixture of both. So what else could they name their son—who does indeed soon come to them, as God had ordained—if not *Yitshaq* (Isaac) meaning

"He Laughs" or "He Will Laugh"? Isaac had brought them happiness beyond description, especially after they had lost all hope of ever enjoying offspring of their own. And having parents who are both close to a century old is arguably rather funny. Parenthetically, God also thereby gave Jews the greatest gift of all: a sense of humor.[6] They would come to need it more than they knew.

The holy ritual of circumcision came later, eight days after Isaac's birth. Known as *brit* (Hebrew for "Covenant") the ceremony that marks the sacred trust between God and the child's father lays the foundations for the child's sense of belonging to a continuing tradition. Explains Rosenblatt, "With this Covenant, God shifted the ancient Near Eastern tribal practice of circumcision from puberty to the eighth day after birth and thereby from sexual to spiritual significance. . . . Echoing His first lesson to Adam and Eve, God's lesson to Abraham as part of the Covenant is a lesson for every male: with fatherhood comes responsibility."[7] Presumably, Sarah already knew that with motherhood comes responsibility, for pregnancy and child-rearing are manifestly difficult and even life-threatening—especially in ancient times.

Much more needs to be said about Sarah and Abraham, whose story is complex and fascinating, but for our purposes, it is enough to summarize the importance of their relationship, whose fundamental strength set the tone for generations to come. Again, Rosenblatt explains eloquently and succinctly:

> Just as Adam and Eve left the Garden of Eden together on their way to a brave new world, Abraham and Sarah left their comfortable old world for the land promised them by God. Eve took risks in seeking wisdom; Sarah took risks in entering the Covenant. . . . Despite the burdens imposed on them, Sarah and Abraham were dedicated to a surprisingly monogamous partnership within a polygamous society. It is impossible to think of one without the other. More than any other marriage in the Bible, that of Sarah and Abraham was a lifelong bond based on devotion to each other and a loyalty to a shared faith and vision. To the end of their life together, Sarah, at times passionate and unyielding, at times courageous and stoic, was the partner Abraham loved—and whom God sanctioned. They were inseparable.[8]

The first Jews, Sarah and Abraham, are equally revered by the followers of Christianity and Islam. If Adam and Eve had been the first humans, Abraham and Sarah were the first historically documented quasi-mythical biblical spouses, followers of the monotheistic creed.

Their tumultuous and complex life, fraught with obstacles both external and psychological, is a source of inspiration and hope for all subsequent generations of every sect.

Joseph and Mary

Now the origin of Christ was in this wise. When Mary his mother had been betrothed to Joseph, before they came together, she was found to be with child by the Holy Spirit. But Joseph her husband, being a just man, and not wishing to expose her to reproach, was minded to put her away privately. But while he thought on these things, behold, an angel of the Lord appeared to him in a dream, saying, "Do not be afraid, Joseph, son of David, to take to thee Mary thy wife, for that which is begotten in her is of the Holy Spirit."
Matthew, *1:18–20*

So Joseph, arising from sleep, did as the angle of the Lord had commanded him, and took unto him his wife. And he did not know her till she brought forth her firstborn son. And he called his name Jesus.
Matthew, *1:24–25*

The fact that Joseph and Mary had been betrothed before she was visited by the Holy Spirit is no coincidence. Lest Mary be castigated and vilified as an unwed mother, the divinely conceived Jesus had to be considered Joseph's legal son. Joseph himself proved no less pious than Mary, having trusted God's Word at every step. His original hesitation to marry his betrothed had simply reflected their times: premarital pregnancy being prohibited by law, Joseph was in a quandary. As a "just man," he could not break the law; thus private divorce, or dissolving the engagement (described euphemistically as "putting away"), seemed the best solution. Yet after God's messenger angel assures Joseph that since his fiancée was carrying the Lord's child no man had touched her, Joseph is instantly convinced. Without hesitation, he proceeds with the marriage with a clear conscience, sparing Mary both shame and penury.

Not that the marriage implies consummation: the fact that Joseph is said not to have known her "till she brought forth her firstborn son" in no way implies that he knew her *afterward*. Nor does the fact that Jesus is described as her firstborn imply that she had any other children later,[9] since among the Jews this appellation was also commonly given to an only child.[10] While their marriage was never technically consummated, this does not imply that they were never "really" husband and wife. In the first place, God's messenger urged Joseph to proceed with the ceremony rather that merely be there for her, by her side. Far more important than legality, they were certainly helpmates in a profound, intimate way. They were more than friends—they shared one another's life and were deeply devoted to one another and to the God they trusted equally. Not only did Mary and young Jesus need Joseph's indispensable practical help on several crucial occasions; considering Joseph's unflinching faith, the couple were above all genuine soulmates, capable of understanding the great mystery that had created their holy child.

Joseph and Mary were the first married Christians. Before anyone else, Joseph had believed the angel's words, unquestioningly. Even though he heard them during the course of a dream, he did not dismiss it as mere nocturnal fantasy but proceeded to obey God and did not abandon Mary. Though we are told nothing about their life together, it is impossible to imagine any discord between them, given their common consciousness of their privileged chosen status. We do learn that after the Magi's journey to Bethlehem, Joseph was again visited by an angel in a dream and was told to take child and mother away to Egypt, whereupon he should await further instructions. Those instructions came as promised—God's angel appearing once more, after Herod's death, to tell Joseph that he should at last feel free to lead the family to the land of Israel: "for those who sought the child's life are dead" (*Matthew*, 2:20). This Joseph duly proceeded to do, though after receiving one more piece of divine intelligence in a dream which informed him that Herod's son Archelaus was reigning in Judea, Joseph heeded the warning and took his family into Galilee, where they settled in Nazareth (*Matthew*, 2:23). Pious, courageous, and devoted to his family as much as to the Lord, Joseph was clearly the ideal husband for Mary.

Why, then, was he so little known throughout most of history? Though he had been Mary's exemplary helpmate and the recipient of angelic directives, which he obeyed unflinchingly and faithfully, it was not until 1399 that the Franciscans adopted a feast day dedicated to Joseph. Among his supporters were church leaders like Jean Gerson, who tried at the Council of Constance in 1416 to have Joseph elevated to a rank next to Mary, with a universal feast to celebrate The Marriage of Mary and Joseph, but did not succeed. He was later added to the Roman Breviary in 1479—which was not made compulsory for the whole Catholic church until 1621. He was finally declared to be the patron saint and protector of the Catholic church (along with Saint Peter) by Pope Pius IX in 1870. In 1955, Pope Pius XII declared May 1 *the Feast of St. Joseph the Worker.* This was in part to counteract May Day, primarily a workers' and socialists' holiday, but the name does reflect what many Christians genuinely believe: that Saint Joseph is the patron and "model" of workers. Few people know that Joseph is also the patron saint of the United States.

There are some who wonder about another possible holy alliance: what about Jesus himself? Was he ever married? For the vast majority of Christians, the question is simply preposterous, indeed outright blasphemous. Others, however, find it at the very least fascinating, not to mention lucrative.

Jesus and Mary of Magdala (??)

Now when Jesus was risen early the first day of the week, he appeared first to Mary Magdalene, out of whom he had cast seven devils.
Mark 16:9

Ultimately, perhaps, the story of Mary Magdalene is woven of thin strands of legends and allusions, many of which say more about the cultural aspirations of the milieu that created them than about the historical Mary.
Richard Smoley, Forbidden Faith

In recent years, the speculation that Jesus and Mary Magdalene had known each other in what is euphemistically described as "the biblical sense" has proven mighty profitable. Notable among the beneficiaries is Dan Brown, the author of the wildly popular novel *The Da Vinci Code,* published in 2003, which immediately climbed to first place on the *New York Times* best-seller list and remained there for over a year. It is still selling strong. What is most disturbing, however, is that while obviously fictitious, Brown's characters make historical claims whose veracity the author specifically endorses in a pre-prologue audaciously—and irresponsibly—titled FACT: "All descriptions of artwork, architecture, documents, and secret rituals in this novel are accurate."[11]

Which includes, presumably, the following statement: "the marriage of Jesus and Mary Magdalene is part of the historical record." This preposterous claim is made by a character named Teabing, whose alleged source is *The Gnostic Gospels*, which he touts as being among the recently discovered Dead Sea Scrolls. With an air of authority, he tells his reportedly awestruck audience:

> Fortunately for historians, some of the gospels that [Emperor] Constantine attempted to eradicate [in the fourth century A.D.] managed to survive. The Dead Sea Scrolls were found in the 1950s hidden in a cave near Qumran in the Judean desert. And, of course, the Coptic [a language spoken by Christians in Egypt] Scrolls in 1945 at Nag Hammadi. In addition to telling the true Grail story, these documents speak of Christ's ministry in very human terms.[12]

The unsuspecting reader may be forgiven for not immediately recognizing this for what it is: sheer nonsense. Bart D. Ehrman, chairman of Religious Studies at the University of North Carolina, sets the record straight:

> (1) Constantine did not attempt to eradicate any of the earlier Gospels. (2) The Dead Sea Scrolls do not contain any Gospels, or in fact any documents that speak of Christ or Christianity at all; they are Jewish. (3) Their (initial) discovery was in 1947, not the 1950s. (4) The Coptic documents at Nag Hammadi were in book form, they were not scrolls (an important distinction for the history of early Christian books). (5) Neither these nor the Dead Sea Scrolls ever speak of the Grail story. (6) Nor do they speak of Jesus's ministry "in very human terms"; if anything, Jesus is portrayed as more divine in the Nag Hammadi sources than he is in the Gospels of the New Testament. (7) The Vatican had nothing to do with covering up either of these discoveries.[13]

What is most astonishing about Brown's "research" is not so much his disregard for the truth as his sloppiness, which seems to imply an unflattering assessment of his readers' respect for accuracy.

But let us focus on the alleged marriage of Jesus and Mary Magdalene. It is once again the fictional Teabing who proposes it, by citing the following passage which is said to be from the *Gospel of Philip*:

> And the companion of the Savior is Mary Magdalene. Christ loved her more than all the disciples and used to kiss her often on her mouth. The rest of the disciples were offended by it and expressed disapproval. They said to him, "Why do you love her more than all of us"[14]

Another character, Sophie, perceptively observes that the passage "says nothing of marriage," but Teabing will have none of it. "*Au contraire,*" protests the Englishman (in *French*? that alone should have been a tip-off); "as any Aramaic scholar will tell you, the word companion, in those days, literally meant spouse." He then directs her to read a few other passages that, lo and behold "to Sophie's surprise, clearly suggested Magdalene and Jesus had a romantic relationship."[15]

"Clearly suggested"? That is very hard to believe. For only one thing from the silly episode cannot be denied: the passage cited by Teabing is indeed from the *Gospel of Philip*. But that's the best one can say about this would-be scholar's erudition. Continues Ehrman:

> It is wrong to say that when the Gospel of Philip calls Mary Jesus' "companion" that the Aramaic word means "spouse." For one thing, the word that is used is not Aramaic. The Gospel of Philip is Coptic. And even though the word used there for "companion" actually is a loan word from another language, the language, again, is not Aramaic but Greek. In other words, Aramaic has nothing to do with the saying. And to cap it all off, the Greek word that is used (*koinonos*) in fact means not "spouse" (or "lover") but "companion" (it is commonly used of friends and associates).[16]

In brief, this is pseudo-scholarship—that is, complete nonsense. So why bring up such drivel? Having sold an astronomic number of copies hardly justifies mentioning it here, were it not for the fact that *The Da Vinci Code* seems to have struck an important cord. Just two decades earlier, Michael Baigent, Richard Leigh, and Henry Lincoln had speculated in their book *Holy Blood, Holy Grail* that a marriage between Mary Magdalene "would have constituted an important dynastic alliance and one filled with political consequences."[17] The conjecture was based on the assumption that she was from the Tribe of Benjamin, and Jesus from the Tribe of David—though the authors admit that there is "no indication of the Magdalene's tribal affiliation."[18] As to the idea that Jesus would have been interested in a "dynastic alliance," that too is bizarre. Nevertheless, as Richard Smoley, a highly regarded scholar of Gnostic religion, correctly points out, the fact that "the past generation has seen a great resurgence of interest in Mary Magdalene" indicates that "the rediscovery and rehabilitation of this powerful but elusive figure reflects shifts in the spiritual mores of our time."[19]

Smoley suspects that the appeal of Brown's book reflects at least in part a widespread desire to reinstate the Divine Feminine that preceded patriarchal monotheism. He acknowledges that the book's presumed evidence in favor of the Divine Feminine may represent "a coping mechanism for our contemporary discomfort" whose symptoms include what some psychologists call "compensation." The term refers to the theory that, if virtues associated with femininity such as caring, beauty, and compassion are trampled down in the culture at large, they reappear in the unconscious.

But Smoley thinks the problem goes even deeper, reflecting "a widespread sense . . . that something is missing in Christianity."[20] For after all, one could argue that it would not matter if Jesus was married or not: weren't Abraham and Sarah given a son by God through a miracle? As my mother might have said, if Jesus was truly a man and he was meant to go through all the sufferings of humans, why would God had spared him the experience of putting up with a cranky wife going through menopause? In all seriousness, the fact that Jesus could never be conceived as married, that his mother's virginity represents an essential part of her virtue, and the fact that nuns are meant to consider themselves the spiritual spouses of Jesus, demonstrate ultimately the problematic role of sexuality at the very heart of Christianity. The late John Paul II would address this issue in his monumental set of lectures known collectively as *The Theology of the Body*, to which we will turn in the next chapter. But first, we must examine the last of the three biblical religions: Islam.

Mohammed and Khadija

If Islamic exegesis has seen Sara as scripturalist prefiguration of or for a later sacred time, it has done so in terms of Sara's role as her husband's first follower and supporter, an image that links Sara with Muhammad's wife Khadija.
Barbara Freyer Stowarsser, Women in the Qur'an—Traditions, and Interpretation

There has never been any doubt that Mohammed adored his first wife, Khadija Bint Khuwaylid, whose death at age sixty-five left him inconsolable. Though he eventually remarried, no other woman meant the same to him—not even the young and lovely Aisha. Though she was much beloved by Mohammed, Aisha once thoughtlessly lashed out against Khadija's memory, evidently irked by the obvious power of Mohammed's love for his first wife and soulmate, referring to her as "the toothless old woman," for whom Allah had given a better replacement—namely, of course, Aisha herself.[21] This appears to have upset Mohammed so deeply that, deadly earnest, he set her straight in the sternest tone: "He has not given me a better one. She believed in me when no one else did. She considered me to be truthful when the people had left me nothing. Allah gave me children from her while he gave me none from the other women" [82, VI, 117].[22] So there; take that, young lady.

Khadija had been Mohammed's employer and coworker when she asked him to marry her. He had just turned twenty-five; she was forty-two. Twice widowed, the mother of two had used the agency of another woman to propose—a practice not unknown in those days. Mohammed accepted with alacrity; having lost his mother at an early age, the well-respected and wealthy Khadija was quite a catch. He loved her for her generosity and kindness to him, which he felt was God's gift. He writes of himself in the Quran, *Sura* 93:6: "Did He not find thee an orphan and give (thee) a home?" followed, in verse 8, by: "Did He not find thee poor, and enrich thee?"[23] Of the seven children that Khadija bore him, four survived—all daughters.

Even more critical was her spiritual understanding and unflinching faith in him. After receiving his first revelation, she offered him moral support. Shocked by that psychic experience, apparently outright terrified, Mohammed doubted himself, but Khadija stood by him unflinchingly. She prayed with him in secret and became his first follower at a time when others mocked Mohammed, considering him not a little daft. This explains how Mohammed could write:

God has made dear to me from your world
Women and fragrance,
And the joy of my eyes is in prayer.[24]

His love for Khadija certainly gave him joy. And despite the fact that he married several women after her death, a practice not unknown at the time, the fact is that all his wives as well as other women during his lifetime enjoyed unprecedented freedom and respect. No one deserves greater credit for Mohammed's remarkable attitude than Khadija.

For this reason, according to Annemarie Schimmel, "it is impossible to overestimate [the role she] played in defining the woman's place in Islam. . . . Khadija rightfully bears the two honorary titles Mother of Believers and The Best of Women."[25] She had loved Mohammed as deeply as he evidently loved her; she was not only his helpmate at a time when he was very much in need of material and psychological assistance, she was his spiritual pillar when even his faith was being severely tried.

In conclusion, all three of the couples who founded their respective branches of biblical monotheism demonstrated an extraordinary degree of mutuality on all levels: practical, spiritual, and emotional. All three couples had weathered life-threatening challenges together, facing social opprobrium and ostracism, and expressed love that transcended sexuality. While the latter was most obvious in the case of Joseph and Mary who were simply living together side by side, Abraham and Sarah's marriage was never threatened by either of their extramarital sexual episodes—all prompted more by necessity than by the slightest diminution in their mutual, exclusive love. As for Mohammed's marriages that followed the death of his beloved Khadija, all of which ended up being childless, none detracted in any way from his unswerving exclusive devotion to her as his true soulmate and mother of his only children. Although all the first couples of the great Abrahamic religions had been engaged in caring for offspring, there is little doubt that all three were first and foremost spiritual and emotional *soulmates*.

In the introduction to their wonderful anthology *Wing to Wing, Oar to Oar: Readings on Courting and Marrying*, Amy and Leon Kass set marriage in its biblical context:

> According to the story of the Garden of Eden, our humanization is coincident with the recognition of our sexual nakedness and all that it implies: shame at our needy incompleteness, unruly self-division, and finitude; awe before the eternal; hope in the self-transcending possibilities of children and a relationship to the divine. For a human being to treat sex as a desire like hunger—not to mention as sport—is to live a deception.[26]

The satisfaction of sexual desire certainly constitutes one of the principal motivations for couples to live together, but mutual love and friendship are the real basis for marriage. The authors continue, "Not by mistake did God create a woman—rather than a dialectic partner—to cure Adam's aloneness."[27] Even though camaraderie can and often does occur between two individuals of either gender, as does sexual intercourse (variously thus defined), the exemplary closeness of the heterosexual married couples who founded each one of the major biblical sects may well be considered prototypical, indeed archetypal. No, *Genesis* is not homophobic; though some have sought to use as an excuse to condemn homosexuality. Rather, the biblical story of creation simply underscores the place of procreation—and hence the life-giving power within each person that requires two in symbiosis to consummate the conception—within a soul-nourishing relationship of mutuality and love.

Notes

1. Cited in R. W. B. Lewis, *The American Adam*, 60.
2. Naomi Rosenblatt, *After the Apple*, 27.
3. Leon Kass, *The Beginning of Wisdom*, 288.
4. She may not have been a "maid" at all. The story of Hagar is itself complex and fascinating. See especially Savina J. Teubal's *Ancient Sisterhood: The Lost Traditions of Hagar and Sarah*, and Charlotte Gordon's *The Woman Who Named God: Abraham's Dilemma and the Birth of the Three Faiths*.
5. This is Naomi Rosenblatt's reading; see *After the Apple*, 36. Note that God says: "As for your wife Sarai, you shall not call her Sarai but her name shall be Sarah. I will bless her; I will give you a son by her" (*Genesis* 17:15).
6. For a wonderful book on the spiritual no less than practical importance of laughter, see Peter *Berger's Redeeming Laughter: The Comic Dimension of Human Experience*.
7. *After the Apple*, 36.
8. Ibid., 50.
9. In the canonical Gospel accounts Jesus is described as being the brother of James, Joses (Matthew has the spelling: Joseph, Mark has Joses), Judas, and Simon, and of sisters whose names, however, are not mentioned. Catholic tradition, as taught by Saint Jerome and the Fathers of the Church, teaches that the term "brother" in biblical times had a broader meaning and included cousins and other more distant relatives as well.
10. *Holy Bible*, "The New Testament," 2. The note to verse 25, moreover, clarifies that "the apostolic doctrine of Mary's perpetual virginity is in no way denied by these words."
11. Dan Brown, *The Da Vinci Code*, 1.
12. Ibid., 234.
13. Bart D. Ehrman, *Truth and Fiction in the Da Vinci Code: A Historian Reveals What We Really Know About Jesus, Mary Magdalene, and Constantine*, 25–26.
14. Ibid., 248.
15. Ibid.
16. Ehrman, *Truth and Fiction in the Da Vinci Code*, 143–44.
17. Michael Baigent, Richard Leigh, and Henry Lincoln, *Holy Blood, Holy Grail*, 347.
18. Ibid.
19. Richard Smoley, *Forbidden Faith: The Gnostic Legacy—From the Gospels to the DaVinci Code*, 28.
20. Ibid., 199.

21. Wiebke Walther, *Women in Islam: From Medieval to Modern Times*, 104.
22. Ibn Hanbal, A., Musnad, G. 1–6. *Misr.* 1313, cited in ibid., 104 and 246.
23. *The Koran*, 420.
24. See Annemarie Schimmel, *And Muhammad is His Messenger: The Veneration of the Prophet in Islamic Piety* 51.
25. Annemarie Schimmel, *My Soul Is a Woman: The Feminine in Islam*, 26.
26. Amy A. Kass and Leon R. Kass, *Wing to Wing, Oar to Oar: Readings on Courting and Marrying*, 15.
27. Ibid., 16–17.

10

Modern Man in Search of a Soulmate

You must have a Soulmate, as well as a House or Yokemate.
Robert Samuel Coleridge, Letters and Conversations, 1822

This is hardly the way one might have expected the idea of a soul-mate to have been introduced into the English language—by grudg-ingly, even disparagingly, acknowledging its necessity, likening him or her to a cotenant who lessens the burdens of housework and rent, a mere fellow beast of burden. *Yoke-mate*, or the more frequently used *yokefellow*, reminds one of *yokel*—a country bumpkin. As a contriv-ance for joining together a pair of draft animals, usually oxen, the yoke has traditionally denoted servitude, subjection. So understood, then, a soulmate is a thinly veiled oxymoron, a mongrel, improbable cross between the immortal and the base, the metaphorical equivalent of a (barren) mule. While this last renders it especially appropriate as a euphemism for the activities routinely found in the barnyard, also used to indicate X-rated Web sites, it tends to be shunned by those who think the two component words not merely antagonistic but mutually exclusive. Most computers' spell-check features will balk at the word, contemptuously flagging it with the electronic equivalent of the expletive: the red underline. (They tolerate its hyphenated twin, soul-mate, presumably for displaying the common decency at least to underscore the hybrid, if not outright contradictory, nature of the bastard word.)

Modern man—to say nothing of woman—deserves better. One definition provided by a dating service, which helpfully appears when typing in "soulmate," at www.solvedating.com, defines the term in the lingo of "love economics"—which, if you must know, is a discipline "based on probabilities, calculations, population statistics, and empirical research." Looking for precision? You got it: "Soulmate ratio = Total Love Benefit/Total Love Cost." It follows logically that your soulmate is "the person who will maximize your soulmate ratio and vice versa."[1] This is presumably not a joke (at least not consciously).

Such a perfunctory nod to what passes for the scientific method among the uninitiated may be seen as subtly and deliberately mocking the pretense of precision. But far more likely, it is symptomatic of a profound malaise that permeates our culture, testimony to the ancient, God-given—and God-shared—desire for companionship. If answers to the most vital existential questions are not accessible through computer search engines, those questions will still be asked, in every way possible. Modern man, rightly proud of his many accomplishments, seems to have underestimated his fundamental spiritual kinship to his admittedly technologically challenged ancestors. Like it or not, we are no less hungry for intimacy, empathy, and meaning now than we have always been—and, God willing, always will be. Writes Thomas Moore, the justly celebrated best-selling author and former Catholic monk, in his book *Soul Mates: Honoring the Mysteries of Love and Relationships*: "It is no wonder that in an age of telecommunications—which, by the way, literally means 'distant connections'—we suffer symptoms of the loss of soul. We are being urged from every side to become efficient rather than intimate."[2]

Modern man seems to have forgotten that the ability to reach out to another soul is inextricably linked to establishing a link to his own. But where—and what—*is* his soul? Has he lost it in the shuffle, between the entertainment-consumerist culture and the pursuit of *ersatz*-happiness? Until modern man can fathom the depth of such a loss and the great challenge of reconnecting to himself through another human being, the quest will keep running into a dead end. Modern man's soul is in danger of being trampled upon by the very disciplines allegedly devoted to its study, under the heavy boots of neurophysiology along with the other social "sciences."

The problem began at least as early as the Scientific Revolution, whose otherwise felicitous legacy degenerated into a simplistic view of the universe and of man that eventually led to a pernicious materialism. In the eighteenth century, the age of Isaac Newton, Gottfried Wilhelm von Leibniz, and Johann Kepler, geniuses to whom we owe the theory of gravitation, the calculus, and accurate measurements of the planetary orbits, man's rational powers seemed all but universal. (It might even have included woman's rational faculties, but at the time, no one said so explicitly.) The Laws of Reason and those of Nature were believed to coincide, and a benevolent God was assumed to exercise His Will through such laws, which could—and were meant to—be understood by man, through a God-given faculty expressly designed for that very purpose: his quasi-divine intellect. Though not deliberately intended to render faith and its handmaiden, theology (the erstwhile queen of the sciences) superfluous, the net effect was to deliver a near-lethal blow to the humanities, unceremoniously degraded to mere outlets for passion, sensibility, and the all-too dangerous imagination.

Little wonder that an antithesis soon emerged: Romanticism took off with a vengeance, declaring the supremacy of Spirit, emotion, feeling, mind—in German, *Seele*. That too would soon be replaced, with dialectical necessity, as thesis is inexorably succeeded by antithesis (and hence extremism in the opposite direction), by what we may call the modern worldview. Dominant for well over a century, the mind-set currently in vogue considers the physical universe simply redundant: concepts like mind, consciousness, and spirit are linguistic shortcuts, thoroughly explicable, at least theoretically, in terms of concrete, material forces, and particles. Its scientific legitimacy in tatters, henceforth the soul would be relegated to the pulpit and the sanctuary, as a condescending concession to the tender-hearted.

In his influential *Modern Man in Search of a Soul*, C. G. Jung expresses his dismay at the vast popularity of the pernicious scientism that has infected the Western world. Distressed that the concept of soul has been lost, Jung blames an unduly rigid ideological pendulum, which had irresponsibly swung 180 degrees, in an overreaction to nineteenth century Romantic idealism. The modern replacement of a metaphysics of soul (a.k.a. "psyche," "mind," and "spirit") "by a metaphysics of matter" in the aftermath of the Scientific Revolution, argues Jung, amounts to nothing less than a monumental, seismic "revolution in man's outlook upon the world":

> Just as formerly the assumption was unquestionable that everything that exists takes its rise from the creative will of a God who is spirit, so the nineteenth century discovered the equally unquestionable truth that everything arises from material causes.[3]

Modern man as a "newly formed human being" has "suffered an almost fatal shock, psychologically speaking, and as a result has fallen into profound uncertainty."[4] There is but one word to characterize him: "solitary."[5]

Having lost the teleological certainties of his medieval brother, modern man replaced them with the ideals of material security. Those ideals, however, are little more than a mirage, its aftereffects eventually lethal. Jung understands that "modern man begins to see that every step in material 'progress' adds just so much force to the threat of a more stupendous catastrophe . . . . Let man but accumulate his materials of destruction and the devil within him will soon be unable to resist putting them to their fated use."[6] The book was prescient, more than even its author realized. Published in 1933, it coincided with Hitler's rise to power.

Once the Nazis took over, psychology all but disappeared from the European continent. After the war, largely by default, American psychoanalysis came to dominate the field. This development was of enormous consequence, for in the United States, the discipline was but a branch of medicine: practitioners of psychoanalysis were required to be licensed physicians. This had been strongly opposed by Sigmund Freud, who did not conceal his utter contempt for what he called "the obvious American tendency to turn psychoanalysis into a mere housemaid of Psychiatry."[7] After an inauspicious trip to the United States, Freud is reported to have concluded that "America is gigantic, but it is a gigantic mistake."[8] His younger colleague Bruno Bettelheim, like Freud, a Jew and a Viennese exile, speculates that "his views must have been influenced by what he regarded as the American commitment to materialism and technological accomplishments, which excluded those cultural—one may say spiritual—values that were most important to him."[9]

After emigrating in 1939 and joining the University of Chicago, Bettelheim had a chance to see firsthand the tragic implications of this decision. To his dismay, Bettelheim found that his highly trained staff at Chicago's Orthogenic School failed miserably to help disturbed children afflicted with severe psychiatric disorders. The reason was not their lack of theoretical knowledge; it was the exclusion of *all else*. Explains Bettelheim, "It was a reasoned-out, emotionally distant understanding. What was needed was emotional closeness based on an immediate sympathetic comprehension of all aspects of the child's soul . . . what Freud occasionally spoke of explicitly but much more often implicitly: a spontaneous sympathy of our unconscious with that of others, a feeling response of our soul to theirs."[10]

This attitude, argues Bettelheim, is clearly reflected in the dismally inaccurate translations of Freud's works in the English language, which have systematically failed to render his use of the German *Seele* as "soul." Freud's enormous influence on modern psychology thus became a double-edged sword: while reviving an interest in the psyche, it did so on terms that sabotaged his intent, leading to interpretations that would have been anathema to him. Bettelheim's verdict is chilling:

> If American psychoanalysts had shared Freud's concern for the soul, and his disregard for adaptation or adjustment to the requirements of society [which were to "cure mental illness"], then the history of psychoanalysis in the United States would be entirely different, since psychoanalysis would have had to transcend the narrow confines of medicine. But, of course, if this had happened, psychoanalysis might not have been successful in the United States.[11]

It is only adding insult to injury to blame Freud for dispensing with the soul, reducing it to an obsession with mere sexuality, when in fact it had been his translators who trivialized and misrepresented Freud's sophisticated insights.

Few people today realize that the word "psychoanalysis" itself had been coined by Freud deliberately to reference the story of Psyche and Eros. Freud, like the rest of his Viennese colleagues, had been steeped in the classical tradition. It was the narrative itself that impressed Freud, who took the story very seriously indeed. Bettelheim speculates that Freud may have found it particularly attractive "because she [Psyche] had to enter the underworld and retrieve something there before she could attain her apotheosis. Freud, similarly, had to dare to enter the underworld—in his case, the underworld of the soul—to gain his illumination."[12] And it was the underworld of the unconscious that Freud had sought to explore, believing it unwise to ignore its power and potential fury instead of mastering it, in order to benefit both the self and mankind.

Freud knew that Psyche eventually won over her young lover from the clutches of his jealous mother goddess by her fresh beauty and fragility no less than her courage to dare to know him by looking at him despite his admonition to the contrary. Freud had always been fascinated by Greek mythology, which he studied with great interest; he was an avid collector of Greek, Roman, and Egyptian statues. He also knew that Psyche was sometimes depicted with delicate wings, reminiscent of butterflies—symbols of the soul in many cultures.

215

Bettelheim explains the rationale: a butterfly is perfectly suited "to emphasize [the soul's] transcendental nature. These symbols invested the word 'psyche' with connotations of beauty, fragility, and insubstantiality—ideas we still connect with the soul—and they suggest the great respect, care, and consideration with which Psyche had to be approached, because any other approach would violate, even destroy her."[13] Psyche, like Eve, had represented an archetypal aspect of the human spirit; ignoring its place in the common memory of our civilization is to fundamentally misunderstand the so-called science of the mind, precluding it from helping modern man in his pressing spiritual quest.

Translation from German to American English is only part of the problem; no less important is the cultural setting of the word "soul." In America, the word is most commonly used in a more or less religious sense; in secular contexts, we are more likely to turn to "mind" when we mean to emphasize the intellect, and "heart," "feelings," or "instincts" when at issue is emotion. "Soul" may even be used synonymously with "spirit," a term whose empirical credentials are minimal at best, hence thought ill-suited for public purposes outside the confines of the church. This, Bettelheim assures us, was not the case in Freud's Vienna and is not the case in all German-speaking countries today:

> In German the word *Seele* has retained its full meaning as man's essence, as that which is most spiritual and worthy in man . . . [By contrast,] the translators have relegated [this essence] entirely to the I, the thinking and reasoning part of man. They have disregarded the nonthinking, the irrational world of the unconscious and of the emotions.[14]

Yet that, above all, is what Freud was especially concerned to unveil. The concept of soul is of course notoriously vague. But Bettelheim suspects that, far from a reason to reject it, this is precisely *why* Freud chose the term, so as to embrace all three aspects of man's ambiguous and complex essence. The human psyche reflects warring levels of consciousness simultaneously; thus, to explore that essence, we need metaphors, myths, dreams, jokes—in short, every tool of communication at our disposal.

The ultimate paradox of Freud's emphasis on total self-examination, on exploring the depths of the unconscious, hidden undercurrent of emotion, is that he is often thought to have been responsible for modern man's loneliness—the product of obsessive self-absorption, sexual gratification, and self-fulfillment. Nothing could be further from the truth. Well acquainted with the original myth of Narcissus, Freud never encouraged such an attitude. The young Greek who tragically fell in love with his own reflection had been no role model: Narcissus's infatuation with himself proved not only perverse but suicidal. It stands to reason that Freud would choose him to name the all too ubiquitous malady—precisely in order to stigmatize, not applaud it.

Narcissism as Suicide in the West versus Suicide as Narcissism in Islam

Narcissus: *A beautiful youth, son of Cephisus and Liriope, was inaccessible to the feeling of love; and the nymph Echo, who was enamored of him, died of grief. But Nemesis [Fate], to punish him caused him to see his own image reflected in a fountain, whereupon he became so enamoured of it, that he gradually pined away, until he was metamorphosed into a flower that bears his name.*
The Wordsworth Classical Dictionary, *1852*

It has become a cliché, thanks largely to Hollywood, that American culture is essentially narcissistic. Selfishness, individualism, not *qua* healthy self-regard but a narrow, ugly egotism—having one's way no matter what anyone else may wish or feel—are ubiquitous. So is an alarming decline in civility. This is by no means true only in America, but it seems more apparent here because the popular media disproportionately highlights and rewards these traits with notoriety. Bettelheim observes sadly: "It seems that quite a number of Americans, in their efforts to attain the good life, have made themselves their prime love object, advocating self-assertion over concern for others, looking out for Number One" with apparent disregard of any other numerals. It was precisely this mind-set that Freud considered unhealthy, and chose to call it narcissism to help us understand that egocentricity is not merely harmful to oneself but indeed dangerous.

Freud applied the term to the first stage of human development, the infant whose utter helplessness requires that he howl the moment he is hungry or otherwise uncomfortable, at all times of day or night, oblivious to his exhausted parents. Freud sought to warn us against the destructive force of narcissism; writes Bettelheim, "He knew that caring only for oneself is self-defeating, that it alienates one from others and from the real world, and eventually, from oneself, too." That is the recipe for meaninglessness, the surest path to suicide.

Though allegedly based on a diametrically opposed ideology—God's will in the interest of the community of believers—the case of terrorist Islamist fundamentalism, known also as jihadism and totalitarian Islamism, is far more lethal, since it extends to justifying the murder of innocents. Those who engage in suicidal attacks on presumed infidels are praised by their fellow extremists as heroes and true Muslims, promised a place in heaven. Their families are often provided with large sums of money by way of compensation, and their "sacrifice" hailed as holy. To die while killing others—or intending to do so, in the case of unsuccessful attackers—is as honorable as it had been for the ancient Greek hero to be slaughtered during battle while defending his city. Except that the ancient Greeks did not outright *seek* death, they merely did not fear it—a very different proposition indeed. What is more, the Greeks fought battles against other soldiers rather than target defenseless civilians who meant no harm.

While the Quran categorically forbids suicide, it does allow what has come to be known as martyrdom. This term, however, is ordinarily associated with nonviolence and passive resistance: Christ and his early disciples are the quintessential *martyrs* in the Western tradition. Since *martys* originally meant "witness" in Greek, the paradigmatic martyrs considered themselves witnesses to the true God. The grandson of Mohammed, the third Imam Husayn, killed in 680 by followers of a rival caliph (leader of the Islamic state), was not only the son of Ali who founded Shi'ism but in many ways the founding figure of Islamic martyrdom.

Not widely appreciated, especially in the West, is that using Husayn's death as an example of martyrdom in the aggressive, jihadist sense of the term is a very recent development. A book entitled *The Immortal Martyr*,[15] published in Iran under the sponsorship of the Ayatollah Khomeini and his religious followers, portrays Husayn not as a victim but as having launched a "wholly rational and fairly well-planned attempt—indeed, a revolution,"[16] seeks to justify deliberate self-killing in the interest of the Muslim community, in a radical departure from the original intent.

A parallel metamorphosis was taking place elsewhere in Islam, notably among the Sunni of Egypt, the Tamils of Sri Lanka, and the Wahabbis of Saudi Arabia. What had been unleashed was *A Fury for God*, the title of Malisse Ruthven's book in which she singles out the Egyptian Islamist Sayyid Qutb as the most influential proponent of violent extremism in the name of Islam. Ruthven claims that Qutb's radicalization was prompted in part by revulsion against the sexual debauchery he witnessed even before landing on the American shore, during his transatlantic voyage in 1949. "Qutb's visit to the United States," writes Ruthven, "deserves to rank as the defining moment or watershed from which the 'Islamist war against America' would flow."[17] It is no accident that the word *fitna*, meaning strife or disorder, is used for sexual misdemeanors as well as civil wars within the Muslim community. Sexuality plays a crucial role in Muslim extremism.

In their highly acclaimed book *The Age of Sacred Terror*, Clinton-administration terrorism officials Daniel Benjamin and Steven Simon agree with Ruthven that the principal ideologist of the new, militaristic interpretation of the Muslim's mission in this world, who first inspired terrorists targeting Americans worldwide, was Sayyd Qutb. Write Benjamin and Simon:

> These men are descendants of Sayyid Qutb, who recoiled from the woman who accosted him aboard the ocean liner and who at a church social saw a "hall swarmed with legs." All these jihadists react to the taint or seduction they felt by espousing a violent Islamism, as though that overcorrection would erase the sin of their earlier lives.[18]

This is no exaggeration. The men responsible for suicide attacks such as the horrific 1998 bombing of the U.S. Embassy in Dar Es Salaam, Tanzania, firmly believed that great rewards awaited them in heaven.

Most commonly, the rewards are billed as above all aesthetic. Dr. Adel Sadeq, professor of psychiatry at Cairo's 'Ein Shams University, for example, characterizes the self-described martyr as undergoing "an act of transition to another, beautiful world, and he knows very well that within seconds he will see the light of his Creator. He will be as close as he can possibly be to the Creator."[19] While this inducement may satisfy the more refined killer, others require a more direct approach. Recognizing that some people are reluctant to fight merely "for the sake of Allah," verses from the Quran are invoked to indicate that "Verily, of the faithful hath God bought their persons and their substance, on condition of Paradise for them in return: on the path of God shall they fight, and slay, and be slain: a promise for this is pledged in the Law, and in the Evangel, and in the Koran—and who more faithful to his engagement than God?" (*Sura* 9:112).[20] This is interpreted by jihadists to imply that their lives are not really theirs at all but Allah's—hence He can do what He deems best, in exchange for a reserved place in heaven. In any event, those who die for His sake are not really dead: "Repute not those slain on God's path to be dead. Nay, alive with their Lord, are they richly sustained . . ." (*Sura* 3:163).[21]

Of particular interest to those disproportionately prone to sin, such holy death "on God's path" is supposed to wash away all previous transgressions. Immediate access to the highest pleasures of paradise, moreover, spares the martyr the inconvenient torments of the grave. And since the Quran is said to illustrate those pleasures specifically (e.g., the infamous "black-eyed virgins"), it is hardly surprising that such promises have proved highly successful in recruiting jihadists throughout the Middle East.

The chief mufti of the Palestinian Authority police, Sheikh 'Abd Al-Salam Abu Shukheydem, lists an even more impressive list of rewards awaiting a martyr:

> From the moment he sheds the first drop of blood, he does not feel the pain of his wounds, and he is forgiven all his sins; he sees his seat in Paradise; he is spared the torment of the grave and the great horror of Judgment Day; he marries the black-eyed [virgins]; he vouches for 70 of his family members; he receives a crown of honor inlaid with a precious stone that is more valuable than this entire world and everything in it.[22]

No wonder that prior to their martyrdom, the future warrior-murderers often visit various and sundry X-rated establishments: it is the last splurge, harmless because automatically forgiven along with all previous sins and crimes, no matter how heinous. It explains the seemingly paradoxical pre-attack debauchery of the 9/11 terrorists, who visited porno shops just before their impending suicide motivated by absolute devotion to Allah's will. A letter of instructions found in the vehicle of jihadist Nawaf al-Hazmi includes the following memo-to-self: "Do not show signs of discomfort and anxiety, be relaxed and happy . . . . Know that Paradise has been bedecked with the finest decorations in anticipation of your coming, and that the black-eyed [virgins] are calling to you."[23]

This kind of brainwashing takes place from a very early age. The children in the Hamas system, for example, are told beginning in kindergarten about the martyrs' posthumous reward of choice— seventy-two virgins in paradise. While touring Hamas schools in

Gaza, the American journalist Jack Kelley heard an eleven-year-old boasting in front of his class: "I will turn my body into a bomb that will tear the flesh of the Zionists, the sons of apes and pigs . . . I will tear their bodies into little pieces and cause them more pain than they could have ever imagined." The teacher, far from chastising the young sadist, wishes him success in the afterworld: "May the virgins give you pleasure!" Kelly also had a sixteen-year-old youth confess that "most boys cannot stop thinking about the virgins of Paradise."[24]

According to the Saudi researcher Sa'ad Al-Sowayan, writing in the Saudi daily *Al-Iqtisadiyya*, religious cassettes that are widely available throughout Saudi Arabia advocate jihad by emphasizing the sexual rewards awaiting the lucky martyr in paradise. Writes Al-Sowayan, "this kind of propaganda 'reduces the lofty objective of spiritual martyrdom to mere lust and a selfish search for sexual pleasure, regardless of what martyrdom can achieve for the public interest or for upholding Allah's word.'"[25] So we seem to have come full circle, from the materialist Western narcissist to the Islamist sex-obsessed suicide bomber. Al-Sowayan explains the reason for the obvious appeal of such rationale to young men whose hormones act roughly the same everywhere:

> The sweetest thing for a teenager, especially in a conservative society like ours, is sex, and the discourse of the religious cassettes is directed toward these very youngsters in their sexual peak of life. They reach these youth through the *hoor al-hen* [virgins], just as how the youth of our time were drawn to slide pictures of actresses and female singers.

He then explains the ideology behind the cassettes:

> They first divide the world into two parts: one belonging to God, which you are for, and the other to Satan, which you are against. The next step is to step up the value of the myth and draw the recipient into a world of mythical thinking in which rational thinking stops and the mind becomes receptive to suggestions and irrationalism.[26]

Yet mythical thinking is unavoidable: such is the nature of emotion that it reaches for any instrument of communication, anything that helps capture and convey its mysteries. Rational thinking, of course, need not be its enemy—on the contrary, it can and should reinforce the wisdom of intuition. But Al-Sowayan is absolutely right to denounce the Manichean picture of a world divided into "us" versus "them,"

221

where violence, even against oneself, is recommended on grounds that are little more than raw selfishness and a very stupid version at that.

The Search for Meaning

Freud and the divergent therapists made it clear that myths are the essential language in psychoanalysis. I speak of the Cry for myths because I believe there is an urgency in the need for myth in our day . . . . Many of the problems of our society, including cults and drug addiction, can be traced to the lack of myths which will give us as individuals the inner security we need in order to live adequately in our day. . . . The approach of a new period in history stimulates us to take stock of our past and to ask the question of the meaning we have made and are making in our lives.
Rollo May, The Cry for Myth

The celebrated psychiatrist Viktor E. Frankl, less fortunate than his erstwhile Viennese colleague Sigmund Freud who died just days after Hitler invaded Poland in 1939, spent three unimaginable years at Auschwitz and other Nazi houses of torture. This is two years more than Bettelheim, who had spent "only" a year in the concentration camps of Dachau and Buchenwald before his emigration to the United States. And yet, it was there, in the very bowels of hell on earth, that Frankl attained the sublime insights that were to guide and nourish him the rest of his life. Frankl reveals how he came to understand the holiest of human experiences: an awareness of one's own soul through that of another. In his case, this was literally life-giving.

Frankl recounts in his powerful autobiographical book *Man's Search for Meaning* how the revelation came to him on one of those horrific death marches that spelled the end of so many emaciated prisoners forced to walk against an icy wind, feet numb with pain, from one concentration camp to another. Since stumbling would be rewarded with a bullet in the head, most prisoners wouldn't make it to destination; Frankl had every reason to think it his last trip. Defying the threat of execution for daring to say anything, someone whispered, just loud enough for Frankl to hear: "If our wives could see us now! I do hope they are better off in their camps and don't know what is happening to us." Which suddenly reminded him of his own wife; Frankl records the experience:

A thought transfixed me: for the first time in my life I saw the truth as it is set into song by so many poets, proclaimed as the final wisdom by so many thinkers. The truth—that love is the ultimate and the highest goal to which man can aspire. Then I grasped the meaning of the greatest secret that human poetry and human thought and belief have to impart: *The salvation of man is through love and in love.* I understood how a man who has nothing left in this world still may know bliss, be it only for a brief moment, in the contemplation of his beloved. In a position of utter desolation, when man cannot express himself in positive action, when his only achievement may consist in enduring his suffering in the right way—an honorable way—in such a position man can, through loving contemplation of the image he carries of his beloved, achieve fulfillment. For the first time in my life I was able to understand the meaning of the words, "The angels are lost in perpetual contemplation of an infinite glory."[27]

Frankl's epiphany is not unique: the conviction that God manifests Himself through love lies at the basis of every religion. To be sure, not all love is sexual—and Frankl fully recognizes this. That said, a cherished image of a human being such as one's spouse or soulmate is especially potent. If we are lucky and as wise as poets, we may be granted a vision of the truth understood as "contemplation of an infinite glory." Angels have the capability of enjoying this bliss on a "perpetual" basis; we are given mere occasional glimpses. But in such a moment, we know that bliss is a vision of magic as the loving partners become one.

The marriage relationship is the paradigmatic fusion into one meta-phorical "flesh." As Robert Davidson, professor of Old Testament at the University of Glasgow, writes in the essay on *Genesis* published as part of the series *The Cambridge Bible Commentary*, in this context "flesh" evidently means more than "the physical side of life; it is the medium through which the whole personality communicates its varied emotions, longings, joys and fears." Davidson observes that, while in most cultures it is of course the woman who actually has to leave *her* home in order to be united with a man to whom she is married, in the case of the *Genesis*, "the narrator is neither lawyer nor sociologist. He is grappling on a religious level with the need and loneliness of man."[28] Hence his description of the union in "one flesh" is entirely appropriate precisely *because* the figure of speech is primarily metaphorical.

In fact, the rather grotesque image from Plato's *Symposium* of lovers actually merging into a previously spliced four-legged creature, described earlier in chapter 3, which a literal interpretation of "one flesh" might suggest, is precisely the opposite message of *Genesis*. After tasting the forbidden fruit, Adam and Eve both recognize their *otherness*, which is not primarily, certainly not merely, sexual. They

223

are suddenly aware of being capable of (and, conversely, subject to) admiration as well as contempt: the other is a separate individual endowed with the power to evaluate.

The consequence of this new realization is that they become "ashamed"—a feeling inconceivable to a creature incapable of normative judgment. Both Adam and Eve are suddenly concerned that the other might find something wrong in their appearance; they need some distance, not only in order to understand and appraise one another fairly but to conceal what might be a source of potential embarrassment. C. S. Lewis observes in his perceptive little book *The Four Loves* that "naked" is a passive verb with good reason: clothing being a form of protection, to be "made naked" is a serious proposition. The recognition of nakedness represents an awareness of vulnerability—one's own as much as another's. In that sense, it represents consciousness of the potential for evil, whether toward oneself or another, as well as the possibility of mutual protection. We become one flesh when that mutuality is not only understood but welcomed: another person is simultaneously known to be different and accepted as such—not despite but *because* of his (or her) otherness. Once the difference is not only noticed but embraced, love becomes possible. After all, without awareness and appreciation of otherness, love is little more than a form of reciprocal narcissism—*narcissisme a deux.*

This is the ultimate message of the myth of Psyche and Eros, recounted by Apuleius in *The Golden Ass,* whose motif has been found in a large number of folktales spanning the spectrum of cultural traditions. Jungian psychologist Erich Neumann highlights the antiquity of one particular theme:

> The idea that the human soul is not passively cleansed and purified, but actively imposes the same purification upon the loving Eros, is prefigured in the folk tale and achieves its full meaning in the myth of Psyche. Here it is not Psyche alone who is transformed; her destiny is indissolubly intertwined with that of Eros, her partner. We have then a myth of the relation between man and woman.[29]

It had been Psyche who, by seeking to see her lover's face, had first dared to want more than a sexual relationship. It was she who descended into the underworld and carried out difficult tasks imposed by a jealous Aphrodite, though it was Eros who eventually persuaded Zeus to let them be together—whereupon Zeus elevated Psyche to the status of goddess. The Soul or Psyche and Love or Eros have since been inexorably connected: thus is Soul inseparable from Love, and their child is blissful, sublime Pleasure.

Choosing to Be Together, However Briefly

> *Son of Laertes, versatile Odysseus,*
> *After these years with me, you still desire*
> *Your old home? . . . Can mortals*
> *Compare with goddesses in grace and form?*
> *"My lady goddess, here is no cause for anger.*
> *My quiet Penelope—how well I know—*
> *Would seem a shade before your majesty,*
> *Death and old age being unknown to you,*
> *While she must die. Yet, it is true, each day*
> *I long for home, long for the sight of home.*
> Homer, The Odyssey

> *After all these years, I see that I was mistaken about Eve in the begin-*
> *ning:* it is better to live outside the Garden with her than inside it
> without her. *At first I thought she talked too much; but now I should be*
> *sorry to have that voice fall silent and pass out of my life. Blessed be the*
> *chestnut [forbidden fruit] that brought us near together and taught me*
> *to know the goodness of her heart and the sweetness of her spirit!*
> Mark Twain, Adam and Eve (emphasis added)

The epic story of Odysseus captures dramatically the stark choice before the celebrated hero: a gorgeous, eternally young, ravishing mistress versus his own aged wife. How can he possibly make the immortal Calypso understand that her beauty, however stunning, is no match for his dearest soulmate? Odysseus tries by explaining that in his own mind, Penelope *is his home*: he can almost hear her soft voice calling him to the table, and he yearns for the moment when he will be able to share his improbable adventures with her. When he finally does so, they cannot stop talking. Calypso could never know what it is like to grow old with someone. She lacks man's most important treasure: the terrible luxury of ephemeral joy.

In the myth of Psyche and Eros, the God of Love chooses a mortal precisely because she is richer than any deity, capable of bestowing the ultimate gift to the one she loves: her life. Writes Erich Neumann:

> Through Psyche's sacrifice and death the divine lover is changed
> from a wounded boy to a man and savior, because in Psyche he
> finds something that exists only in the earthly human middle zone
> between heaven and underworld: the feminine mystery of rebirth
> through love. In no goddess can Eros experience and know the

miracle that befalls him through the human Psyche, the phenomenon of a love which is conscious, which, stronger than death, anointed with divine beauty, is willing to die, to receive the beloved as bridegroom of death.[30]

It is for that willingness that she is resurrected in the Greek tale, transposed into the realm of myth to illustrate the mystery of love. Neumann interprets this as evidence "that the soul's individual ability to love is divine and that transformation by love is a mystery that deifies . . . . It is the experience of mortality, the passage through death to rebirth and resurrection to Eros, that makes Psyche divine in a mystery of transformation . . . ."[31]

C. S. Lewis rightly defines the essence of Eros as aiming not at pleasure narrowly understood, nor at happiness as mere mirth: "For it is the very mark of Eros that when he is in us we had rather share *unhappiness* with the Beloved than be happy on any other terms."[32] Even though erotic love alone is obviously not *the* quintessential Love that leads to spiritual union, neither is it to be disparaged. That higher union is the product of all four kinds of love, which Lewis identifies as Affection, Friendship, and Charity—all at least if not *more* important than the fourth and final, Eros. Erotic love alone is never sufficient— Homer's Odysseus and Mark Twain's Adam both fully appreciate this. And yet, of the four kinds of love, Eros can transport us, as can no other emotion, into a realm beyond the self. It is through Eros that most of us can reach that ultimate, Higher Love, which C. S. Lewis calls "Love Himself."

That said, emotion is by no means the most reliable foundation on which to base the deepest relationship among two individuals, the principle most conducive to morality and mutual respect. Reason alone can grasp that no man may treat another as a means to his own selfish ends, that each person must respect another as an end in himself—in other words, that every human being is spiritually on a par with every other. Inequalities among us inevitably abound, for humans differ greatly in qualities and assets. And yet, no matter how shortsighted, selfish, and congenitally prone to choosing hastily and unwisely, imperfect men and women are mercifully endowed with sufficient insight to appreciate what it means for God to have created us in His own image.

The fortunate may be graced to find a soulmate who mirrors, however faintly, the love between ourselves and our Creator. But hardly anyone goes through life without feeling very close to some other human being—often more than one, each in a different way but still close. In this larger—largest—sense, we are all soulmates, our temporary sojourn on this earth rendered more bearable by the thought that we can rejoice in one another to lighten the burden of knowledge.

Notes

1.   Admittedly, there is a catch: "only after you finished the research phase *and had been in love for many years* can you determine if the person you are with is indeed your soulmate" (Italics added). www.solvedating.com/soulmates-definition.html.

2.   Thomas Moore, *Soul Mates: Honoring the Mysteries of Love and Relationships*, xvii.

3.   C. G. Jung, *Modern Man in Search of a Soul*, 175.

4.   Ibid., 200.

5.   Ibid., 197.

6.   Ibid., 204.

7.   Bruno Bettelheim, *Freud and Man's Soul*, 36.

8.   Ibid., 79. Cited in Ernest Jones, *Free Associations*

9.   Ibid.

10.   Ibid., 5.

11.   Ibid., 40.

12.   Ibid., 12.

13.   Ibid., 15.

14.   Ibid., 76.

15.   Hamid Enayat, *Modern Islamic Political Thought*, 191.

16.   Ibid., 194.

17.   Malisse Ruthven, *A Fury for God*, 76.

18.   Daniel Benjamin and Steven Simon, *The Age of Sacred Terror*, 165.

19.   Clip no. 927, April 25, 2002, *Martyrdom*, MEMRI, 98.

20.   *The Koran*, 129.

21.   Ibid., 46.

22.   Al-Hayat Al-Jadida (Palestinian Authority), September 17, 1999. Cited in *Inquiry and Analysis* No. 411, MEMRI, Dec. 2007

23.   Al-Sharq Al-Awsat (London), September 30, 2007. Cited in ibid., *Inquiry and Analysis*, No. 411.

24.   *USA Today*, June 26, 2001.

25.   Special Dispatch No. 1032, November 23, 2005, Ibid., 123.

26.   Ibid., 124.

27.   Viktor E. Frankl, *Man's Search for Meaning: An Introduction to Logotherapy*, 60–61.

28.   R. Davidson, *Genesis 1–11*, 38.

29.   Erich Neumann, *Amor and Psyche: The Psychic Development of the Feminine*, 158.

30.   Ibid., 125.

31.   Ibid., 136.

32.   C. S. Lewis, *The Four Loves*, 107 (emphasis added).

11

I–Thou

*The life of human beings is not passed in the sphere of transitive verbs
alone. It does not exist in virtue of activities alone which have some
thing for their object. I perceive something. I am sensible of something.
I will something. I feel something. I think something. The life of human
beings does not consist of all this and the like alone. This and the like
together establish the realm of It. But the real of Thou has a different
basis. When Thou is spoken, the speaker has no thing for his object . . . .
The primary word I–Thou establishes the world of relation.*
Martin Buber, I and Thou

The realm of *It*, as Buber explains, consists of objects and, more
to the point, object-like people who mean little to one another. They
include the fellow passengers on the metro, whose names we don't
(and have no wish to) know. They include waiters who bring us cof-
fee, hairdressers, and valets, whom we reward with tips for their
good service. Most of life involves such relations; without them, we
could not live. *I–It* relationships are necessary, but to live fully, we
must seek and nurture reciprocal, mutually reinforcing connections.
Buber's word: *I–Thou.*

A little grammatical housekeeping, however, may be in order.
Brushing up on some elementary rules of English usage could help
us better understand what Buber means by living in the sphere of
transitive verbs. The root of the word "transitive" is "transaction"—
indicating a kind of *exchange* between an actor and a recipient of action.
(I will coin, if I may, the awkward word "actee.") Where the exchange
is unidirectional, the actor is the agent, while the actee is passive:
for example, the transitive verb "to murder" refers to the action of a
criminal against his victim. Where the relationship is asymmetrical,
both have some degree of power, but it is usually unequal. A transitive
relationship might be considered relatively symmetrical if both subject
and object have something to gain from the interaction no matter who
originally "initiated" it: for example "to guide" is transitive, as are "to

paint" and "to heal," because in each case, there is a subject and an object who both "profit" from the exchange. When we hire guides, painters, or doctors, what makes the relationship asymmetrical or symmetrical is context: the putative employee may well be the net gainer in a tight-enough market.

But enough of transitivity. What mainly differentiates a transitive from an intransitive verb is that the latter may NOT take object: most obvious examples are "to awaken" and "to die." Intransitivity, that is, can and often does take place in solitude, with no witnesses. But here's the catch: if intransitivity dooms us to aloneness, transitivity does not necessarily save us from it. In an *I–It* relationship, we are still objects to one another.

Put differently, an *I–It* transitive relationship maintains distance between the linked objects, no matter who initiates or even controls the interaction, and no matter who is supposed to "profit" from the exchange. For at a most fundamental level, at the end of the day, an *I–It* relationship is spiritually barren. "It" refers to something fundamentally foreign to the self, something that could be in-human, or perhaps a-human, but certainly not human-as-I-am. In contrast to an *I–It* exchange, a relationship that involves personal insight and empathy is something entirely different—it is thereby transformative. No longer a mere relationship but a communion, where neither party is merely an object: this is what Buber means by as *I–Thou*.

Thou refers to a personal-other, a being like oneself, no less a child of God. Hence *I–Thou* captures intimacy, mutuality, soul connection. It involves, ideally, both respect and love. To be sure, we not only do but indeed must interact with most people in a nonintrusive manner, but can we even imagine what it would be like to have never felt empathy for another? Someone for whom other people are nothing but objects is dubiously human. Buber puts it pithily: "without *It* a man cannot live; but he who lives with *It* alone is not a man."[1]

The word "marry" offers a perfect example. A quintessentially transitive verb, it may describe a standard *I–It* relationship if a marriage is little more than a contract, with each side reaping benefits—sexual, social, economic, even political, as in the case of some (actually, most) royal couplings—which may in fact be roughly equal, though often one side benefits more than the other. Insofar as the marriage partners are mere "objects" to one another, however, the two agents are involved in a strictly *I–It* relationship. Contractual arrangements, no matter how voluntary, are *I–It*.

It may be tempting to think that reciprocated romantic love constitutes the paradigmatic *I–Thou* relationship, its very apogee: Don't two infatuated lovers seem to merge with one another? Doesn't the biblical expression referring to Adam's instant recognition that Eve was his counterpart, leading to their becoming "as if one flesh," capture precisely that image? Ah yes, love at first sight! The spectacle of two starstruck lovers gazing into one another's eyes, oblivious to the rest of the world, is many people's idea of the perfect fusion of two hearts. The perennial story that never seems to go out of fashion is centered on yearning for the ultimate merger. Surely that is *I–Thou* writ large, where two sexually attracted individuals, body and soul, seek satisfaction in one another, is it not? Well—yes, maybe . . . and maybe not.

The selfish nature of lustful passion is easily camouflaged when both parties share the same goal, when sexual satisfaction is what they are both after. In a dance of reciprocal hunger, the difference between the two individuals seems to become gradually obliterated. At first, as each *I* believes to have possessed the other, the resulting synthesis expands the self into an apparent doubling—not unlike Plato's hermaphrodite sphere resulting from two reunited halves. Except that here, each half is an emotional carbon copy of itself, each perceives the other as the incarnation of what he or she desires, incapable of—and (unbeknownst to either) not especially interested in—transcending beyond the self. The urgency once quenched, what looked like absolute ecstasy all too soon proves to be no more than counterfeit gold, concocted by a self-deceptive alchemy. Once it dawns on the two ephemerally mesmerized individuals how divergent their perceptions of the universe really are, the original mirage gradually evaporates.

An *I–Thou* relationship involves not merely a mutually satisfactory relationship, no matter how "total" and even spiritual it may seem. Rather, the *I–Thou* relationship refers to a profound appreciation of another's deepest essence, another's core being, another's very soul. Whether or not that appreciation is reinforced by physical—including sexual—interaction is, if not irrelevant, certainly secondary. Thus Adam and Eve were "like one flesh" quite apart from whether or not they actually "knew" each other in a sexual sense. But were they *soulmates-at-first-sight*? Were they the paradigm example of an *I–Thou* relationship, always empathetic? Not likely. After all, they were . . . only human.

I for Thee

My beloved is mine and I am his.
Song of Songs *2:16*

Immediately after having been created, Adam and Eve may be assumed to have been harmoniously interrelated in a pristine *I–Thou* relationship, where both desire the same thing as the other at all times, and there is no discord. Admittedly, they do not actually seem to have desires as such: they simply do everything that God tells them and nothing else, without seeming to realize that there is any other option. It is not even clear that they are aware of such a thing as desire. Even Adam's loneliness was discerned by God rather than by himself. Adam did not ask for a helpmate; it was God who sought it for him, and not finding a "fitting" one, He created it metaphorically from Adam's own flesh.

The moment that God forbade the first couple to eat from the Tree of Knowledge, the possibility of choice awakened in the two humans an awareness, as yet unconscious, of their own individual desires and interests upon which they may or may not act in accordance with God's commandment. "Do not" means "you might—but mustn't." The prohibition—God's first—was a lesson: the first humans were being confronted with the experience of freedom. They were made to *feel* what it means to deliberate, decide, and—of course—err.

When the serpent's crafty arguments in favor of indulging Eve's curiosity (and appetite) contradict God's advice, the woman ponders the additional evidence and, in the end, decides to trust her own judgment rather than God's. She thus implicitly *judges* that it is she, not God, who knows what is in her best interests. She then *chooses* to taste the fruit and thereby taking a chance at making a mistake. When the fruit turns out to taste delicious, she encourages Adam to taste it as well, which he does, with no seeming hesitation. They both soon realize that they had both been *wrong*: they had made a decision that turned out badly. This taught them that what may *seem* desirable is not always *truly* good, a fact that is not always immediately obvious but depends on future *consequences*.

The momentous event is, I submit, more appropriately called *the Spring* rather than *the Fall* because it inaugurates a life of seasons and change (though—minor detail—it appears to have followed a kind of endless summer in balmy, verdant Eden). What is more, Adam and Eve now know that they are distinct individuals, who suddenly "sprung" (pun definitely intended) into existence with separate identities and interests, however intertwined their fates would always remain. Once they notice they are naked, they feel ashamed. Yet to be ashamed is to fear some sort of harm. We are ashamed if we have done something wrong or fear that we may have exposed too much of ourselves (physically or otherwise). (For that reason, I cannot feel ashamed before someone who cannot evaluate me: I may be afraid of a lion, but certainly not ashamed. When I feel ashamed, I am conscious of being judged imperfect in some way and potentially humiliated by disapproval.)

Adam and Eve proceed to hide their nakedness from one another by stitching together fig leaves. At the same time, they become aware that they could also . . . seduce one another. With clothing came the added allure of imagination and expectation, of delayed gratification and enhanced sexual attraction, the rich possibilities of culture and mystery. Given the simultaneous consciousness of one's ability to tease, frustrate, and deceive, clothing would be both blessing and calamity. Sex would become, well, interesting.

In brief, this is the first necessary condition for a genuine *I–Thou* relationship: only when another is perceived as indeed altogether *other* than a relationship of complete love and respect is even possible. *I* and *Thou* do not and should not literally merge: they become *as if* one flesh but they *are* not one and must not think of themselves as such. After eating the forbidden fruit, that is precisely what happened to Adam and Eve: they come to see each other, as if for the first time, as individuals in their own right. Their eyes are opened to their separateness.

As individuals, they are simultaneously terrified of God's wrath and overwhelmed by the instinct for self-preservation—that primal, selfish drive we share with all the animals. Thus when God interrogates Adam about the circumstances of his disobedience, Adam explains that he was following in Eve's footsteps: it was *she*, really, who decided to eat it, she disobeyed first, while he was just following along. She was the "decider," not him: "The woman you gave me . . . she gave me fruit." (*Genesis* 3:12). In his desperation, he even takes on his own Creator: he blames God for having created his helpmate! This is not just *chutzpa*; it is blasphemy. Then, temporarily forgetting that his accuser happens to be omniscient, Adam tries to shift the blame to Eve—testifying against her, as it were.

To her credit, Eve simply blames the serpent, pleading gullibility: "He duped me, so I ate it." (*Genesis* 3:13). After all, she *could* have said (not that she *should* have, mind you!), "Well, You, God, told only Adam not to eat the fruit, remember? You did not actually speak to me. I only learned about this from him, and wasn't sure whether the dunce—he is a *guy*, after all—may have misunderstood or even mis-spoken, so in a way Adam is more to blame than me . . ."—or words to that effect. Though she was obviously in no position to save her brother-husband, at least she acted as his "keeper" by not trying to harm him further. While God's omniscience obviously rendered both pleas irrelevant in the Edenic pseudo-trial, they do indicate an awareness of culpability, representing the first appeal in history to "mitigating circumstances."

In sum, the experience of eating from the forbidden tree taught Adam and Eve that something may be good or bad for us, though we as mere humans may not know it, even—indeed especially—when we are convinced that we do. Eve's judgment was just as flawed as Adam's, and they both paid for their mistake. Most important, the couple realized that they are both fallible with regard to one another as well as themselves. These are all critically significant distinctions. In this instance, the fruit had calamitous consequences for both of them; in other cases, what might be good for one may well be harm-ful to another. Eve did not mean to hurt Adam by suggesting he too eat of the fruit; on the contrary, she thought it would be beneficial for him as well as herself. She thought he would like it as much as she did. Intentions, however, are not enough. Sometimes they are in fact positively harmful.

The philosopher Michael Novak uses the term *caritas* to describe the highest form of love as willing "not what you wish for the other, nor what the other wishes, but the real good."[2] In other words, this requires us "to will the good of the other as other"—a proposition altogether different from supporting what someone else wishes, no matter what it may be. That is clearly not real love: my beloved may be unwittingly self-destructive. But it is very important to re-member that just because I *think* I know what another really wants or needs—whether he or she is aware of it—does not mean that I am right.

In some cases, it is relatively easy to demonstrate with reasonable certainty that a particular choice is unwise: for instance, that ingesting a certain substance would produce side-effects that are harmful enough to override other, all too fleeting advantages. The morning-after hangover following a night of carousing is not typical—most situations are far more problematic. Warning (to all mothers, but especially to Jewish mothers of adult children): you may be wrong to think yourself in a better position to know another person's *real* interests, no matter how much love you might feel. In a genuinely reciprocal relationship, you should not—*must* not—presume to decide for another.

God teaches Adam and Eve (and for that matter, the serpent) the relevant lesson of freedom: each receives his and her respective punishment so each may recognize his and her individual *responsibility*. Yet at the same time, God impresses upon them how much they are loved, clothing them before they are sent away, to the east of Eden. While angry with them, God does not cease to protect them. To be sure, outside Eden, the first humans would have to care for one another amid dangers and hardship. They could not count on God to make their decisions. But they could always count in His love. God cannot decide for mankind without obliterating freedom, which dignity requires as a prerequisite. Moreover, without freedom, without the ability to evaluate our own actions and that of others, without an appreciation for what constitutes good and evil, mankind could not behold the universe and see, as had God, that it is *good*—which is the reason why God created mankind in the first place.

In sum, an *I–Thou* relationship must not be confused with an *I for Thee* situation, where one person either subsumes his will to another or, conversely, presumes to will for another (in the latter's presumed benefit). For both to subsume their wills to the other is theoretically impossible, as children discover when they play the game of "I'll go where you want to go:" they end up immobile, stuck in paradox. What is far from impossible, however, is to will selflessly, to take another's feelings and desires into consideration. What is clearly *not* compatible with an *I–Thou* relationship, for it destroys the essential requirement of complete mutuality, is placing one's own interests above those of another to the point of hurting him or her, thus treating *Thou* as an *It*.

I–Thou as Moral Imperative

Man is without qualification equal even to higher beings in that none has the right to use him according to pleasure. This is because of his reason—reason considered not insofar as it is a tool to the

*satisfaction of his inclinations, but insofar as it makes him an end in
himself.*
Immanuel Kant, The Critique of Practical Reason

The bachelor German philosopher Immanuel Kant, a pillar of
modern liberalism, is best known for his monumental (if utterly
incomprehensible to all but the most persistent students of philosophy) *Critique of Pure Reason* (1781) and the shorter but still rather
opaque *Foundations of the Metaphysics of Morals* (1785). Far more
accessible is a virtually forgotten, intriguing little essay published in
1786 under the title "Conjectural Beginning of Human History." A
kind of allegory based on the first two chapters of *Genesis*, this highly
unusual piece is perfectly serious. (The closest Kant ever came to
displaying a sense of humor was in naming his essay on international
law *Perpetual Peace*.)

Why would Kant write about *Genesis*? At the outset, Kant begs his
reader to favor him "with the permission to use, as a map for [his] trip,
a sacred document," proposing to show that such a "trip—undertaken
on the wings of the imagination, albeit not without a clue rationally
derived from experience—may take the very route sketched out in
that document."[3] He recommends (again, without a trace of droll-
ery) consulting it, to check "at every point" how perfectly the road
"which philosophy takes with the help of concepts coincides with
the story told in [the] Holy Writ."[4] In other words, Kant proposes to
demonstrate that the path of biblical narrative leads to the same end
as that of Reason Herself—presumably the highest compliment that
the sovereign of eighteenth-century Enlightenment could pay to the
nearly eclipsed monarch discipline, Theology.

Kant concedes the story's intrinsic advantage over irresponsible
quasi-scientific conjectures regarding man's beginnings: human reason
simply cannot derive "the existence of man" from prior natural causes.
Genesis is also perfectly applicable to ethical theory, which assumes
the moral agent to be an adult capable of making his own decisions. In
addition, the first humans must obviously be a pair so as to procreate
and thereby constitute a social unit. But the unit must be kept to only
one couple, "in order that war should not originate at once, what with
men being close to each other and yet strangers." Finally, man would
also have to be able to speak, indeed in coherent concepts, which is
to say he must be capable of thinking and deliberation. Since all these
assumptions are contained in *Genesis*, it seems ideally suited to Kant's

philosophical inquiry, which is "to consider the development of manners and morals in his way of life."

That development, in Kant's view, started as soon as man tasted the forbidden fruit, which amounted to "the first attempt at a free choice." Its effect would be cataclysmic:

> He discovered in himself a power of choosing for himself a way of life, of not being bound without alternative to a single way, like the animals. Perhaps the discovery of this advantage created a moment of delight. But of necessity, anxiety and alarm as to how he was to deal with this newly discovered power quickly followed; for man was a being who did not yet know either the secret properties or the remote effects of anything. He stood, as it were, at the brink of an abyss. Until that moment, instinct had directed him toward specific objects of desire. But from these there now opened up an infinity of such objects, and he did not yet know how to choose between them. On the other hand, it was impossible for him to return to the state of servitude (i.e., subjection to instinct) from the state of freedom, once he had tasted the latter.[5]

That freedom, in other words, was double edged. On the one hand, man could no longer fail to see that his actions had consequences, some desirable and some not, while at the same time he could discern that he had it in his power to postpone some immediate goods in exchange for others that were more distant but perhaps more desirable. The moral agent could appreciate moreover that delay sometimes augments gratification—in no other domain as obviously as in that of sexuality. By means of the imagination, pleasure can be immeasurably increased as well as sublimated.

This is why, according to Kant, the fig leaf to which Adam and Eve were said to have resorted upon noticing each other's nakedness "was a far greater manifestation of reason" because "it reflects consciousness of a certain degree of mastery of reason over impulse. Refusal was the feat which brought about the passage from merely sensual to spiritual attractions, from mere animal desire gradually to love." So the first advance over the brutes was to recognize that mere sensuality is inferior to something higher, more spiritual, which more properly deserves to be called love. Nor is that all: "in addition, there came a first hint at the development of man as a moral creature. This came from the sense of decency, which is an inclination to inspire others to respect by proper manners, i.e., by concealing all that which might arouse low esteem. Here, incidentally, lies the real basis of all true sociability." The desire for respect is at the basis of all civilization—as is the ability and willingness to confer it upon others.

What Kant calls merely a small beginning was nevertheless irreversible, soon to be followed by the step which raised man altogether above the animals. That step took place arrived the moment he understood,

> however obscurely, that he is the true end of nature, and that nothing that lives on earth can compete with him in this regard. The first time he ever said to the sheep, "nature has given you the skin you wear for my use, not for yours"; the first time he ever took that skin and put it upon himself (*Genesis* 3:21)—that time he became aware of the way in which his nature privileged and raised him above all animals.[6]

So God allowed man to use everything in nature for his own ends, with one exception: other humans. It may be worth noting that Kant in no way condones thereby the inhumane treatment of animals. Even less does he rule out close relationships with our linguistically challenged creatures, who—as anyone whose alarm clock is a face-licking kitten, and any dog owner who is treated like the canine equivalent of Zeus, will readily testify—often deserve to be treated better than many humans. But the ethical relationship is, logically speaking, different. We should treat animals with kindness; we must treat human beings with respect.

Here is, in brief, Kant's summary of the moral lesson of human creation:

> Thus man had entered into a relation of equality with all rational beings, whatever their rank (*Genesis* 3:22), with respect to the claim of being an end in himself, respected as such by everyone, a being which no one might treat as a mere means to ulterior ends. So far as natural gifts are concerned, other beings may surpass man beyond all comparison. Nevertheless, man is without qualification equal even to higher beings in that none has the right to use him according to pleasure. This is because of his reason—reason considered not insofar as it is a tool to the satisfaction of his inclinations, but insofar as it makes him an end in himself. Hence this last step of reason is at the same time man's release from the womb of nature, an alteration of condition which is honorable, to be sure, but also fraught with danger.[7]

Being created in God's image is no small honor, though it comes with exceptional burdens, among which knowledge of one's own death is by far the heaviest. That knowledge, when fully realized, is the ultimate loneliness. Against that loneliness, and the certainty of its verdict, man has sought, and sometimes even found, a modicum of solace. When such solace is felt as a spiritual, perhaps even mystical, experience, it is often described as boundless, joyful peace.

I–Thou as Spiritual Bond

Only those into which Love Himself has entered will ascend to Love Himself.
C. S. Lewis, The Four Loves

The categorical imperative severed from emotion by the steely knife of logic is certainly a useful moral precept. It liberates the agent from having to base his actions either on religious faith or on personal inclination; instead, he can rely on Reason. Universal and subject to our control, Reason is reliable: we can all understand what it means to treat another as an end and never as a means. Personal inclination, by contrast, is fickle: we may not be capable of loving our neighbor as ourselves, or care about him (or her) at all. We might even hate the wretched neighbor, as Cain did his own brother Abel. And yet, we have no right to harm, let alone kill someone simply out of dislike. No one man is entitled to set himself above another. Abel upset Cain enough for Cain to want him out of the way: thus did Abel become an *It* for Cain, a nonhuman noxious object, to be eliminated like a fly or another irksome beast. It is no accident that terrorists show contempt for their victims by referring to them as pigs or monkeys, that Nazis declared Jews to be an inferior race of cockroaches, and that communist dictators speak of exterminating their political opponents as one talks of eradicating filthy rats.

To treat another as a *Thou* requires first, as indicated in the previous section, complete respect regardless of personal feelings. But to engage in an *I–Thou* relationship is an additional step, far more difficult since it assumes affective—emotionally, though unselfishly, experienced—spiritual mutuality. Martin Buber describes it in aphoristic, poetic, prose:

The primary word *I-Thou* establishes the world of relation . . . . .
The *Thou* meets me through grace—it is not found by seeking . . . . .
The *Thou* meets me. But I step into direct relation with it. . . . .
The primary word *I-Thou* can be spoken only with the whole being.
The relation to the *Thou* is direct. No system of ideas, no foreknowledge, and no fancy intervene between *I and Thou*. . . . .

No aim, no lust, and no anticipation intervene between *I and Thou.* . . . .
Only when every means has collapsed does the meeting come about.[8]

It is exceptionally difficult to grasp the idea that every *I–Thou* relationship, often described by the simpler but more fluid and ambiguous
word "love," is in effect a reflection of God's love for us. Again C. S.
Lewis finds words to capture this notion eloquently: "We were made
for God. Only by being in some respect like Him, only by being a
manifestation of His beauty, loving-kindness, wisdom or goodness,
has any earthly Beloved excited our love."[9]

Practically the same sentiment is expressed by Michael Novak,
who suggests that God should be understood as "radiating his presence throughout creation, calling unworthy human beings to be his
friends, and infusing into them his love so that they might love with
it."[10] *Caritas,* or an I–Thou relationship of spiritual communion, "is our
participation in a way of loving not our own. It is our participation—
partial, fitful, hesitant, imperfect—in his own loving."[11]

Writes Martin Buber, "Every particular *Thou* is a glimpse through
to the eternal *Thou*; by means of every particular *Thou*, the primary
word addresses the eternal *Thou*."[12] Through the relationship of I-
Thou, respect linked to love, man is able to catch a glimpse of God's
love for him. That relationship is first known in Eden, between Adam
and Eve. Once they notice one another's separateness, nakedness,
and ability to harm one another, they also become aware of God's
otherness, while realizing that no human being can presume to
know what is best for him—neither his own self nor that of another.
Yet there is great comfort in knowing that God cares, that there is
at least in principle the idea of good, even if none of us may ever
grasp it. The best we can do is allow one another to make our own
mistakes, though love and caring necessarily impel us to try to help
others when we feel they make the wrong choice. And no, we are not
one another's keeper in the sense of having the right to decide FOR
someone else. That said, we most certainly are prohibited—as Cain
learned too late—from hurting anyone. "Am I my brother's keeper"
is plainly answered, "No, not literally. But yes, you may not hurt him
lest you become less than human."

I through Thee

> *Through the Thou man becomes I.*
> *Martin Buber,* I and Thou

We come at last to the reason why God created man and woman for each to *be* through the other and, thereby, for both to truly *be*, through Him. Through their mutual love, made possible through the grace of God, Adam and Eve come to understand *themselves*: not as solitary beings, in competition with one another in a hostile natural environment, but as partners in beholding each other's soul and the wonder of creation.

At last, Psyche and Eros are united through one another's devotion, strengthened by their ordeal following their separation. Writes Martin Lowenthal:

> According to the myth, your unique contribution to the whole, the result of the alchemical marriage at the end, comes, not so much from what you are given—the beauty, royal birth, and fame that both Eros and Psyche have—but from the wounds you receive, the difficulties you confront, your surrender and service to what seems terrifying but is simply unknown and mysterious to you, and the steadiness of your intention to pursue what you love.[13]

None of this is possible without the spiritual dimension, love as a manifestation of something transcending any one individual, indeed the world itself. The myth, he continues,

> integrates passion and love with the spiritual, calling on us to live all of life intimately and erotically. This marriage of aliveness and love in the context of the sacred constitutes the erotic, where we experience everything, not only sex, with wholehearted intimacy and engagement. The greater, sacred meaning of the erotic animates the core of this story [of Eros and Psyche], suggesting that the divorce of our sensory and passionate nature from our spiritual nature can lead to despair and distortions in the way we live.[14]

A surprisingly similar message may be found in a rather unexpected source: the sermons of John Paul II. The Polish Pope, as he was affectionately known, explained that sexuality "is by no means something purely biological, but concerns the innermost being of the human person as such. It is realized in a truly human way only if it is an integral part of the love by which physical self-giving would be a lie if it were not the sign and fruit of a total personal self-giving, in which the whole person, including the temporal dimension, is present."[15]

"In that complete mutuality," he says, "God is necessarily present." "God loves His people . . . . [and is] proclaimed through the living and concrete word whereby a man and a woman express their conjugal love. Their bond of love becomes the image and the symbol of the covenant which unites God and his people."[16]

Through love for another, I find myself, God willing. But does this mean that I find God too? That I feel God's love for man? No one can ever be certain; C. S. Lewis confesses, "God knows, not I, whether I have ever tasted this love. Perhaps I have only imagined the tasting."[17] To imagine a taste is still far from experiencing the taste itself. But it is certainly a start. To wonder about something one may have never known is, at a minimum, to feel its absence. And thus, continues Lewis, "if we cannot 'practice the presence of God,' it is something to practice the absence of God, to become increasingly aware of our unawareness till we feel like men who should stand beside a great cataract and hear no noise, or like a man in a story who looks in a mirror and finds no face there, or a man in a dream who stretches out his hand to visible objects and gets no sensation of touch"—which, in some ways, is already everything. "[T]o know that one is dreaming is to be no longer perfectly asleep."[18] To awaken takes courage, and it takes trust. It takes believing that we are here for a reason, and we are not alone. It means that we are blessed with consciousness and the ability to appreciate that the world is good.

Whatever we may choose to call Him, whether Yawheh or Allah or Christ, we can still awaken. Writes Buber, "Men have addressed their eternal Thou with many names. In singing of him who was thus named, they always had the Thou in mind: the first myths were hymns of praise." To praise His creation is to enter into the ultimate relation, whether we know it or not. In fact, even he "who abhors, and believe himself to be godless," Buber insists, if he "gives his whole being to addressing the Thou of his life, as a Thou that cannot be limited by another, he addresses God."[19] Ultimately we must admit to ourselves that God is beyond human conception.

Theologian Paul Tillich, who was close to Buber, expresses this most dramatically when he suggests that man, if he is honest to himself, realizes that God's truly spiritual nature is forever elusive: then and only then can man find the courage to be what he was meant to be, through the ability to truly love another and himself. "The ultimate source of the courage to be is the 'God above God' .... the object of all mystical longing, but mysticism also must be transcended in order to reach him," writes Tillich. "*The courage to be is rooted in the God who appears when God has disappeared in the anxiety of doubt.*"[20]

Notes

1. *The Writings of Martin Buber,* "I and Thou," 55.
2. Michael Novak, "The Love that Moves the Sun," in *A Free Society Reader,* 100.
3. Immanuel Kant, *On History,* 54.
4. Ibid.
5. Ibid., 56.
6. Ibid., 58.
7. Ibid., 59.
8. *The Writings of Martin Buber,* 45.
9. C. S. Lewis, *The Four Loves,* 139.
10. Michael Novak, *Free Society Reader, t*99.
11. Ibid.
12. *The Writings of Martin Buber,* 55.
13. Martin Lowenthal, *Alchemy of the Soul: The Eros and Psyche Myth as a Guide to Transformation,* 51.
14. Ibid., 52.
15. Pope John Paul II, *Familiaris Consortio,* Part Two, "Man, the Image of the God Who is Love," sec. 11.
16. Ibid., sec. 12.
17. C. S. Lewis, *The Four Loves,* 140
18. Ibid., 141.
19. Buber, *The Writings of Martin Buber,* 55.
20. Paul Tillich, *The Courage to Be,* 188–90.

Epilogue

What we call the beginning is often the end
And to make an end is to make a beginning.
The end is where we start from.
With the drawing of this Love and the voice of this Calling
We shall not cease from exploration
And the end of all our exploring
Will be to arrive where we started
And know the place for the first time.
Through the unknown, remembered gate
When the last of earth left to discover
Is that which was the beginning.
T. S. Eliot, Four Quartets

The end is where we start: from dust we come and to dust we return. From Love we emerge, helpless and naked, and in Love we find our home. The gate we closed behind us once we departed the Eden of our innocence is *unknown* not only because we didn't see it at the time but because it cannot be seen. And yet (poetry allows us to admit the paradox), it is, without doubt, also intensely and constantly *remembered*: for it is always before us—both the paradise of nostalgia and the promise beyond, the yearning.

Which is why it will be rediscovered when we arrive; we will return, in that sense, where we started. Though not exactly. In truth, we will understand the place for the first time, as we could never have done before embarking upon the journey. We will have realized that all along we had been drawn there by Love, the Calling—the voice that we did not always hear, for we were too busy exploring.

The word "end" is ambiguous, referring both to purpose and finality—and for that very reason, perfectly suited to address the profound human craving to explain one's own mortality. What is the point of departing "dust" if at the end we each return to it in the end? What sort of end—purpose—is that? The simple answer is that along the way we are graced to discover that man is privileged to realize

245

how much more he is than mere dust, appearances to the contrary notwithstanding. In the end, therefore, every man and woman sees the beginning—of Adam and Eve, and of all creation—and knows the place truly for the first time.

But none of us can do it alone.

Beyond Genesis

> *O humanity,*
> *revere your Lord*
> *who created you from one soul*
> *and created likewise its mate,*
> *and from these two*
> *spread countless men and women.*
> *Revere God*
> *through Whom you ask of each other,*
> *and revere the wombs [that bore you];*
> *for God is watching over you. (Sura 4:1)*
> *It is God who has produced you all*
> *From a single self;*
> *So here is an abode, and a lodging. (Sura 98)*
> *Indeed, be they Muslims,*
> *Jews, Sabians, or Christians,*
> *those who believe in God*
> *and the final day*
> *and who do good,*
> *have nothing to fear*
> *and they will not grieve. (Sura 62)*

Only the last of the three Abrahamic religions would be in a position to spell out explicitly the unifying spirit of the *Genesis* narrative. It was Mohammed who reiterated the common sanctity of all people whom God had created in His image, "from one *soul*—and created likewise its mate" from that same soul. The metaphor is then explicitly spelled out to include "all who do good," be they Jews, Christians, or indeed any other person who does no harm. The Lord reassures those who fear the torment of fire: "I certainly do not overlook the work of any worker among you, male or female: you come from one another" (*Sura* 195). But he expects respect and reverence for His work, His love, and our very existence.

Should we need proof of His existence, it is easy enough to find:

Truly in the creation
Of the heavens and the earth,

And the alternation of the night and day
Are signs for those of heart . . . (*Sura* 190)

"Those of heart," however, must be capable of compassion and respect, of love for another—which captures the *I–Thou* relationship.

It is true that in *Genesis* itself, the feelings between Adam and Eve
are not specifically described as love. For a fuller description of that
sentiment, we must turn to another part of the Old Testament, the
redoubtable *Song of Songs*. This sensuous poem is undoubtedly the
most astonishing anomaly in all of scripture.

Consider the intense eroticism of a dream that is described in
chapter 5:

I was asleep but my heart stayed awake.
Listen!
my lover knocking:
"Open, my sister, my friend,
my dove, my perfect one!
My hair is wet, drenched
with the dew of night."
"But I have taken off my clothes,
how can I dress again?"
I have bathed my feet,
must I dirty them?"
My love reached in for the latch
and my heart
beat wild.[1]

Small wonder that early audiences took such verses literally. "My
sister, my friend, my dove," seemed innocent enough, yet the wild
beating of the heart was unmistakably erotic—especially in light of
other, far more graphic passages. Rabbi Simeon ben Gamaliel, for
example, writing in the first century CE, recounts that twice a year,
on the fifteenth of Av and even on the solemn Day of Atonement
(improbably enough), the young women of Jerusalem would dress in
white and go out to dance in the vineyards, reciting verses from the
Song of Songs.[2]

Naturally, this had to change, and it did: for twenty centuries thereafter, the *Song* would be declared allegorical. The most prominent
among the first proponents of its loftier interpretation was the great
Rabbi Akiva in the second century, who argued that the deceptively
profane object of longing was the love of God expressed by the pious
people of Israel—a view later adopted by renowned Jewish commentators Rashi in the eleventh century and Ibn Ezra in the twelfth.
Christianity did the same: following Origen (who died in 254 CE), it

247

adapted the religious reading to the relationship between Christ and his Bride the Church, or Christ and the soul of the believer. Both Jews and Christians took their cue from the Bible—from the Old Testament metaphor of God's marriage to Israel, and also from the New Testament image of Christ as Bridegroom.

Rather more ambiguous is the interpretation of mystics—Jewish (such as the Kabbalists), Christian (notably Saint Teresa of Avila and Julian of Norwich), as well as Muslim (especially in the Sufi tradition)—all of whom used unmistakably erotic language to describe their divine adoration. Saint Bernard of Clairvaux, in the twelfth century, for example, wrote eighty-six sermons on the *Song* in this vein: "O strong and burning love, O love urgent and impetuous, which does not allow me to think of anything but you."[3] No less passionate are these verses dedicated to the Creator by Rabi'a al-'Adawiyya, an eighth century woman who became a major saint of Islam and a central figure in the Sufi tradition:

My joy—
My Hunger—
My Shelter—
My Friend—
My Food for the journey—
My Journey's End—
You are my breath,
My hope,
My companion,
My craving,
My abundant wealth.
Without You—my Life, my Love—
I would never have wandered across these endless countries.
You have poured out so much grace for me,
Done me so many favors, given me so many gifts—
I look everywhere for Your love—
Then suddenly I am filled with it.[4]

Notwithstanding this passionate sentiment, however, religious mystics, particularly Christian and Muslim, have been celibate, proudly proclaiming their love for God as greater than—and replacing—all others. Rabi'a's response, upon being asked how she was able to "climb so high" in her holiness, was uncompromising: "I did it by saying: 'Let me hide in You from everything that distracts me from You'"— to the point that "ever since the first day You brought me back to life, the day You became my Friend, I have not slept . . ."[5] This is no idle claim; indeed, several of her poems are about keeping all-night vigils. Camille Adams Helminski explains, "In line with Islamic tradition, she practiced the ancient technique of combating spiritual sleep by avoiding physical sleep—of sitting up on the roof all night, while the lights are out and the consensus of the day is asleep, watching the Universe turn."[6] Her asceticism even extended to eschewing food and water, strongly reminiscent, if not surpassing, her Christian counterparts.

But asceticism is not what the *Genesis* story is mainly designed to convey. Instead, it is human love, most vividly captured by the first couple, that offers the most plausible interpretation of the *I–Thou* relationship among souls. That relationship is meant to mirror, though certainly not replicate, our reciprocal relationship to the Creator. God Loves us differently than we love Him. He created us and all the world. We, by contrast, cannot even imagine Him without somehow conjuring up anthropomorphic characteristics. But in our arrogance, we have presumed to know better than our fellow humans God's "true" nature and have claimed to be acting in God's name when persecuting others who disagreed with us on the matter. As a result, the most monstrous crimes have been committed in the name of the Lord.

The universal significance of the creation narrative described in *Genesis* is too easily forgotten. In the twenty-first century, despite mankind's spectacular recent advances in knowledge, the Abrahamic family continues to be shredded by fratricide. The verses in the Quran that express God's love, which urge us to remember that "to God belong the East and the West . . . For God is omnipresent, all knowing" (*Sura* 115), are dismissed by jihadists while other, belligerent passages are given precedence, by distorting historical context and proportion.

And so we are all transformed from soulmates to enemies, from being our brothers' keepers to being marked by an indelible stain like Cain, which protects us neither from others nor from ourselves—least of all from God. Revenge feeds upon revenge in a whirlwind of evil that may yet end in a self-inflicted, mad fire.

The Resurrected Eve

There's a lesson in the Kabbalah about the oneness of all of us, the connectedness—it's like a connective tissue. We are all connected by a membrane of light. In fact, that is an American Indian concept, too, the idea of the wedding basket: You have a connectedness between mates, that there are membranes of light that tie you to the other . . . We were given the imprint on our soul of God. There is God in all of us.
Dr. Gail Gross

So there is indeed. Connectedness is beautifully captured by the image of translucent light. A little wedding basket, which ties us to one another, is also such a simple and delicate symbol: the imprint of God on our soul comes from a luminous breath that warms us to our common fate. We have so little time together, why would we want to harm one another? Why would we hurt ourselves by hurting one another? Why is it so difficult to embrace one another and recognize that we share the spark of divinity? Why do we presume to know *for* another, know what is good and evil, and even destroy the life of another presuming to act in God's name? Are we so desperate in our desire to come even close to tasting the fruit of the Tree of Life that we would anoint ourselves as gods?

That fruit was not to be tasted. For whatever promise there may be of another Garden after our journey upon his earth, whatever form the soul might take, gods we shall never be. Nor should we wish it. For the gift of beauty, and the sublime pain at its brevity, renders this sojourn awesome enough. Along the path, as the Sufi poet of the thirteenth-century Rumi reminds us, let's notice:

There is a community of the spirit.
Join it, and feel the delight
of walking in the noisy street,
and *being* the noise . . .
Why do you stay in prison
when the door is so wide open?
Move outside the tangle of fear-thinking.
Live in silence.
Flow down and down in always
widening rings of being.[7]

There, to open the door, will be Eve, outside the tangle of fear-thinking, embracing you in her arms like a child she would never abandon, the father she could not have, and the husband who would help her create soulful life: a new beginning in the widening rings of being. Quoth Eliot:

Dawn points, and another day
Prepares for heat and silence. Out at sea the dawn wind
Wringles and slides. I am here
Or there, or elsewhere. In my beginning.[8]

Notes

1. *Song of Songs*, 83.
2. The authors note that "these rabbinic passages are the earliest testimony we have about the popular understanding of the Song." Ibid., 30.

3. "Sermon 79," in *Bernard of Clairvaux: On the Song of Songs*, trans. Irene Edmonds, Cistercian Fathers Series, No. 40; cited in *Song of Songs*, Ibid., 32.

4. Camille Adams Helminski, *Women of Sufism: A Hidden Treasure—Writings and Stories of Mystic Poets, Scholars and Saints*, 33–34.

5. Ibid., 32–33.

6. Ibid., 28.

7. Cited in Dean Ornish, M. D., *Love and Survival: The Scientific Basis for the Healing Power of Intimacy*, 257.

8. T. S. Eliot, "East Coker," *Collected Poems*, 183.

Bibliography

Books

A Modern Narrative for Muslim Women in the Middle East: Forging a New Future (Washington, DC: American Islamic Congress, 2010).

Muhammad Abdel Haleem, *Understanding the Quran: Themes and Style* (London and New York: I.B. Tauris & Co., 2010).

Leila Ahmed, *Women and Gender in Islam* (New Haven, CT: Yale University Press, 1992).

Ayaan Hirsi Ali, *Infidel* (New York: Free Press, Simon & Schuster, Inc., 2007).

Tamim Ansary, *Destiny Disrupted: A History of the World Through Islamic Eyes* (New York: Public Affairs, 2010).

Karen Armstrong, *The Great Transformation: The Beginning of Our Religious Traditions* (New York: Random House, 2007).

Saint Augustine, *Confessions*, trans. with an introduction by R. S. Pine-Coffin (Baltimore, MD: Penguin Books, 1961).

Michael Baigent, Richard Leigh, and Henry Lincoln, *Holy Blood, Holy Grail* (New York: Dell Publishing, 1983).

Anne Baring and Jules Cashford, *The Myth of the Goddess: Evolution of an Image* (New York: Arkana, Penguin Books, 1993).

Mojdeh Bayat and Mahammad Ali Jamnid, *Tales from the Land of the Sufis* (Boston and London: Shambhala Publications, 1994).

Daniel Benjamin and Steven Simon, *The Age of Sacred Terror: Radical Islam's War against America* (New York: Random House, 2003).

Peter Berger, *Redeeming Laughter: The Comic Dimension of Human Experience* (Berlin, Germany: Walter de Gruyter, 1997).

Bruno Bettelheim, *The Uses of Enchantment: The Meaning and Importance of Fairy Tales* (New York: Random House, 1977).

———, *Freud and Man's Soul* (New York: Alfred A. Knopf, Inc., 1983).

Ariel Bloch and Chana Bloch, *The Song of Songs* (New York: Random House, 1995).

Harold Bloom, *The American Religion: The Emergence of the Post-Christian Nation* (New York: Simon & Schuster, 1992).

Jean Shinoda Bolen, *Goddesses in Everywoman: A New Psychology of Women*, foreword by Gloria Steinem (New York: Harper & Row, 1985).

Leila Leah Bronner, *From Eve to Esther: Rabbinic Reconstructions of Biblical Women* (Louisville, KY: Westminster John Knox Press, 1994).

Geraldine Brooks, *Nine Parts of Desire: The Hidden World of Islamic Women* (New York: Random House, 1995).

Dan Brown, *The DaVinci Code* (New York: Doubleday, 2003).

P. Brown, *The Body and Society: Men, Women and Sexual Renunciation in Early Christianity* (New York: Columbia University Press, 1988).

Thomas Bulfinch, *The Age of Fable* (Philadelphia, PA: Running Press Book Publishers, 1990).

L. H. Butterfield, Marc Friedlaender, and Mary-Jo Kline, eds., *The Book of Abigail and John: Selected Letters of the Adams Family 1762–1784* (Cambridge, MA and London: Harvard University Press, 1976).

John Calvin, *Commentary on Genesis* (Grand Rapids, MI: Eerdmans, 1948).

Joseph Campbell, *Myths to Live By* (New York: Bantam Books, 1972).

Willa Cather, *My Antonia* (Boston: Houghton Mifflin Co., 1977).

Karen Chase, *Eros and Psyche: The Representation of Personality in Charlotte Bronte, Charles Dickens, George Eliot* (New York and London: Methuen & Co., 1984).

Thomas Cleary, ed., *The Essential Koran: The Heart of Islam* (Edison, NJ: Castle Books, 1998).

Francis S. Collins, *The Language of God: A Scientist Presents Evidence for Belief* (New York: Free Press, 2007).

Jim Cullen, *The American Dream: A Short History of an Idea that Shaped a Nation* (Oxford: Oxford University Press, 2003).

Dennis Danielson, ed., *The Cambridge Companion to Milton* (Cambridge, UK: Cambridge University Press, 1989).

Andrew Delbanco, *The Puritan Ordeal* (Cambridge, MA: Harvard University Press, 1989).

William G. Doty, *Mythography: The Study of Myths and Rituals* (Tuscaloosa, AL: University of Alabama Press, 1986).

John P. Dourley, *The Psyche as Sacrament: A Comparative Study of C. G. Jung and Paul Tillich* (Toronto, ON: Inner City Books, 1981).

Alan Dundes, *The Study of Folklore* (Englewood Cliffs, NJ: Prentice-Hall, Inc., 1965).

Lee R. Edwards, *Psyche as Hero: Female Heroism and Fictional Form* (Middletown, CN: Wesleyan University Press, 1984).

Bart D. Ehrman, *Truth and Fiction in The Da Vinci Code: A Historian Reveals What We Really Know about Jesus, Mary Magdalene, and Constantine* (Oxford: Oxford University Press, 2006).

Riane Eisler, *The Chalice and the Blade: Our History, Our Future* (New York: HarperOne, 1988).

Mircea Eliade, *Patterns in Comparative Religion* (New York: The New American Library, Meridian Books, 1958).

_____, *Cosmos and History: The Myth of the Eternal Return* (New York: Harper & Row, 1959).

_____, *The Sacred and the Profane: The Nature of Religion* (New York: Harper & Row, 1959).

_____, *The Quest: History and Meaning in Religion* (Chicago: University of Chicago Press, 1975).

_____, *Mitul Rentegrarii* (Bucharest: Humanitas Press, 2003).

Hamid Enayat, *Modern Islamic Political Thought* (London and New York: I.B. Tauris & Co., 2005).

Clarissa Pinkola Estes, *Women Who Run with the Wolves: Myths and Stories of the Wild Woman Archetype* (New York: Random House, 1995).

Elizabeth Warnock Fernea, *In Search of Islamic Feminism: One Woman's Global Journey* (New York: Random House, 1998).

Stanley E. Fish, *Surprised by Sin: The Reader in Paradise Lost* (Berkeley, CA: University of California Press, 1971).

F. Scott Fitzgerald, *The Great Gatsby* (New York: Charles Scribner's Sons, 1925).

Viktor E. Frankl, *Man's Search for Meaning: An Introduction to Logotherapy* (New York: Beacon Press, 1971).

Antonia Frazer, *The Weaker Vessel* (New York: A. A. Knopf, 1984).

Sir James George Frazer, *The Golden Bough* (New York: Macmillan Publishing, 1963).

Northrop Frye, *The Great Code: The Bible and Literature* (Orlando, FL: Harcourt Brace Jovanovich, 1983).

_____, *Fables of Identity: Studies in Poetic Mythology* (Orlando, FL: Harcourt Brace Jovanovich, 1984).

Tikva Frymer-Kensky, *In the Wake of the Goddesses: Women, Culture, and the Biblical Transformation of Pagan Myth* (New York: The Free Press, 1992).

Andrew George, trans., *The Epic of Gilgamesh: The Babylonian Epic Poem and Other Texts in Akkadian and Sumerian* (New York: Penguin Books, 1999).

Louis H. Ginzberg, *Legends of the Jews*, Vol. I (Philadelphia: The Jewish Publication Society of America, n.d.).

B. Z. Goldberg, *The Sacred Fire: The Story of Sex in Religion* (New York: Gold Press, Inc., 1962).

James Gollnick, *Love and the Soul: Psychological Interpretations of the Eros and Psyche Myth* (Waterloo, ON: Wilfred Laurier Press, 1992).

Charlotte Gordon, *The Woman Who Named God: Abraham's Dilemma and the Birth of the Three Faiths* (New York: Little, Brown & Co., 2009).

Cyrus H. Gordon and Gary A. Rendsburg, *The Bible and the Ancient Near East*, 4th ed. (New York: W. W. Norton & Co., 1997).

Robert Graves, trans. from Apuleius, *The Transformations of Lucius, Otherwise Known as The Golden Ass* (New York: Farrar, Straus & Giroux, 1996).

David Greene and Frank Connor, eds. and trans., *A Golden Treasure of Irish Poetry, 600–1200* (London: Macmillan, 1967).

Gary S. Gregg, *The Middle East: A Cultural Psychology* (Oxford: Oxford University Press, 2005).

Shasha Guppy, *The Secret of Laughter: Magical Tales from Classical Persia* (London: I.B. Tauris & Co., 2008).

Husain Haddawy, trans., based on the text ed. by Muhsin Mahdi, *The Arabian Nights* (New York: W. W. Norton & Co., 1990).

Shira Halevi, *Adam and Havah: A Targum of Genesis 1:26–5:5* (Northvale, NJ: CreateSpace, 2009).

Edith Hamilton and Huntington Cairns, eds., *The Collected Dialogues of Plato, Including the Letters* (Princeton, NJ: Princeton University Press, 1969).

Nathaniel Hawthorne, *The Scarlet Letter* (New York: Penguin Books, 1999).

_____, *The New Adam and Eve*, http://www.gutenberg.org/ebooks/9227.

_____, *Mosses from an Old Manse* (New York: Random House, 2003).

Camille Adams Helminski, *Women of Sufism: A Hidden Treasure— Writings and Stories of Mystic Poets, Scholars, and Saints* (Boston and London: Shambhala Publications, 2003).

Will Herberg, ed., *The Writings of Martin Buber* (New York: Meridian Books, 1967).

Hesiod, *Theogony, Works and Days* (Oxford: Oxford University Press, 1988).

Azizah al-Hibri, ed., *Women and Islam—Women's Studies International Forum*, Vol. 5, no. 1 (Oxford, New York: Pergamon Press, 1982).

Gilbert Highet, *The Classical Tradition: Greek and Roman Influences on Western Literature* (New York and Oxford: Galaxy Book, Oxford University Press, 1959).

James Hillman, *The Soul's Code: In Search of Character and Calling* (New York: Random House, 1996).

Samuel Huntington, *The Clash of Civilizations: Remaking of the World Order* (New York: Simon & Schuster, 1998).

Washington Irving, *Tales of the Alhambra* (Madrid, Spain: Granada Press, n.d.).

Harriet Jacobs, *Incidents in the Life of a Slave Girl—Written by Herself* (New York and London: Penguin Books, 2000).

E. O. James, *The Ancient Gods* (Edison, NJ: Castle Books, 2004).

Henry James, *Daisy Miller and Other Stories* (Hertfordshire, UK: Wordsworth Editions, 1994).

Robert A. Johnson, *She: Understanding Feminine Psychology— An Interpretation Based on the Myth of Amor and Psyche and Using Jungian Psychological Concepts* (New York: Harper & Row, 1977).

Thomas H. Johnson, ed., *Final Harvest: Emily Dickinson's Poems* (Boston and Toronto: Little, Brown & Co., 1961).

Ernest Jones, *Free Associations: Memories of a Psychoanalyst* (New York: Basic Books, 1959).

C. G. Jung, *Modern Man in Search of a Soul* (New York: Harcourt Brace Jovanovich, 1933).

_____, *Psyche and Symbol* (Princeton, NJ: Princeton University Press, 1991).

Immanuel Kant, *On History*, ed. Lewis White Beck (New York and London: Macmillan Publishing Co., 1963).

_____, *Critique of Pure Reason* (Cambridge: Cambridge University Press, 1998).

_____, *Foundations of the Metaphysics of Morals* (Cambridge: Cambridge University Press, 1998).

Amy A. Kass and Leon R. Kass, *Wing to Wing, Oar to Oar: Readings on Courting and Marrying* (Notre Dame, IN: University of Notre Dame Press, 2000).

Leon R. Kass, *The Beginning of Wisdom: Reading Genesis* (Chicago: University of Chicago Press, 2003).

G. S. Kirk, *Myth: Its Meaning and Function in Ancient and Other Cultures* (Berkeley, CA: University of California Press, 1973).

James L. Kugel, *The Bible as It Was* (Cambridge, MA: Harvard University Press, 1997).

Kristen E. Kyam, Linda S. Schearing, and Valarie H. Ziegler, eds., *Eve and Adam: Jewish, Christian, and Muslim Readings on Genesis and Gender* (Bloomington and Indianapolis, IN: Indiana University Press, 1999).

George Lakoff and Mark Johnson, *Metaphors We Live By* (Chicago: University of Chicago Press, 2003).

Harriet Lerner, *The Dance of Connection: How to Talk to Someone When You're Mad, Hurt, Scared, Frustrated, Insulted, Betrayed, or Desperate* (New York: Harper-Collins Publishers, 2002).

C. S. Lewis, *Till We Have Faces: A Myth Retold* (Grand Rapids, MI: William B. Eerdmans Publishing Co., 1956).

_____, *The Great Divorce* (New York: Macmillan Publishing Co., Inc., 1974).

_____, *The Four Loves: The Much Beloved Exploration of the Nature of Love* (New York: Harcourt Brace, 1988).

_____, *The Pilgrim's Regress* (Grand Rapids, MI and Cambridge, UK: Wm. B. Eerdmans Publishing Co., 1992).

R. W. B. Lewis, *The American Adam: Innocence, Tragedy, and Tradition in the Nineteenth Century* (Chicago, IL: University of Chicago Press, 1955).

Sinclair Lewis, *Lewis at Zenith, A Three-Novel Omnibus—Main Street, Babbitt, Arrowsmith* (New York: Harcourt, Brace & World, Inc., 1961).

John Locke, *Second Treatise of Government*, edited by C. B. Macpherson (Indianapolis, IN and Cambridge, UK: Hackett Publishing Company, Inc., 1980).

Herbert London, *America's Secular Challenge* (New York: Encounter Books, 2008).

Martin Lowenthal, *Alchemy of the Soul: The Eros and Psyche Myth as a Guide to Transformation* (Berwick, ME: Nicolas-Hays, Inc., 2004).

Melani McAlister, *Epic Encounters: Culture, Media and U.S. Interests in the Middle East, 1945–2000* (Berkeley and Los Angeles, CA: University of California Press, 2001).

Fatima Mernissi, *Beyond the Veil: Male–Female Dynamics in Modern Muslim Society*, rev. ed. (Bloomington and Indianapolis, IN: Indiana University Press, 1987).

_____, *Dreams of Trespass: Tales of a Harem Girlhood* (Reading, MA: Addison-Wesley Publishing Co., 1994).

_____, *Scheherazade Goes West: Different Cultures, Different Harems* (New York: Simon & Schuster, Inc., 2002).

Edna St. Vincent Millay, *Renascence and Other Poems* (New York: Dover Publications, 1991).

James E. Miller, Jr., *Whitman's "Song of Myself"—Origin, Growth, Meaning* (New York and Toronto: Dodd, Mead & Co., 1964).

John Milton, *Paradise Lost* (New York: Penguin Books, 2000).

Mansoor Moaddel and Kamran Talattof, eds., *Modernist and Fundamentalist Debates in Islam: A Reader* (New York: Palgrave Macmillan, 2002).

Thomas Moore, *Soul Mates: Honoring the Mysteries of Love and Relationships* (New York: Harper Perennial, 1994).

Maureen Murdock, *The Heroine's Journey* (Boston and London: Shambhala Publications, 1990).

Cullen Murphy, *The Word According to Eve: Women and the Bible in Ancient Times and Our Own* (Boston and New York: Houghton Mifflin Co., 1994).

Azar Nafisi, *Reading Lolita in Tehran: A Memoir in Books* (New York: Random House, 2003).

Erich Neumann, *Amor and Psyche: The Psychic Development of the Feminine* (Princeton, NJ: Princeton University Press), 1971.

Carol A. Newsom and Sharon H. Ringe, eds., *The Women's Bible Commentary* (London, England and Louisville, Kentucky: Westminster/ John Knox, 1992).

Michael Novak, William Brailsford, and Cornelis Heesters, eds., *A Free Society Reader: Principles for The New Millennium* (Lanham, MD: Lexington Books, 2000).

Michael B. Oren, *Power, Faith and Fantasy: America in the Middle East 1776 to the Present* (New York: W. W. Norton & Co., 2007).

Martha Lee Osborne, *Woman in Western Thought* (New York: Random House, 1979).

Rosalie Osmond, *Imagining the Soul: A History* (Phoenix Mill, UK: Sutton Publishing, 2003).

Ovid, *The Metamorphoses* (New York: New American Library, 1960).

———, *The Art of Love* (New York: Stavron Publishers, 1963).

Camille Paglia, *Sexual Personae: Art and Decadence from Nefertiti to Emily Dickinson* (New York: Random House, 1991).

———, *Sex, Art, and American Culture: Essays* (New York: Random House, 1992).

Raphael Patai, *The Arab Mind* (New York: Charles Scribner's Sons, 1973).

———, *The Hebrew Goddess*, 3rd enlarged ed. (Detroit: Wayne University Press, 1990).

Jaroslav Pelikan, *Whose Bible Is It? A History of the Scriptures through the Ages* (New York: Penguin Group, 2005).

Kathrin Perutz, *Beyond the Looking Glass: A Glimpse into America's Beauty Culture* (New York: William Morrow & Co., 1970).

John A. Phillips, *Eve: The History of an Idea* (New York: Harper & Row, 1984).

David Price-Jones, *The Closed Circle: An Interpretation of the Arabs* (New York: Harper & Row, 1989).

Naomi Harris Rosenblatt, *After the Apple: Women in the Bible—Timeless Stories of Love, Lust, and Longing* (New York: Hyperion, 2005).

Naomi H. Rosenblatt and Joshua Horwitz, *Wrestling with Angels: What Genesis Teaches Us About Our Spiritual Identity, Sexuality, and Personal Relationships* (New York: Dell Publishing, 1995).

Leo Rosten, *The Joys of Yiddish* (New York: Pocket Books, 1991).

Richard E. Rubenstein, *Aristotle's Children: How Christians, Muslims, and Jews Rediscovered Ancient Wisdom and Illuminated the Middle Ages* (Orlando, FL: Houghton Mifflin Harcourt, 2003).

Helge Rubinstein, ed., *The Oxford Book of Marriage* (Oxford: Oxford University Press, 1990).

Malise Ruthven, *A Fury for God: The Islamist Attack on America* (London: Granta Books, 2002).

Annemarie Schimmel, *My Soul Is a Woman: The Feminine in Islam* (New York and London: Continuum Books, 1997).

_____, *And Muhammad Is His Messenger: The Veneration of the Prophet in Islamic Piety* (Chapel Hill, NC: University of North Carolina Press, 1985).

Carl C. Schlam, *Cupid and Psyche, Apuleius and the Monuments* (Pennsylvania: American Philosophical Association, 1976).

Gershom G. Scholem, ed., *Zohar: The Book of Splendor—Basic Readings from the Kabbalah* (New York: Schocken Books, 1972).

M. V. Seton-Williams , *Egyptian Legends and Stories* (New York: Fall River Press, 1988).

Roger Shattuck, *Forbidden Knowledge: From Prometheus to Pornography* (New York: St. Martin's Press, 1996).

Leonard Shlain, *The Alphabet versus the Goddess: The Conflict between Word and Image* (New York: Viking, 1998).

Richard Smoley, *Forbidden Faith: The Gnostic Legacy—From the Gospels to the DaVinci Code* (New York: HarperOne, 2006).

John Steinbeck, *East of Eden* (New York: The Viking Press, 1952).

Barbara Freyer Stowasser, *Women in the Qur'an, Traditions, and Interpretation* (Oxford: Oxford University Press, 1994).

Tanakh—A New Translation of the Holy Scriptures According to the Traditional Hebrew Text (Philadelphia and Jerusalem: The Jewish Publication Society, 1985).

Rabbi Joseph Telushkin, *Jewish Literacy: The Most Important Things to Know About the Jewish Religion, Its People and Its History* (New York: William Morrow & Co., 1991).

Savina J. Teubal, *Ancient Sisterhood: The Lost Traditions of Hagar and Sarah* (Athens, OH: Swallow Press/Ohio University Press, 1990).

The Holy Bible—the Douay Version of the Old Testament, First published in 1609 (New York: P.J. Kenedy & Sons, 1950).

Henry David Thoreau, *Walden and Civil Disobedience* (New York and London: Penguin Books, 1986).

Bruce Thornton, *Greek Ways: How the Greeks Created Western Civilization* (San Francisco: Encounter Books, 2000).

Paul Tillich, *The Courage to Be* (New Haven and London: Yale University Press, 2000).

Janet Todd, ed., *Mary Wollstonecraft, Mary and Maria; Mary Shelley, Matilda* (London and New York: Penguin Books, 1992).

Phyllis Trible, *God and the Rhetoric of Sexuality* (Philadelphia, PA: Fortress Press, 1978).

Mark Twain, *Diaries of Adam and Eve* (Lawrence, KS: Coronado Press, 1971).

Paula Uruburu, *American Eve: Evelyn Nesbit, Stanford White, the Birth of the "It" Girl, and the Crime of the Century* (New York: Riverhead Books, 2008).

Amina Wadud-Muhsin, *Qur'an and Woman* (Kuala Lumpur: Penerbit Fajar Bakti Sdn. Bhd., 1994).

Barbara G. Walker, *Women's Spirituality and Ritual* (Gloucester, MA: Fair Winds Press, 1990).

Wiebke Walther, *Women in Islam: From Medieval to Modern Times* (Princeton, NJ: Markus Wiener Publishers, 1995).

Montgomery Watt, *Muhammad at Mecca and Muhammad at Medina* (Oxford: Oxford University Press, 1981).

Simone Weil, introduction by T. S. Eliot. *The Need for Roots* (New York: Harper & Row, 1952).

Eudora Welty, *One Writer's Beginnings* (New York: Warner Books, 1984).

———, *The Robber Bridegroom* (Orlando, FL: Harcourt Brace Jovanovich, 1987).

Edith Wharton, *A Backward Glance* (New York: Charles Scribner's Sons, 1964).

———, *Summer*, with an introduction by Marilyn French (New York: Macmillan Publishing Co., 1981).

———, *The Age of Innocence* (New York: Charles Scribner's Sons, 1986).

Deborah Gray White, *Ar'n't I a Woman? Female Slaves in the Plantation South* (New York: W. W. Norton, 1985).

Walt Whitman, *Leaves of Grass* (Oxford: Oxford University Press, 1998).

Anna Wierzbicka, *Semantics, Culture, and Cognition: Universal Human Concepts in Culture-Specific Configurations* (Oxford and New York: Oxford University Press, 1992).

James Q. Wilson, *The Moral Sense* (New York, The Free Press, 1993).

Virginia Wolf, *A Room of One's Own* (Orlando, FL: Harcourt Brace Jovanovich, 1957).

Cynthia Griffin Wolff, *A Feast of Words: The Triumph of Edith Wharton* (Reading, MA: Addison Wesley Publishing Co., 1995).

Mary Wollstonecraft, *A Vindication of the Rights of Woman* (London: Orion Publishing Group, 1995).

Theodore Zeldin, *An Intimate History of Humanity* (New York: HarperCollins Publishers, Inc., 1994).

Articles

Nabia Abbott, "A Ninth Century Fragment of the 'Thousand Nights': New Light on the Early History of the Arabian Nights," *Journal of Near Eastern Studies*, 8, no. 3 (July 1949): 129–64.

S. M. Adams, "Hesiod's Pandora," *The Classical Review* (November 1932): 193–96.

W. F. Albright, "Gilgames and Engidu, Mesopotamian Genii of Fecundity," *Journal of the American Oriental Society* 40 (1920): 307–35.

John A. Bailey, "Initiation and the Primal Woman in Gilgamesh and Genesis 2–3," *Journal of Biblical Literature* 89, no. 2 (June 1970): 137–50.

E. F. Beall, "Hesiod's Prometheus and Development in Myth," *Journal of the History of Ideas*, 52, no. 3 (July–September 1991): 355–71.

Daniel Beaumont, "'Peut-on . . .': Intertextual Relations in the Arabian Nights and Genesis," *Comparative Literature* 50, no. 2 (Spring 1998): 120–35.

Ernest D. Burton, "Spirit, Soul, and Flesh—in Greek Writers from Homer to Aristotle," *The American Journal of Theology* 17, no. 4 (October 1913): 563–98.

C. M. Cady, "The Use of Mythical Elements in the Old Testament, II," *The Biblical World*, 194–202.

David Carr, "Gender and the Shaping of Desire in the Song of Songs and Its Interpretation," *Journal of Biblical Literature* 119, no. 2 (Summer 2000): 233–48.

Gregory Chaplin, "'One Flesh, One Heart, One Soul': Renaissance Friendship and Miltonic Marriage," *Modern Philology* 99, no. 2 (November 2001): 266–92.

Leigh N. B. Chipman, "Mythic Aspects of the Process of Adam's Creation in Judaism and Islam," *Studia Islamica* 93 (2001): 5–25.

Tikva Frymer-Kensky, "Review of *Genesis: The Beginning of Desire* by Avivah Gottlieb Zornberg," *The Journal of Religion* 76, no. 4 (October 1996): 611–12.

Meyer I. Gruber, "Review of Tikva Frymer-Kensky, *In the Wake of the Goddesses: Women, Culture, and the Biblical Transformation of Pagan Myth*," *The Jewish Quarterly Review*, LXXXVI, nos. 1–2 (July–October 1993): 213–16.

———, "Review of Nehama Aschkenasy, Woman at the Window: Biblical Tales of Oppression and Escape," *The Jewish Quarterly Review*, SCII, nos. 3–4 (January–April 2002): 589–93.

Gustave E. von Grunebaum, "Greek Form Elements in the Arabian Nights," *Journal of the American Oriental Society* 62, no. 4 (December 1942): 277–92.

"Heb. 'Soul,'" *The American Journal of Semitic Languages and Literatures* 32, no. 2 (January 1916): 141–42.

Morris Jastrow, Jr., "Adam and Eve in Babylonian Literature," *The American Journal of Semitic Languages and Literatures*, XV, no. 4 (July 1899): 193–214.

W. F. Kirby, "The Forbidden Doors of the *Thousand and One Nights*," *The Folk-Lore Journal* 5, no. 2 (1887): 112–24.

Samuel Tobias Lachs, "The Pandora-Eve Motif in Rabbinic Literature," *Harvard Theological Review* 67 (1967): 341–45.

Arthur O. Lovejoy, "Milton and the Paradox of the Fortunate Fall," *A Journal of English Literary History* 4, no. 3 (September 1937): 161–80.

Henry Malter, "Personifications of Soul and Body. A Study in Judaeo-Arabic Literature," *The Jewish Quarterly Review*, New Series 2, no. 4 (April 1912): 453–79.

Ahmed Mansour, "The Right of Women to Rule an Islamic State," November 20, 2008, http://www.ahl-alquran.com/English/show_article.php?main_id=2932 (Accessed April 3, 2011).

Patricia A. Marquardt, "Hesiod's Ambiguous View of Woman," *Classical Philology* 77, no. 4 (October 1982): 283–91.

D. D. McGibbon, "The Fall of the Soul in Plato's Phaedrus," *The Classical Quarterly*, New Series 14, no. 1 (May 1964): 56–63.

Wayne A. Meeks, "The Image of the Androgyne: Some Uses of a Symbol in Earliest Christianity," *History of Religions* 13, no. 3 (February 1974): 165–208.

David L. Miller, "Polytheism and Archetypal Theology: A Discussion," *Journal of the American Academy of Religion* 40, no. 4 (December 1972): 513–20.

J. Maxwell Miller, "In the 'Image' and 'Likeness' of God," *Journal of Biblical Literature* 91, no. 3 (September 1972): 289–304.

J. A. Montgomery, "Soul Gods," *The Harvard Theological Review* 34, no. 4 (October 1941): 321–22.

William L. Moran, "The Epic of Gilgamesh: A Document of Ancient Humanism," *Bulletin, Canadian Society for Mesopotamian Studies* 22 (1991): 15–22.

George W. E. Nickelsburg, "Review of Michael E. Stone, *A History of the Literature of Adam and Eve*," *The Journal of Religion* 74, no. 1 (January 1994): 94.

Simo Parpola, "The Assyrian Tree of Life: Tracing the Origins of Jewish Monotheism and Greek Philosophy," *Journal of Near Eastern Studies* 52, no. 3 (July 1993): 161–208.

Olga Raggio, "The Myth of Prometheus: Its Survival and Metamorphoses up to the Eighteenth Century," *Journal of the Warburg and Courtauld Institutes* 21, nos. 1/2 (January–June 1958): 44–62.

Nawal El Saadawi, "Woman and Islam," *Women's Studies International Forum* 5, no. 2 (1982): 193–207.

D. Shepardson, "The Biblical Element in the Quran," *The Old and New Testament Student* 10, no. 4 (April 1890): 207–12.

Larry D. Shinn, "The Goddess: Theological Sign or Religious Symbol?" *Numen* 31, Fasc. 2 (December 1984): 175–98.

Jane L. Smith and Yvonne Y. Haddad, "Eve: Islamic Image of Woman," *Women's Studies International Forum* 5, no. 2 (1982): 135–44.

D. A. Spellberg, "Writing the Unwritten Life of the Islamic Eve: Menstruation and the Demonization of Motherhood," *International Journal of Middle East Studies* 28 (1996): 305–24.

James Stambaugh, "'Life' According to the Bible, and the Scientific Evidence," *Creation Ex Nihilo Technical Journal* 6, no. 2 (1992): 98–121.

W. E. Staples, "The 'Soul' in the Old Testament," *The American Journal of Semitic Languages and Literatures* 44, no. 3 (April 1928): 145–76.

Index

Abraham, x, xviii, 38, 192, 196-199, 205-208; Abrahamic ix, 39, 24, 28, 29, 38, 41, 42, 66, 73, 76, 77, 87, 89, 97, 101, 112, 115, 192, 207, 208, 246, 249, 255
Adam, x-xvi, xx, 12, 19-21, 29-54, 63, 72, 77, 85, 87-90, 95-101, 103, 105, 106, 107, 110, 114-5, 114-121, 126, 151-3, 156, 184, 191, 195, 207; and Eve, ix, xi, xiv, xvi, xx, 37, 44, 50-4, 72, 77, 87, 90, 107, 110, 121, 129-30, 134, 136, 153, 158, 160, 166, 184, 186, 187, 196, 199, 223-26, 231-35, 237-241; and Lilith, 99, 101; created in God's Image, xx, 19, 34, 237, 241; *adamah*, 29, 35; American, 147-149, 156, 163, 171, 208; *See also* Creation, Eve, Human, Man, Mankind
Adams, Camille, 248
Aeschylus, 54, 56
Ahmed, Leila, 23, 25, 67, 70
Aisha, 205-6
Akkadian, 75, 78,9, 90, 182
Allah, ix, ixx, 42, 134, 206, 219-21, 242. *See also* Author, Creator, God
Allegory, 40, 73, 236
Ali, Ayaan Hirsi, xviii, 137, 142
America(n), x, 71, 129, 139, 145-68, 214, 216-7, 219; culture, 41, 217; psycho-analysis, 215-6; women, x, 17; view of Islam, 139, 143. *See also* New World, United States
American Islamic Congress, 123
Androgyny, 51-4; androgynous, 32-4, 176; androphilia, x; androphobia, x
Angel, 24, 150, 166, 200-1
Animal(s), 20-1, 29-30, 36-7, 45-6, 55, 74, 76, 80, 82, 136, 211, 233, 237-8

Anthropomorphic, xvii, 19, 73, 102, 185, 249
Aphrodite, xi, 32, 57-8, 73, 163, 224. *See also* Goddess of love and beauty, Venus
Apple, 28, 107. *See also* Fruit, Forbidden Fruit, Fruit from the Tree of Knowledge, Original Sin
Apuleius, Lucius, 57, 69, 224
Arab, 66, 122-3, 125, 133, 138; Arabic, 24, 110, 112,130-1, 133
Archer, Newland, 158-9
Archetype, 62, 186, 255; archetypal, 59, 83, 85, 116, 123, 132, 165, 184, 208, 216. *See also* Jung, Carl G.
Aristotle, 28, 123, 145
Aristophanes, 32, 56
Armstrong, Karen, 14, 25
Ascetic, 125-6; asceticism, 124, 229. *See also* Virgin
Assyrian, 6, 75
Augustine, Saint, 64-5, 70, 72, 105-7, 117
Author, xvii, 4, 9, 17, 28, 34, 39, 40, 50. *See also* Creator, God, Goddess, Lord
Averroes (Ibn Rushd), 119

Babylon(ian), 15-6, 18, 41, 79-80, 85, 90, 179, 182. *See also* Mesopotamia(n)
Balkhi, Din Mohammad. *See also* Rumi
Baring, Anne and Cashford, Jules, 79, 102, 117, 179, 183-4, 193
Beauty, xi, 13, 17, 32, 34, 50, 52, 57-9, 66, 71-3, 86, 149, 159, 163-4, 197, 205, 215-6, 226, 240-1, 250; American, 167-8; female, 71-3, 113, 135, 141, 165-70; 235, and love, 57-9, 71, 165-7;

medieval, 71; Muslim (or Islamic), 24, 109-10, 112-23, 127-33, 248; Quranic, 65; rabbinic, 98, 100; Sufi, 248; Sumerian, 181

Trible, Phyllis, 20-1, 25

Twain, Mark, xiv, 22, 37, 88, 225

Underworld, 15, 83-4, 180, 215, 224-5. *See also* Hell

United States, x, xiv xviii, 33, 116, 136, 202, 214-5, 219, 222

Universe, 4, 11, 134, 16-7, 28, 40, 76, 182, 185, 188, 190, 191, 212-3, 231, 235, 279. *See also* Creation, World

Uruburu, Paula, 165

Uta-napishti, 77, 84

Van Gogh, Theo, 137

Venus, xi, 57-8, 176-7. *See also* Aphrodite, Goddess of love and beauty

Virgin(s), 105, 125-6, 131, 135-6, 145, 157, 168, 184, 186-7, 220-1; black-eyed (or virgins of Paradise), 220-1; the Virgin (also Virgin Mary, Mary), 101, 134, 162, 184

Voltaire, 88

Wadud-Muhsin, Amina, 42, 44,110

Walther, Wiebke, 70, 128

Wharton, Edith, xiv, 157, 159, 171

Whitman, Walt, xiv, 146, 151-5, 157, 171

Wife, 20-3, 32, 42, 60, 66, 73, 77, 81, 8406, 89, 95, 110, 107, 110, 113-4, 123-4, 126, 130-1, 133, 148, 180, 161, 168-70, 195-201, 205-6, 108, 222, 225; wives, x, 25, 39, 66, 104, 125, 181, 196, 206, 222

Wisdom, 3, 5, 17-8, 32, 36, 49, 52, 56, 60, 63-4, 69, 76, 79-80, 82, 111, 138, 178, 183, 186, 199, 221-2, 240. *See also* Sophia

World, xvii, xix, xx, 3-5, 13-6, 21, 24, 27-30, 34, 40, 43, 47, 50-2, 58, 60, 62, 65-6, 68, 77, 85-6, 88, 95, 97, 99-100, 102, 108, 111-2, 116, 120, 125, 129, 137-8, 148, 153, 158, 165, 170, 180, 190-1, 199. 206, 213, 216-7, 219, 220-1, 223, 229, 231, 239, 241-2, 249; Muslim, x, xix, 68, 110, 121-3, 125, 127, 138. *See also* New World, Creation, Universe

Woman. *See also* Eve, Female, Feminine.

Zeldin, Theodore, 88

Zeus, xvii, 55-6, 73, 86, 153, 224, 238

Zohar, 35, 44

Zulaikha, 125, 130